Still Harping
on Daughters

Still Harping on Daughters

Women and Drama in the Age of Shakespeare

LISA JARDINE

COLUMBIA UNIVERSITY PRESS
NEW YORK

Columbia University Press Morningside Edition 1989
Columbia University Press
New York

Copyright © 1983, 1989 by Lisa Jardine

Library of Congress Cataloging-in-Publication Data

Jardine, Lisa.
    Still harping on daughters : women and drama in the age of
Shakespeare/Lisa Jardine. — Columbia University Press Morningside
ed.
        p.   cm.
    Reprint, with new pref. Originally published : Sussex, England :
Harvester Press : Totowa. N.J. : Barnes & Noble. 1983.
    Bibliography: p.
    Includes index.
    ISBN 0-231-07062-4. —ISBN 0-231-07063-2 (pbk.)
    1. English drama—Early modern and Elizabethan, 1500–1600—History
and criticism. 2. Women in literature. 3. English drama—17th century—
History and criticism. 4. Shakespeare, William, 1564–1616—Characters—
Women. 5. Feminism and literature. 6. Women—England—
History—16th century. 7. Women—England—History—17th century.
I. Title.
PR658.W6J37   1989
822'.3'09352042—dc19   89–745
                                                                                                      CIP

♾

Printed in the United States of America
p 10 9 8 7 6 5 4 3 2

Contents

Preface to the Morningside Edition

A great deal has happened in the fields of feminist and historical criticism of Shakespeare since *Still Harping on Daughters* was first published in 1983. It is remarkable how rich the resources in feminist Shakespeare criticism now are. Then I maintained that existing feminist Shakespeare criticism was disappointing *as* criticism, and maintained that 'just concentrating on the female characters, or protesting as political feminists at the sexist views expressed by the male characters, will not get us very far with a feminist Shakespeare criticism appropriate to the 1980s'. That is now entirely inadequate as a verdict on the varied and methodologically sophisticated body of work available.

If I were to attempt to add now to what I wrote in my first preface, therefore, I would be bound to write another book, which would be an entirely new contribution to the field – one which would build on all I have now learned. This is not the place for such fresh effort, though inevitably the temptation is there. I should love to be able to put the record straight on all those places in *Still Harping on Daughters* where I now find myself critically in disagreement with what I wrote. Participants in many seminars since the book was published have seen to it that I have been made well aware of the need further to expand on many of the points I tried to make – there is nothing like able colleagues (particularly graduate students) for teaching one lessons in humility.

When I wrote *Still Harping on Daughters* I conceived of my task as one of bringing historical material to bear upon the texts of the drama of Shakespeare's age in an original way. I thought of this as the particular contribution that I could make to feminist Shakespeare criticism, as someone whose own research work is in intellectual history, but who was now thinking about

English Renaissance literature. It is not an entirely welcome discovery to find that one's own supposedly thoroughly idiosyncratic intellectual commitments are part of a general trend. So it was with mixed feelings that I found myself, almost immediately the book was published, listed as part of a critical movement, 'loosely called the "new history" and flourishing both in Europe and America'.[1] But the perception of a critical grouping was a shrewd one. The 'turn to history' has indeed shaped much recent Renaissance text criticism, and there is no doubt in my own mind that being thrown together with those of distinct critical and political persuasions who share that historical focus in their work has been extremely valuable – even when, as in a number of the platform encounters between 'new historicist' and 'feminist' Shakespeareans, the vital component in the exchange has been passionate disagreement.

For it has inevitably turned out that those of us who struggle to position ourselves between the disciplines of history, cultural studies, and text criticism have a variety of objectives in mind. I am now clear that, in my case, the move *forwards* towards a new fusion of methodologies and material from cultural history and text studies was made in order to retrieve *agency* for the female subject in history – in all periods women have acted as well as been acted upon, but it is strikingly a feature of some recent text criticism to appear to erase that active participation in the historical process. I consider that this urge to retrieve lost participants in the historical process is one which I share with the 'new social history' of the early modern period, 'in which a deliberate effort has been made to recover the experience of the mass of . . . people, to rediscover them as members of a distinct and vigorous culture and to understand their part in the making of their history'.[2] Just as the social historian combs his or her archival material for the textual trace of those on the margins, so I have dredged the documents for textual evidence of the presence of women in the early modern community.

Furthermore, insofar as I have been successful in giving back to her a place in contemporary events, this retrieval of agency has been achieved by my treating the individual female subject in the drama as a 'cultural artifact', a methodological move which I now recognise that I share with 'new' social anthropology.[3] Like the anthropologist, I look for the subject in history at the intersection of systems of behaviour, customs, beliefs, out of which, I consider, personal identity is constructed. The past is another culture; its subjects are accessible to us only in the cultural forms which gave recognisable public shape and expression to individualised participation in events in their community.

Every feminist and historicist critic like myself is, I believe, in the process of developing an individual methodological position in a new interdisciplinary area somewhere strategically between history, text criticism and social anthropology. It is this methodology in process which determines our own angle of address on the canonical texts which provide the occasion for our intellectual activity. When I took issue with the feminist Shakespeare criticism of others in my original preface, I now see that it was the specific nature of my own intellectual goals and objectives which prevented my responding adequately to their critical achievements. If I was bemused by the direction taken by Shakespearean psychoanalytical criticism it was because individual subjectivity was not on my own agenda; and in their turn, those Shakespeare critics committed to psychoanalytic theory and techniques would certainly be bound to feel that external social relations, and the primacy of material conditions were too much on mine. With the benefit of hindsight I now consider that the variety of approaches which have been, and continue to be attempted by feminist critics of the plays of Shakespeare and his contemporaries have all contributed – even in their oppositions and disagreements – to the methodological subtlety, as well as to the continuing engagedness with real issues, which distinguish the most recent work.

So, finally, this is an opportunity to set the record straight in one important way. In Spring 1984 I was invited to take part in a seminar session on 'Women and Shakespeare' at the annual meeting of the Shakespeare Association of America, in Boston. It was my first encounter face to face with the extensive and thriving group of North American feminist Shakespeare critics about whose work – from my insular English position – I had been so confidently disparaging in my original preface. Within that group it was individual critics with whose work I had taken issue – in particular Carol Neely and Coppélia Kahn – who welcomed me most vigorously, with whom I engaged in the most stimulating and exciting debate, and who have supported and encouraged me on every subsequent occasion (and there have been many) on which we have met. I owe them an enormous intellectual debt, but beyond that, they taught me an important, and I hope a lasting lesson in generosity. This new preface allows me publicly to thank them, and all the other feminist critics at Boston in 1984, and, two years later, at Berlin, for all they have taught me about open intellectual exchange, and about cooperative feminist endeavour.

Lisa Jardine
1989

Notes

1 J. E. Howard, 'The new historicism in renaissance studies', *English Literary Renaissance 16* (1986), 13–43; 13. The very first time I heard myself described, from a public platform, as a 'new historicist' was by Coppélia Kahn at the Boston SAA meeting in Spring, 1984.

2 Keith Wrightson, *English Society 1580–1680* (Hutchinson, 1982).

3 See first of all Clifford Geertz, *The Interpretation of Cultures* (Basic Books, New York, 1973), 51; then Stephen Greenblatt, *Renaissance Self-Fashioning* (University of Chicago Press, Chicago & London, 1980), 3.

Introduction

Hamlet   Have you a daughter?
Polonius I have my lord.
Hamlet   Let her not walk i' th' sun. Conception is a blessing. But as your
            daughter may conceive – friend look to 't.
Polonius How say you by that? (Aside) Still harping on my daughter.[1]

It was almost inevitable that feminist criticism, even before it had
begun to clarify its ideas of peculiarly feminist approaches to the
literature of the nineteenth and twentieth centuries, would try its
teeth on that most patriarchal body of texts, the works of William
Shakespeare. It was as predictable, I suppose, that the collection
of studies which emerged would be fragmentary, confusing and
contradictory. What was less expected was that feminist studies
of Shakespeare would be so predictable *as* criticism – that they
would be marked, almost without exception, by an all too familiar
sameness in their reverence for the realism of Shakespeare's
plays. The present work was written on a growing tide of
personal irritation at the apparent inability of such critics to
break with the conventions of orthodox Shakespeare criticism,
except in their single-minded preoccupation with the female
characters in the plays, and their hostility to the chauvinistic
attitudes the plays incorporate. Just concentrating on the female
characters, or protesting as political feminists at the sexist views
expressed by the male characters, will not get us very far with a
feminist Shakespeare criticism appropriate to the 1980s.

There appear currently to be two main lines of approach to
Shakespeare's drama within a feminist perspective (in some cases
it would be more appropriate to dub them 'lines of attack'). The
first assumes that Shakespeare has earned his position at the heart
of the traditional canon of English literature by creating characters who reflect every possible nuance of that richness and variety
which is to be found in the world around us. His female charac-

ters, according to this view, reflect accurately the whole range of specifically female qualities (which qualities are supposed to be fixed and immutable from Shakespeare's own day down to our own). In the words of a prominent female Shakespearean actor:

> From the point of view of an actress, the Shakespearean women are most satisfactory people, for when portrayed they actually seem to feed the artist even when she is giving out the most of herself in the performance of her part. They are so true; their nobility, beauty, tenderness, loveliness, lightheartedness, subtlety, provocativeness, passion, vengefulness, worthlessness, stupidity and a hundred more qualities so entirely right from the feminine point of view that they provide a field the most ambitious artist could scarcely hope to cover.[2]

'Shakespeare's vision of women transcended the limits of his time and sex', even if his inspired vision was dimmed by those who subsequently directed his works on the stage. This means, we are told, that Shakespeare's women characters 'offer insights into women's perceptions of themselves in a patriarchal world'.[3]

Juliet Dusinberre has advanced particularly persuasively the thesis that Shakespeare's genius enabled him to transcend patriarchal partisanship, and to project on stage a spectrum of female qualities which reflected the burgeoning emancipation of the wives of the London bourgeoisie:

> Genius is a process of selecting what to ask as much as, if not more than of deciding what and how to answer. . . . Shakespeare's theatre came magnificently of age in a London where women's influence was sharply felt and attitudes towards them keenly debated. The feminism of the city provided one of those curious catalysts through which genius is crystallised.
>
> Feminism nevertheless sounds a strange bedfellow for poetry, more like a joke in Aristophanes than a serious statement in Shakespeare. Shakespeare was not concerned to register in his plays his own presence as defender of women. . . . But Virginia Woolf was deceived by the poet's own unobtrusiveness when she declared that 'it would be impossible to say what Shakespeare thought of women'. Shakespeare saw men and women as equal in a world which declared them unequal. He did not divide human nature into the masculine and the feminine, but observed in the individual woman or man an infinite variety of unions between opposing impulses.[4]

And this is a view which the prominent Shakespearean Anne Barton appears to share. Shakespeare, according to her, takes a broadly enlightened view of the rich variety of prospects open to individual women, while refusing to be confined to any theoretical platform on 'the woman question':

No other writer challenges the aggressively limited feminist position, the intolerant and rigidly schematized view of human life . . . with such power. At the same time, disconcertingly, no other writer has created so many memorable and sensitively understood women characters.[5]

Shakespeare takes no position on women, any more than on any other issue according to this view. He simply mirrors in a perfectly reflecting glass the varieties of womanhood in contemporary society, or rather, in that sector of society with which his genius felt most closely attuned (London city burghers and their families). Because that sector of society recognised the emancipated woman, female qualities in Shakespeare's plays square conveniently with present-day feminist notions of acceptable womanhood.[6] Queen Elizabeth's own example gave 'a sharpness which survives in Shakespeare's noble ladies'; whilst 'the actual situation of middle-class women in Jacobean society, gave the witty woman noticeable status in the drama'.[7]

The second line of approach assumes quite the opposite. Shakespeare's society is taken to be oppressively chauvinistic – a chauvinism whose trace is to be found in innumerable passing comments on women in the plays:

> *Duke* There is no woman's sides
> Can bide the beating of so strong a passion
> As love doth give my heart; no woman's heart
> So big to hold so much; they lack retention.
> Alas, their love may be call'd appetite –
> No motion of the liver, but the palate –
> That suffer surfeit, cloyment, and revolt;
> But mine is all as hungry as the sea,
> And can digest as much. Make no compare
> Between that love a woman can bear me
> And that I owe Olivia.[8]

Shakespeare's *maleness* therefore makes it inevitable that his female characters are warped and distorted. One may identify, as it were, an aggressive and a non-aggressive strand in this approach. The non-aggressive approach takes it that Shakespeare did his best to be a true reflecting glass, but that contemporary society's limited understanding of women combined with his own male viewpoint have skewed the resulting picture. What the critic interested in retrieving a rounded view has to do is to bring the insights of the *female* critic, or the male critic sympathetic to the female view, to bear on the plays. At its most endearing this approach produces reinterpretations of female characters like the following:

> Gertrude, in Shakespeare's *Hamlet*, has traditionally been played as a sensual, deceitful woman. Indeed, in a play in which the characters' words, speeches, acts, and motives have been examined and explained in myriad ways, the depiction of Gertrude has been remarkably consistent, as a woman in whom 'compulsive ardure . . . actively doth burn. / And reason [panders] will' (III.iv.86–8). Gertrude prompts violent physical and emotional reactions from the men in the play, and most stage and film directors . . . have simply taken the men's words and created a Gertrude based on their reactions. But the traditional depiction of Gertrude is a false one, because what *her* words and actions actually create is a soft, obedient, dependent, unimaginative woman who is caught miserably at the center of a desperate struggle between two 'mighty opposites,' her 'heart cleft in twain' (III.iv.156) by divided loyalties to husband and son. She loves both Claudius and Hamlet, and their conflict leaves her bewildered and unhappy.[9]

Here the critic adopts the familiar tactic of reconstructing the parts of the play which Shakespeare failed to include, and concludes that Gertrude is the 'nurturing, loving, careful mother and wife – malleable, submissive, totally dependent, and solicitous of others at the expense of herself', and that this 'more accurately reflects the Gertrude that Shakespeare created'.[10] This despite the fact that, on the author's own admission, 'Gertrude appears in only ten of the twenty scenes that comprise the play; furthermore, she speaks very little, having less dialogue than any other major character in *Hamlet* – a mere 157 lines out of 4042 (3.8 per cent)'.[11]

The aggressive strand sees Shakespeare's work as out-and-out sexist, and sets out to uncover his prejudices to the reader. For some such critics this is simply a cautionary device: to alert the reader to the limitations of the plays. For others it is coupled with a strenuous denial that Shakespeare any longer deserves the place he occupies at the centre of English literary studies.

Coppelia Kahn argues that Shakespeare's masculinity inexorably colours his drama, but still with a strong insistence that the plays remain worthy of study in spite of, or indeed, possibly because of this. From Shakespeare's centrally representative creative writing the alert critic can learn the implications of the author's sex for his or her perceptions and writing strategies. In Kahn's view, the fundamental difference between a male child's initial separation from the nurturing parent (female) and that of the female child, produces a 'crucial difference between the girl's developing sense of identity and the boy's'.[12] In his plays, according to Kahn, Shakespeare struggles with the difficulties of establishing a male identity within a patriarchal society, and this struggle is reflected in his representations of male and female characters:

Shakespeare's interest in masculine identity centers on this adult struggle to achieve a second birth into manhood. Whatever the details of his own experience, he lived as a man in Elizabethan times and knew at first hand at least some of the male anxieties and fantasies he depicts. Moreover, he lived in a patriarchal society that exacerbated male anxieties about identity. Though he accepts conventional arguments for patriarchy, perhaps because he sees no preferable alternative, he objects to the extreme polarization of sex roles and the contradiction underlying it. In its outward forms, patriarchy granted near-absolute legal and political powers to the father, particularly powers over women. Yet in unacknowledged ways it conceded to women, who were essential to its continuance, the power to validate men's identities through their obedience and fidelity as wives and daughters. Shakespeare's works reflect and voice a masculine anxiety about the uses of patriarchal power over women, specifically about men's control over women's sexuality, which arises from the disparity between men's social dominance and their peculiar emotional vulnerability to women.[13]

Kahn therefore takes the male heroes in Shakespeare's drama as reflecting in turn, and at various stages in Shakespeare's own development, the postures and attitudes of 'man in search of his identity', while the female characters provide a kind of perpetual sounding-board. They 'are' on-stage manifestations of the male anxieties of the hero, which the hero projects outside himself. Gertrude, on this approach, is indeed lewd and lascivious, because that is how both the older and younger Hamlet react to their humiliations at the hands of the world — it is woman's fault in general, the wife/mother's fault in particular.[14]

For Marilyn French, Shakespeare's plays strikingly embody that perpetual polarising of sets of qualities according to cultural notions of gender which she calls 'the gender principle', which characterises all cultural assessment of behaviour, and hence of morality. What is orderly, fixed, structured, is 'masculine', and is to be preferred; what is fluid, vacillating, formless is 'feminine' and less preferable. Maturity, however, lies in recognising the need for a healthy balance between the two, and this Shakespeare demonstrates in his romances. Once again, misguided patriarchal attitudes stamp Shakespeare (and marr subsequent literary works in the Shakespearean tradition); once again, Shakespeare evades, even if he fails to transcend, some of the worst possible consequences of the inevitable 'division of experience'.[15]

Whether the critic decides that Shakespeare's plays contain inspired insights or warped fantasies of womanhood, the two schools seem to agree in their assumption that Shakespeare's characters are susceptible of analysis as *people*. The 'perfectly reflecting glass' school regards these 'people' as sufficiently rounded for the astute critic to read out emancipated insights earlier criticism has missed. The 'distorted masculine view' school believes that the tools of psychoanalysis applied to the male/female relationships in the plays will lay bare a timeless conflict between male and female sexuality.

This study does not start with such an assumption. It tries instead to give the reader a succession of avenues of approach to the representations of women in the drama of the early modern period. We now know a considerable amount about this histori-cal period, in particular about the position of women, and about views concerning women: enough to know that Shakespeare's plays neither mirror the social scene, nor articulate explicitly any of the varied contemporary views on 'the woman question'. In the collection of essays which follows I take as my starting point a series of specific cultural issues of the early modern period which I believe provide useful perspectives on the treatment of women in the drama. Each chapter suggests a way in which 'femaleness' was significant in a network of possibilities for categorising and discriminating experience. I suggest that each of these offers a helpful way of seeing what is going on in stage representation of women, and at what level it might possibly be related to concerns outside the theatre. I maintain that the strong interest in women shown by Elizabethan and Jacobean drama does not in fact reflect newly improved social conditions, and greater possibility for women, but rather is related to the patriarchy's unexpressed worry about the great social changes which characterise the period – worries which could be made conveniently concrete in the voluminous and endemic debates about 'the woman ques-tion'.

Most importantly, I hope, I do not offer a theory, but a practice of feminist interest in literature. I make no pretence at offering definitive or exhaustive statements. Rather, I try to suggest alternative (corrective) possibilities for reading the relationship between real social conditions, and literary representation. My aim, I suppose, is to disrupt a little, to dislodge a few sacred cows which are fast coming to take hold on feminist Shakespeare criticism, as on much other Shakespeare criticism. In this spirit, I begin with a chapter on the boy player – the 'play-boy' – who takes the woman's part and represents femaleness, but who is the object of Elizabethan erotic interest in his own male right.

I hope that in documenting the contexts in which male and female members of the Elizabethan audience brought to the theatre a set of expectations, attitudes and beliefs about significant femaleness (and significant maleness) I make available a fair amount of material which the reader is unlikely to have encountered before. For this reason I have frequently quoted at length from contemporary documents and records, or from less accessible literary works. I hope that students will make free use of these excerpts in their own work, even if they are not always in a position to consult the original source. For the same reason I have tried to give a wide and varied selection of bibliographical references, to secondary works on topics in history, social history, anthropology, art history and intellectual history. On the whole I have chosen the works in these fields which are most accessible (both physically and in terms of approach) to the non-specialist, or which at least give good guidance. I have myself found the existing bibliographies in women's history invaluable as a means of access to areas of research which my own traditional training made entirely unfamiliar to me. I have in fact been startled by how much work already exists, and how many relevant Elizabethan and Jacobean sources have lain neglected on libary shelves – a silent history which alters our picture of the early modern world.

Finally, this book is directed at the reader who comes to Shakespeare's drama with a special interest in his female characters. But I hope very much that such a reader will not necessarily be a female reader, or even a feminist reader, male or female. As I have researched this book I have become increasingly aware of how criticism has regularly treated Shakespeare's female characters with unconscious partisanship, often because of assumptions which can now be shown to be false about contemporary women's lives. If it has done so, then an alternative 'special interest' view such as I offer here ought to broaden the vision of all those who study Shakespeare's plays, and those of his near contemporaries. I offer my own study of Shakespeare's heroic womanhood as part of a future complete view of the heroic in general in the drama of the age of Shakespeare.

Notes

1 *Hamlet* II.ii.181–5. All Shakespeare quotations are taken from and referenced to the Alexander Text (*The Complete Works* (London, 1951, 1971 edn)). I have, however, generally worked with the Arden editions of individual plays, where these are available.

2 Edith Evans, in J. Cook, *Women in Shakespeare* (London, 1980), p. 145.

3 I. G. Dash, *Wooing, Wedding and Power: Women in Shakespeare's Plays* (New York, 1981), p. 6.

4 J. Dusinberre, *Shakespeare and the Nature of Women* (London, 1975), p. 308.

5 A. Barton, 'Was Shakespeare a chauvinist?', *New York Review of Books* (11 June 1981), p. 20.

6 Dusinberre calls Shakespeare a 'feminist' in this context. I do not consider the term appropriate, even if Dusinberre could prove that Shakespeare shows particular insight concerning women's position in society. As a recent sociologist puts in succinctly, defining the limits of useful application of the term 'feminist': 'Any groups that have tried to *change* the position of women, or ideas about women, [deserve] the title of feminist.' O. Banks, *Faces of Feminism* (Oxford, 1981), p. 3.

7 Dusinberre, *op. cit.*, p. 228.

8 *Twelfth Night* II.iv.92–102.

9 R. Smith, 'A heart cleft in twain: the dilemma of Shakespeare's Gertrude', in C. R. S. Lenz, G. Greene and C. T. Neely (eds), *The Woman's Part: Feminist Criticism of Shakespeare* (Urbana, 1980), pp. 194–210, 194.

10 ibid., pp. 207, 208.

11 ibid., p. 199.

12 C. Kahn, *Man's Estate: Masculine Identity in Shakespeare* (Berkeley, 1981), p. 9.

13 ibid., p. 12.

14 ibid., pp. 132–40.

15 M. French, *Shakespeare's Division of Experience* (London, 1982). French's book reveals rather depressingly clearly the common mis-apprehension that to be a literary feminist is adequate qualifications to make one a specialist feminist critic.

I

'As boys and women are for the most part cattle of this colour': Female Roles and Elizabethan Eroticism

Every schoolchild knows that there were no women actors on the Elizabethan stage; the female parts were taken by young male actors. But every schoolchild also learns that this fact is of little consequence for the twentieth-century reader of Shakespeare's plays. Because the taking of female parts by boys was universal and commonplace, we are told, it was accepted as 'verisimilitude' by the Elizabethan audience, who simply disregarded it, as we would disregard the creaking of stage scenery and accept the backcloth forest as 'real' for the duration of the play.[1]

Conventional or no, the taking of female parts by boy players actually occasioned a good deal of contemporary comment, and created considerable moral uneasiness, even amongst those who patronised and supported the theatres. Amongst those who opposed them, transvestism on stage was a main plank in the anti-stage polemic. 'The appareil of women is a great provocation of men to lust and leacherie', wrote Dr John Rainoldes, a leading Oxford divine, (quoting the Bishop of Paris) in *Th' Overthrow of Stage-Plays* (Middleburgh, 1599). And he continues with an unhealthy interest which infuses the entire pamphlet: 'A womans garment beeing put on a man doeth vehemently touch and moue him with the remembrance and imagination of a woman; and the imagination of a thing desirable doth stir up the desire.'[2]

According to Rainoldes, and the authorities with whose independent testimony he lards his polemic, the wearing of female dress by boy players 'is an occasion of wantonnes and lust'.[3] Sexuality, misdirected towards the boy masquerading in female dress, is 'stirred' by attire and gesture; male prostitution and perverted sexual activity is the inevitable accompaniment of female impersonation.

There is, of course, a hysterical edge to Rainoldes' argument which we should not necessarily consider appropriate to less commitedly anti-stage members of the Elizabethan public. (Possibly the fact that the pamphlet was printed abroad indicates that it was exceptionally vitriolic, and recognised as likely to provoke.) Nevertheless, I begin with the extreme position to draw the reader's attention to the lively possibilities available for sexually ambiguous play on 'female parts' in Elizabethan and Jacobean drama, and in comedy in particular. In support of a widespread sense of possibility for gratiutous titillation in drawing attention to the role-playing of the boy player, there is a curious poem by Thomas Randolph (himself a minor dramatist), entitled 'On a maide of honour seene by a schollar in Sommerset Garden':

> As once in blacke I disrespected walkt,
> Where glittering courtiers in their Tissues stalkt,
> I cast by chaunce my melancholy eye
> Upon a woman (as I thought) past by.
> But when I viewed her ruffe, and beaver reard
> As if *Priapus*-like she would have feard
> The ravenous *Harpyes* from the clustred grape,
> Then I began much to mistrust her shape;
> When viewing curiously, away she slipt,
> And in the fount her whited hand she dipt,
> The angry water as if wrong'd thereby,
> Ranne murmuring thence a second touch to fly,
> At which away she stalkes, and as she goes
> She viewes the situation of each rose;
> And having higher rays'd her gowne, she gaz'd
> Upon her crimson stocking which amaz'd
> Blusht at her open impudence, and sent
> Reflection to her cheeke, for punishment.
> As thus I stood the Gardiner chaunce to passe,
> My friend (quoth I) what is this stately lasse?
> A maide of honour Sir, said he, and goes
> Leaving a riddle, was enough to pose
> The crafty *Oedipus*, for I could see
> Nor mayde, nor honour, sure noe honesty.[4]

The poem is a riddle, to which the answer is (like the riddle posed to Oedipus), 'a man': the 'maide of honour' is 'nor mayde' (not female), 'nor honour' (not courtly), 'sure noe honesty' (certainly not chaste) because 'she' is a boy player 'transvestied' – a travesty of a woman. Somerset House was used for play performances before Charles I and his queen throughout the 1630s, and we might even conjecture that the occasion for Randolph's poem was twelfth night, 1634, when the queen arranged for the King's Company to perform Fletcher's *The Faithful Shepherdess* for Charles, which 'the King's Players acted in the Robes she and her Ladies acted their Pastoral in the last year'.[5] What more decadent than a boy dressed as a woman in the very clothes worn by an actual 'maid of honour' to the queen on a previous occasion?

Whether or not there was an actual performance corresponding to the subject of Randolph's verse, it is clearly meant to be erotic (and was omitted from Randolph's published poems in 1638). Priapus is the god of fertility associated with the penis; the Harpies (whom the maid of honour outdoes in predatoriness) were hideous birds with women's faces who preyed on the blind prophet Phineus: in Henry Peacham's Emblem Book, *Minerva Britanna* (London, 1612), they represent 'extortionists and sycophants' ('In repetundos, et adulatores').[6] Randolph's Harpy-like predator threatens with her sexuality (Priapus), reinforced by her ruff (frequently seen by contemporary moralists as a symbol of sexual licence)[7] and her erect 'beaver' (a hat, also alluded to as unseemly for its ambiguous use by men and women, and its 'cocky' assertiveness). His/her crimson stockings and the ornamental 'roses' on her fancy shoes confirm her 'impudence', that is, lack of modesty, immodest boldness. The upshot is, just as Rainoldes predicted, that the dour scholar's interest is translated from curiosity into unhealthy erotic interest in the play-boy.

There is another poem by Randolph which supports this suggestion that the boy player is liable to be regarded with erotic interest which hovers somewhere between the heterosexual and the homosexual around his female attire. This poem is also couched as a riddle: Why does the elderly Lesbia pay through the nose to keep young Histrio, the boy actor, in a manner more fitting for a courtier? Having run through a description of Histrio's extravagances – elaborate dress, gambling, horse-racing – he reaches his facetious conclusion:

> Then this I can no better reason tell;
> 'Tis 'cause he plays the womans part so well.
> I see old Madams are not only toyle;
> No tilth so fruitfull as a barren soyle
> Ah poore day labourers, how I pitty you
> That shrinke, and sweat to live with much adoe!
> When had you wit to understand the right,
> 'Twere better wages to have work'd by night.[8]

Histrio is Lesbia's kept lover, her paid sexual partner. She is prepared to support his wildest extravagances because he is so good in bed: he 'playes the womans part so well' – lewdly, he brings her adeptly to sexual climax. The boy player is by trade a 'player of women's parts', he acts the female roles on stage. And this femaleness is invoked in his sexual relations with his ageing mistress in her name – she is Lesbia, the ancient lesbian lover (whence of course the term derives), so that her young partner is androgynous, female in persona but male in his sexuality. The source of his good fortune with Lesbia is actually (so Randolph implies) that he so ably satisfies her sexual demands (lasciviousness and excess being implied by the fact that she is 'barren soil' – procreation is not the intention). Histrio 'playes the womans part so well' off-stage as well as on.

The ordinary play-goer does not keep constantly in his or her mind the cross-dressing implications of 'boys in women's parts', but it is nevertheless available to the dramatist as a reference point for dramatic irony, or more serious *double entendre*. This *double entendre* adds sexual innuendo, I think, when 'playing the woman's part' is invoked on the stage. In Shakespeare's *Cymbeline*, Posthumus, persuaded that his wife Imogen has been unfaithful, rails against womankind in general:

> Is there no way for men to be, but women
> Must be half-workers? We are all bastards . . .
> Me of my lawful pleasure she restrain'd,
> And pray'd me oft forebearance; did it with
> A pudency so rosy, the sweet view on't
> Might well have warm'd old Saturn; and I thought her
> As chaste as unsunn'd snow. O, all the devils!
> This yellow Iachimo in an hour – was't not?
> Or less! – at first? Perchance he spoke not, but,
> Like a full-acorn'd boar, a German one,
> Cried 'O!' and mounted; found no opposition
> But what he look'd for should oppose and she
> Should from encounter guard. Could I find out
> The woman's part in me! For there's no motion
> That tends to vice in man but I affirm
> It is the woman's part.'

In his rage at Imogen's imputed promiscuousness Posthumus dwells with disturbing explicitness on his wife's sexual behaviour. Her modest reluctance in the face of his husbandly sexual demands was doubly culpable in its counterfeiting. It is to be contrasted with the 'Cried "O!" and mounted' of her sex with Iachimo. And in the progressively obsessive sequence of associations which leads Posthumus from initial outburst to out-and-out abuse of all women, the transition from the 'mounting' to the catalogue of vicious qualities which are 'feminine' is surely made by way of Randolph's pun (the commonplace *double entendre*) on 'the woman's part'. Iachimo encounters no opposition to his assault save the physical obstruction of the female pudenda – 'the woman's part', that which Imogen 'Should from encounter guard'. On this bawdy sense is quickly superimposed that of 'peculiarly female characteristic'. Posthumus attributes vice in mankind in general to those human characteristics which are specific to the female. And this sense again, in a speech on the stage, of a female character indeed acted by a boy, modifies into play-*acting* the woman's part: vice is symbolically represented by the exaggeratedly female posturings of the boy who 'takes the woman's part':

> It is the woman's part. Be it lying, note it,
> The woman's; flattering, hers; deceiving, hers;
> Lust and rank thoughts, hers, hers; revenges, hers;
> Ambitions, covetings, change of prides, disdain,
> Nice longing, slanders, mutability,
> All faults that man may name, nay, that hell knows,
> Why hers, in part or all.[10]

The punning which provides a titillating wittiness in Randolph's poem infuses Posthumus's rant with distorted sexual obsession. All that is potentially evil and disruptive about sexuality is to be asssociated with female roles – women's parts.

A recent feminist critic has described this speech of Posthumus's as 'vehement, doctrinaire, terrified misogyny' which 'painfully degrades women' and 'degrades Posthumus more'.[11] What I want to suggest here is that this is to miss the fact that in the context in which the speech is delivered (on the stage) the faults against which Posthumus rails are woman's 'in part', that is, as she is *acted*. Dubious sex is associated with that female role-playing in a way which would be inappropriate to 'woman': she may be viewed in fantasy as 'More intemperate in her blood / Than Venus, or those pamp'red animals / That rage in savage sensuality',[12] but an added edge of unlawfulness wantonness is gained on stage by the association with the boys who take the women's parts. Posthumus is displaying a warped and distorted view of legitimate sexual relations – behind the 'pudency so rosy' lurks rampant sexuality, perverted concupiscence, 'lust and rank thought'. Whilst these are certainly the views of a misogynist, they are powerfully evoked in the drama by alluding to a familiar area of sub-erotic debate about the morally debilitating effects of cross-dressing on the stage.

The polemicists who attacked cross-dressing as the fundamental depraving feature of the public theatre drew on a rich Biblical and Patristic tradition. When Thomas Thornton wrote to John Rainoldes in 1592 inviting him to attend three Latin plays which were being put on at Christ Church, Oxford (Gager's *Ulysses Redux* on Sunday 5 February, his *Riuales* on Monday 6 February, and an adaptation of Seneca's *Hippolytus* on Tuesday 7 February) it was cross-dressing which Rainoldes gave as his reason for declining. His private letter of reply to Thornton (the first sally in what became a prolonged public battle of words between Rainoldes and the pro-stage pamphleteers) explicitly singles out the Biblical prohibition against 'men in wemens raiment', rather than, for instance, the fact that a secular play was to be performed on a Sunday:

Syr because your curteous inviting of me yesterdaye againe to your plaies dothe shewe you were not satisfied with my answer and reason thereof before geven, why I might not be at them: I have thought good by writinge to open that vnto you which if tyme had served to vtter them by word of mouthe, I doute not but you would have rested satisfied therwith: ffor both I perceaued by that your selfe spake of *men in wemens raiment*, that some of your players were so to be attired: & that you acknowledged, that, if this were vnlawfull, I might iustlie be vnwilling to approve it by my presence. Now for myne owne parte in deed I am perswaded that it is vnlawfull because the scripture saythe *a woman shall not weare that which pertaineth to a man, nether shall a man put on womans raiment: for all that do so are abhomination to the lord thy god*: ffor this being spoken generally of all, and haueing no exception of plaies in the scripture (for ought that I knowe) must be taken generallie, as ment of them also. . . . Nether am I moved by this reason onelie . . . but also by the iudgment of such christian writers, as I dare not dissent from, vnlesse I se them cleerlie convinced of error by the word: *Caluin* as sounde and learned an interpreter of the scriptures as anie synce the apostles times in my opinion after he had shewed the daunger of vnmodest wantonnes and wickednesse for which the Lord forbideth men and wemen to chaunge raiment: *for most true (saith he) is that profane poets saying: Quem prestare potest mulier galeata pudorem* [Juvenal, *Satires* VI.252: what modesty can you expect in a woman who wears a helmet]. In which word sith *Juvenal* condemneth Romane wemen who with helmet on did learne to playe theire warlike parts in games like fensers; and *Caluin* saith that Moses controlleth in both sexes the proportion of that which *Juvenal* doth in one: it followeth that Caluin thought men to be forbidden by the lawe of God, to weare a ffrench hoode or other habiliments of wemen, yea thogh in plaies and enterludes.[11]

The Biblical prohibition to which Rainoldes, and all other polemicists, alludes is Deuteronomy 22.5, and Rainoldes leaves the reader of his *Th' Overthrow of Stage-Playes* in no doubt that the reason why cross-dressing receives such severe Biblical censure ('for all that do so are *abhomination* to the lord thy god') is because of its depraving sexual influence. He links the 'wanton female boys' of stage transvestism with every gradation of unnatural and perverted sexual behaviour:

Nay . . . it is a notorious and detestable euill: as [k]the Spirite sheweth by the words ensuing, *For all that doe so are abomination to the Lord thy God.* And seeing that himself hath giuen this censure, God forbid but we should thinke it most true and iust: although our weake eyesight could discerne no cause, why so small a matter, as flesh and blood might count it, should be controlled so sharpelie. Howbeit, if wee marke with iudgement and wisedome, first, how this precept is referred by learned *Divines* to the commandment [l]*Thou shalt not commit adulterie*, some [m]expreslie making it a point annexed therto, some impliedlie, in that either [n]they knit it to modestie, a parte of temperance, or [o]note the breach of it as ioyned wtth wantonnesse and impuritie: next, among the kindes of adulterous lewdness howe filthie and monstrous a [p]sinne against nature mens naturall corruption and vitiousnes is prone to; the Scripture witnesseth it in [q]*Cananites*, [r]*Jewes*, [s]*Corinthians*, [t]other in other nations, & [u]one with speciall caution, *Nimium est quod intelligitur* [it is more than enough if I have made my meaning clear]: thirdlie, what sparkles of lust to that vice the putting of wemens attire on men may kindle in vncleane affections, as [x]*Nero* shewed in *Sporus*, *Heliogabalus* in himselfe; yea certaine, who grew not to such excesse of impudencie, yet arguing the same in causing their [z]boyes to weare long heare like wemen: if we consider these things, I say, we shall perceiue that hee, who [a]condemneth the female hoore and male, and, [b]detesting speciallie the male by terming him a *dogge*, reiecteth both their offeringes with these wordes that *they both are abomination to the Lorde thy God*, might well controll likewise the meanes and occasions whereby men are transformed into dogges, the sooner, to cutt off all incitements to that beas[t]lie filthines, or rather more then beastlie.

[k]Deut. 22.5. [l]Exod. 20.14. [m]Calv.n. harmon. in lib. Mos. expos. sept. precept. Beza leg. Dei mor. ceremo. & Posit. D. Babingt. exposit. of the command. [n]Procopius in Deut. Thom. Aquin. 2ª.2ᵃᵉ q. 169. art. 2. Hyperius de fer. Bacchan. [o]Cyprian. epi. 61 Chrysost. hom. 38. in Mat. Liran. in Deut. 22.

ᵖRom. 1.27. ۹Gen. 19.5. ʳIud. 19.22. 1 King. 14.24. 2 King. 23.7. ʾ1 Cor. 6.11. ᵗAristot. polit. lib. 2. ca. 9. Senec. epi. 95. ᵛQuintil. lib. 1 cap. 4 & lib. 2 cap. 2. ˣSueton. in Ner. cap. 28. ᵞLamprid. in Heliogab. ᶻHora. carm. lib. 2. od. 5. Catul. in nuptias Iuliae Iuvenal Satyr. 8 Acer si comes. ᵃDeut. 23. verse 17. ᵇver. 18.¹⁴

The references, with characteristic Renaissance coyness, refer the reader to explicit descriptions of sodomy, homosexuality with and without flagellation, dress-swapping, male marriage, and sex between father and son.¹⁵ Genesis 19.5, for instance, gives the story of the men of Sodom attempting to have sex with the angels who have come to visit Lot:

5 And they called unto Lot, and said unto him, Where are the men which came in to thee this night? bring them out unto us, that we may know them.
6 And Lot went out at the door unto them, and shut the door after him.
7 And said, I pray you, brethren, do not so wickedly.
8 Behold now, I have two daughters which have not known man; let me, I pray you, bring them out unto you, and do ye to them as is good in your eyes: only unto these men do nothing.

The 'nimium est quod intelligitur' allusion is referenced to Quintilian, *Institutio oratoria* 1.4 (actually 1.3), in which the author cautions against schoolmasters who take an unhealthy pleasure in beating their boy pupils:

When children are beaten, pain or fear frequently results of which it is not pleasant to speak and which are likely subsequently to be a source of shame. . . . Further if inadequate care is taken in the choices of respectable governors and instructors, I blush to mention the shameful abuse which scoundrels sometimes make of their right to administer corporal punishment. . . . I will not linger on this subject; it is more than enough if I have made my meaning clear.¹⁶

The reference to Aristotle's *Politics* draws the reader's attention to an aside in a serious discussion of the ancient lawgivers, in which he gives a synopsis of the life of Philolaus:

Philolaus of Corinth also arose as lawgiver at Thebes. Philolaus belonged by birth to the Bacchiad family; he became the lover of Diocles the winner at Olympia, but when Diocles quitted the city because of his loathing for the passion of his mother Alcyone, he went away to Thebes, and there they both ended their life.¹⁷

Abuse of dependent boys is the theme of all this covert allusion; boys taking the women's parts in the drama provides the 'meanes and occasions whereby men are transformed into dogges [male whores]'. And Rainoldes enlarges on the stimulus to depravity contained in stage cross-dressing by turning to the gesture and behaviour which accompany female dress:

> Yet the third reason, wherein playes are charged, not for making young men come foorth in hoores attire, like the lewd woman in the *Proverbs*; but for teaching them to counterfeit her actions, her wanton kisse, her impudent face, her wicked speeches and entisements. . . . *Thetis* taught *Achilles* howe to play the woman in gate, in speech, in gesture. . . . *Deidamia* gaue him farder advertisements, howe *he must hold his naked brest, his hands*, & so foorth. These are wemens maners vnseemelie for *Achilles* to imitate: he should not haue done it. Howe much lesse seemely then is it for young men to danse like wemen, though like those who praised God with danses: and much lesse seemelie yet to danse like vnhonest wemen, like *Herodias*? whereby what a flame of lust may bee kindled in the hearts of men, as redie for the most part to conceue this fire, as flaxe is the other, Christian writers shewe in part by *Herodes* example. . . . When *Critobulus* kissed the sonne of *Alcibiades*, a beautiful boy, *Socrates* saide he had done amisse and very dangerously: because, as certaine spiders, *if they doe but touch men onely with their mouth, they put them to wonderfull paine and make them madde: so beautifull boyes by kissing doe sting and powre secretly in a kinde of poyson, the poyson of incontinencie*, as *Clemens Alexandrinus* speaking of vnholy and amatorie kisses saieth: Amatorie embracing goeth in the same line with amatorie kissing, if not a line beyond it. . . . Herewithall if amatorie pangs be expressed in most effectual sort: can wise men be perswaded that there is not wantonnesse in players partes, when experience sheweth (as wise men haue observed) that *men are made adulterers and enemies of all chastitie by comming to such playes?* that *senses are mooved, affections are delited, heartes though strong and constant are vanquished by such players?* that *an effeminate stage-player, while he faineth loue, imprinteth wounds of loue?*[18]

Since the stage-player 'while he faineth love, imprinteth wounds of love', the boy player's female dress and behaviour kindle homosexual love in the male members of his audience. Or rather, he creates a kind of androgyny: for to the Renaissance, the sexuality associated with the effeminate boy – the 'female wanton boy' of stage cross-dressing – is that of Hermaphrodite. With good classical precedent, the sixteenth century's primary understanding of Hermaphrodite is not a figure incorporating both sets of sexual parts (though medical discussions of such individuals do exist),[19] but the erotically irresistible effeminate boy:

> When *Salmacis* behilde
> [Hermaphroditus's] naked beautie, such strong pangs so ardently hir hilde,
> That utterly she was astraught. . . .

He clapping with his hollow hands against his naked sides,
Into the water lithe and baine with armes displayde glydes,
And rowing with his hands and legges swimmes in the water cleare:
Through which his bodie faire and white doth glistringly appeare,
As if a man an Ivorie Image or a Lillie white
Should overlay or close with glasse that were most pure and bright.
    The price is won (cride *Salmacis* aloud) he is mine owne.
    And therewithall in all post hast she having lightly throwne
Hir garments off, flew to the Poole and cast hir thereinto
And caught him fast betweene hir armes, for ought that he could doe:
Yea maugre all his wrestling and his struggling to and fro,
She held him still, and kissed him a hundred times and mo.
And willde he nillde he with hir handes she toucht his naked brest:
And now on this side now on that (for all he did resist
And strive to wrest him from hir gripes) she clung unto him fast: . . .
And pressing him with all hir weight, fast cleaving to him still,
Strive, struggle, wrest and writhe (she said) thou froward boy thy fill:
Doe what thou canst thou shalt not scape. Ye Goddes of Heaven agree
That this same wilful boy and I may never parted bee.[20]

In Golding's version of the Ovid story of Hermaphrodite (which has many affinities with Shakespeare's *Venus and Adonis*), the focus for the representation of Hermaphrodite is the erotic interest of his sexual refusal: the 'wilful boy' who remains obstinately coy under the nymph's assault. The object of attention is the potentially rapeable boy (be the assault by a nymph, or by a male or female god). And this is in accord with late antique models:

There are affinities between hermaphroditism and pederasty. . . . In late antiquity, *androgyne*, with the derogatory overtones which *gynandre* had always had, is often used for either a eunuch, or an effeminate.[21]

Submissiveness, coyness, dependence, passivity, exquisite whiteness and beauty compound in the blushing (yet wilful) boy to create a figure vibrant with erotic interest for *men*. Shakespeare's Adonis, though desired prominently by a female god, is alluring deliberately for male readers:

Over one arm the lusty courser's rein,
Under her other was the tender boy,
Who blush'd and pouted in a dull disdain,
With leaden appetite, unapt to toy:
She red and hot as coals of glowing fire,
He red for shame, but frosty in desire.[22]

Here is the passivity and 'disdain' (a traditionally female trait)
which implies androgyny/homosexuality; the discarding of
'true' masculine gender and its gender attributes, according to
medieval commentators:

> Activi generis sexus, se turpiter horret
> Sic in passivum degenerare genus.
> Femina vir factus, sexus denigrat honorem,
> Ars magicae Veneris hermaphroditat eum.
> Praedicat et subjicit, fit duplex terminus idem,
> Grammaticae leges empliat ille nimis.

[The sex of active genus trembles shamefully at the way in which it
degenerates into passivity. Man is made woman, he blackens the honour of
his sex, the craft of magic Venus hermaphrodites him. He is both predicate
and subject, he becomes likewise of two declensions, he pushes the laws of
grammar too far.][23]

When Rosalind in *As You Like It* adopts male disguise, she
takes the name of Ganymede: Jupiter's boy-lover. (Thomas
Heywood's *Pleasant Dialogues and Drammas, selected out of
Lucian, Erasmus, Textor, Ovid, &c* (London, 1637) includes
amongst commonplace dialogues, Lucian's dialogue between
Jupiter and Ganymede, and the retaliatory dialogue between
Juno and Jupiter.) In *The Two Gentlemen of Verona*, Julia
adopts the name of Sebastian, another homosexual prototype. In
doing so they allude directly to the erotic androgyny which their
boy-dressed-as-girl-dressed-as-boy creates. When Rosalind/
Ganymede describes to her lover Orlando (who does not recognise her as female) how she cured a man mad with love by aping
his lover, she/he combines the terms of the anti-stage attacks and
the wanton effeminacy of the classical Ganymede to intensify the
provocativeness of 'his' exaggerated wooing:

> He was to imagine me his love, his mistress; and I set him every day to woo
> me; at which time would I, being but a moonish youth, grieve, be effeminate,
> changeable, longing and liking, proud, fantastical, apish, shallow, incon-
> stant, full of tears, full of smiles; for every passion something and for no
> passion truly anything, as boys and women are for the most part cattle of this
> colour.[24]

Rosalind *is* just such a boy player/Ganymede, simpering out
feminine affectations in the manner so offensive to moralists like
Rainoldes, and this adds to the piquancy of the speech. In

Shakespeare's source, Thomas Lodge's *Rosalynde: Euphues golden legacie* (London, 1590), the discrepancy between the views of women expressed by Rosalind in her own persona, and those she expresses whilst disguised as the page Ganymede is made explicit. She 'keepe(s) decorum' in slandering women whilst dressed as a man:

> You may see (quoth GANIMEDE) what mad cattell you women be, whose hearts sometimes are made of Adamant that will touch with no impression; and sometime of waxe that is fit for euerie forme: they delight to be courted, and then they glorie to seeme coy; and when they are most desired then they freese with disdaine. . . . And I pray you (quoth ALIENA) if your roabes were off, what mettall are you made of that you are so satyricall against women? Is it not a foule bird defiles the owne nest? Beware (GANIMEDE) that ROSADER heare you not; if he doo, perchance you will make him leape so far from loue, that he wil anger euery vain in your hart. Thus (quoth GANIMEDE) I keepe decorum, I speake now as I am ALIENAS page, not as I am GERISMONDS daughter: for put me but into a peticoate, and I will stand in defiance to the vttermost that women are courteous, constant, vertuous, and what not.[25]

There is no such 'keeping decorum' for Shakespeare's Rosalind. She is the 'peevish boy' with whom Phoebe falls in love, even when most feelingly acting the girl-hero in love; as Ganymede deriding the ways of woman, she is the boy-actor mincing and lisping his way through his 'woman's part'. As Rosalind speaking the Epilogue, she is a little bit of both, saucily provoking the male members of the audience with her problematic sex:

> If I were a woman, I would kiss as many of you as had beards that pleased me, complexions that liked me, and breaths that I defied not. And I am sure, as many as have good beards, or good faces, or sweet breaths, will for my kind offer, when I make curtsy, bid me farewell.[26]

Wherever Shakespeare's female characters in the comedies draw attention to their own androgyny, I suggest that the resulting eroticism is to be associated with their *maleness* rather than with their femaleness. Some dramatists of Shakespeare's day made more direct sexual play on the purely homosexual possibilities. In Lyly's *Gallathea* (1584), the entire plot turns on complicated double-dealing in sexuality brought about by dressing boys as girls and girls as boys (when all the actors are in fact boy children): sexual ambiguity is fundamental to the action. As the editor of the standard edition of Lyly's works summarises the plot:

Neptune, angered by the inhabitants of North Lincolnshire, floods their fields; and is only appeased by a tribute of their fairest virgin to be exposed to the sea-monster Agar every five years. Two fathers, Tyterus and Melebeus, each supposing his daughter (Gallathea and Phillida respectively) to be the fairest, disguise them as boys in order to evade the tribute. So disguised they meet in the woods, and deceived as to each other's sex, fall in love. In the same woods Cupid has assumed the dress of a girl, the better to attack Diana's nymphs, who have defied him. He inspires Telusa with a passion for the disguised Phillida, and Eurota and Ramia with a passion for the disguised Gallathea: but Diana, discovering the mischief, institutes a search, captures the intruder, and sets him to untie love-knots for a punishment. In the end Venus, who has claims on Neptune, persuades him to effect Cupid's ransom from Diana by remitting the virgin-tribute. The natives, who have vainly offered Haebe as a substitute, are pardoned by the gods on the confession of Tyterus and Melebeus; and in order to 'gratify the mutual passion of Gallathea and Phillida, Venus undertakes to change one of them into a boy.[27]

In the opening scene of the play, Tyterus explicitly draws the audience's attention to the 'unlawfulness' of cross-dressing (with which the play is entirely absorbed), and the anti-stage polemicists' accusations of homosexual consequences. He explains to his daughter that the dire circumstances exonerate her from the charge of 'abomination' in her boy's disguise:

Tyterus   I would thou hadst beene lesse faire, or more fortunate, then shouldest thou not repine that I haue disguised thee in this attyre, for thy beautie will make thee to be thought worthy of this God; to auoide therfore desteny (for wisedome ruleth the stars) I thinke it better to vse an vnlawfull meanes (your honour preserued) then intollerable greefe (both life and honor hazarded), and to preuent (if it be possible) thy constellation by my craft. . . .

Gallathea   The destenie to me cannot be so hard as the disguising hatefull.

Tyterus   To gaine loue, the Gods haue taken shapes of beastes, and to saue life art thou coy to take the attire of men?

Gallathea   They were beastly gods, that luste could make them seeme as beastes.[28]

But it is Marlowe who seems most knowingly and gratuitously to exploit the possibilities for androgyne/homosexual innuendo latent in the boy player associations. Not only did Marlowe have a reputation for homosexual practice himself (one of the aphorisms attributed to him by Richard Baines, the spy who testified at Marlowe's posthumous atheism trial in 1593, was 'that they that loue not Tobacco & Boies were fooles'),[29] but he included homosexual themes in two of his plays. In the opening scenes of

Dido Queen of Carthage (c. 1590), Jupiter flirts with a boy
Ganymede in quite explicit fashion:

> Come gentle Ganymede, and play with me;
> I love thee well, say Juno what she will. . . .
> Sit on my knee, and call for thy content,
> Control proud Fate, and cut the thread of Time.
> Why, are not all the gods at thy command,
> And heaven and earth the bounds of thy delight?
> Vulcan shall dance to make thee laughing sport,
> And my nine daughters sing when thou are sad;
> From Juno's bird I'll pluck her spotted pride,
> To make thee fans wherewith to cool thy face;
> And Venus' swans shall shed their silver down,
> To sweeten out the slumbers of thy bed. . . .
> Hold here, my little love; these linked gems
> My Juno ware upon her marriage-day.
> Put thou about thy neck, my own sweet heart,
> And trick thy arms and shoulders with my theft.[30]

Here Marlowe appears to be making an entirely provocative
stage gesture: he opens his play about the all-pervasive consequences of misplaced passion with a celebration of the most extreme of 'unnatural' lusts – homosexuality, and paedophilia at
that. The comic edge to the scene (Ganymede complains that
Jupiter's love does not prevent him getting his ears boxed by
Juno) heightens its deliberate decadence. The 'female wanton
boy'[31] involves the entire tradition of stage wantonness at the very
outset of the play.

In *Edward II*, Marlowe's treatment of Edward's 'unnatural'
passion for his male courtier Gaveston takes particular advantage of the latent sexual deviancy which the anti-stage polemicists associate with the theatre as a whole. Gaveston's 'wooing' of
Edward is represented as performance – as 'play-acting' which
panders (as Rainoldes would have it) to perverted sexual tastes:

> I must have wanton poets, pleasant wits.
> Musicians, that with touching of a string
> May draw the pliant King which way I please;
> Music and poetry is his delight:
> Therefore I'll have Italian masques by night,
> Sweet speeches, comedies, and pleasing shows;
> And in the day, when he shall walk abroad,
> Like sylvan nymphs my pages shall be clad;
> My men like satyrs grazing on the lawns

Shall with their goat-feet dance an antic hay;
Sometime a lovely boy in Dian's shape,
With hair that gilds the water as it glides,
Crownets of pearl about his naked arms,
And in his sportful hands an olive tree
To hide those parts which men delight to see,
Shall bathe him in a spring; and there hard by,
One like Actaeon peeping through the grove,
Shall by the angry goddess be transform'd,
And running in the likeness of an hart,
By yelping hounds pull'd down, and seem to die.
Such things as these best please his majesty.[32]

At the centre of this tableau, the 'lovely boy' dressed as Diana
bathes near-naked in a spring, his olive tree ambiguously shield-
ing 'those parts which men delight to see'. Stage eroticism infuses
the audience's first encounter with the male object of Edward's
uncontrollable passion.

Because the 'wanton female boy' is the open focus of attention
in this play, Marlowe is also able to exploit the stage irony that
Edward's 'natural' love – his queen Isabella – is also, in the event,
a boy. I said that the eroticism of the boy player is invoked in the
drama whenever it is openly alluded to: on the whole this means
in comedy, where role-playing and disguise is part of the genre.[33]
In tragedy, the willing suspension of disbelief does customarily
extend, I think, to the taking of the female parts by boy players;
taken for granted, it is not alluded to. But in *Edward II* attention
is drawn systematically to sexual dalliance, in terms which are
precisely symmetrical for Edward/Gaveston and Edward/
Isabella:

Mortimer Madam, whither walks your majesty so fast?
Isabella   Unto the forest, gentle Mortimer,
            To live in grief and baleful discontent;
            For now my lord the King regards me not,
            But dotes upon the love of Gaveston.
            He claps his cheeks and hangs about his neck,
            Smiles in his face, and whispers in his ears;
            And when I come, he frowns, as who should say,
            'Go whither thou wilt, seeing I have Gaveston.'[34]

Edward   I'll hang a golden tongue about thy neck,
            Seeing thou hast pleaded with so good success.
Isabella   No other jewel hang about my neck
            Than these, my lord, nor let me have more wealth,

> Than I may fetch from this rich treasury. [Kisses him]
> O how a kiss revives poor Isabel.[35]

The stage signs of lascivious passion are 'hanging on the neck', 'kissing on the lips' and 'what you will' in that order. Marlowe puns on this sexual progress in *Doctor Faustus* when he has Pride announce to Faustus:

> I can creep into every corner of a wench: sometimes like a periwig, I sit upon her brow; next, like a necklace, I hang about her neck; then, like a fan of feather, I kiss her lips; and then, turning myself to a wrought smock, do what I list. But fie, what a smell is here![36]

Isabella hanging on Edward's neck, and then kissing him is as sexually tainted as Gaveston. And when Edward rebuffs her crudely with: 'Fawn not on me, French strumpet',[37] her innocent reply ('On whom but on my husband should I fawn?') cannot retrieve her stage innocence. She is 'French strumpet' not merely if she is 'too familiar' with Mortimer, but by virtue of her dubious stage role. Is she Queen, or 'quean' (prostitute)? The answer depends on whether or not we can ignore the fact that 'she' is a boy player, and I think that Marlowe sees to it that we cannot do so.

I am arguing that in the drama the dependent role of the boy player doubles for the dependency which is woman's lot, creating a sensuality which is independent of the sex of the desired figure, and which is particularly erotic where the sex is confused (when boy player represents woman, disguised as dependent boy). It is instructive in this context to turn our attention to the sixteenth-century romance narratives (many of which provide plots for the drama), which also contain the *topos* of the disguised woman, this time without the boy player complication. I referred above to Thomas Lodge's *Rosalynde*, a source for *As You Like It*; one might also pick out Barnaby Riche's tale 'Of Apolonius and Silla', which is a source for *Twelfth Night*, or 'Frederycke of Jennen', source for *Cymbeline*. In each of these tales a virtuous woman adopts male disguise (the disguise of a page or serving lad) out of loyalty to lover or husband, to escape an unlooked for sexual affront at home. Rosalind is banished in case she is preferred as partner by some man above her adoptive station; Silla escapes rape whilst following her lover into battle, and thereafter adopts male dress; 'Frederycke' adopts male dress to escape her husband's assassins, when she is falsely accused of adultery. The loyal woman preserves her 'chaste' self by transposing female dependency into male dependency: page instead of wife or daughter. In this guise she manages to retain her attractive submissiveness, whilst engaging in fantasy 'adventures' which culminate in her triumphantly revealing her true self (and sex) to the beloved, and being reinstated as loving spouse. The shape of these stories is strikingly like that of the cross-dressed female saints of *The Golden Legend* (the mainstay of Christian mythology), who avoid assault on their virginity or reputation, by becoming male monks, reconciled at death as heroic (yet passive) embodiments of female virtue.[38]

One of the digressionary stories in Robert Greene's *Penelope's Web* (1587) provides a fine example of the genre. Greene's work is a narrative treatise on the benefits for women of the three great gifts of obedience, chastity and silence. In the course of it the story is told of the supremely virtuous Cratyna, who disguises herself as a boy worker to avoid the amatory advances of her husband's landlord, and to follow her destitute husband (ruined by the jealous landlord) to work in the mines:

> Cratyna . . . stole secretly from the Pallace, and fled into the Countrey, where in the day tyme hyding her amongst bushes, and in the night trauelling as fast as she could, at last she came to the place where her husband was with the Collyar: & there chaunging her apparell into the attyre of a man, and her head brauely shorne, she became a handsome stripling. The next day coming to the Cole pits she demaunded seruice. The maister Collyar seeing the youth well faced, had pittie of his want, and intertayned him. . . . *Lestio* [the husband] pittying the poore estate of such a young youth, noting narrowly the lyniaments of her face, fell into sighes, and from sighes to teares, for the remembrance of his sweete *Cratyna*.[39]

The husbands and lovers of romance habitually fail to recognise their wives/lovers in such disguise, whilst nevertheless falling to amatory sighs at the memory the youth arouses in them. The *possibility* of associating fond emotion with the boy page derives from the same set of associations which Rainoldes considers to stimulate illicit sexual feeling at the sight of the boy player: the combination of effeminacy, dependence and desirability stirs the affections. In Lestio's case, Cratyna makes herself known to her husband immediately; in tales like 'Frederycke of Jennen' and 'Apolonius and Silla', the disguise is preserved over considerable periods, during which the wife/lover proves herself the faithful and valorous servant before ultimately revealing her true identity and being received back as true spouse. (In Silla's case, she is falsely accused of causing a pregnancy – a fate which befalls a number of female saints in male disguise in *The Golden Legend*[40] – but here her valorousness is displayed in her steadfast behaviour faced with such imputed infamy.)

We are not, I think, to be lured into imagining that such 'romance' cross-dressing matched any contemporary reality. We are in the vein of the 'female hero' of the folk-tale and the saint's life: the sub-erotic female figure whose chastity is strongly figured in the combination of faithful page and resolute/obedient/loyal/ serving daughter or spouse. These are the realms of talismanic female virtue of the kind enshrined in traditional tales like 'Mizilca':

> Time went on, and though Mizilca continued to excel at all knightly pursuits, the Sultan was still not satisfied that she was a man. He went again to the wise woman, and she advised him to have his cook prepare kasha for dinner, and mix a spoonful of pearls into Mizilca's portion. 'If the knight is a maiden,' said she, 'she will pick out the pearls and save them.'
>
> And so it was done. But again Mizilca was too clever for the Sultan. She took the pearls out of the kasha and cast them under the table as if they had been pebbles.
>
> At last the year and a day had passed, and it was time for Mizilca to return home. The Sultan came out to bid her farewell, and said to her, 'Mizilca, you have served me well, and paid the debt your father owed. Before you go, answer me one question. Are you a youth or a maiden?' Mizilca did not answer him, but mounted her horse and rode out through the palace gate. Then she turned and opened wide her shirt so that all could see she was a woman.[41]

In just such a fantasy vein, Silla reveals her true identity to counter the accusation of having caused Iulina's pregnancy:

> And here with all loosing his garmentes doune to his stomacke, and shewed *Iulina* his breastes and pretie teates, surmountyng farre the whiteness of Snowe it self, saiyng: Loe Madame, behold here the partie whom you haue chalenged to bee the father of your childe, see I am a woman the daughter of a noble Duke who, onely for the loue of him, whom you so lightly haue shaken of, haue forsaken my father, abandoned my Countreie, and in maner as you see am become a seruing man, satisfiyng my self, but with the onely sight of my *Apolonius*, and now Madame, if my passion were not vehement, & my tormentes without comparison, I would wish that my fained greefes might be laughed to scorne, & my desembled paines to be rewarded with floutes.[42]

'Effeminacy' and dependence create a composite boy/woman romance figure who is provocatively sensual. In his verse epistle, 'On his Mistris', John Donne fantasises his mistress's transvestism as a sign of love and loyalty in a fashion which strongly suggests his awareness of the erotic edge to the romantic fiction:

> Thou shalt not love by meanes so dangerous.
> Temper, oh faire Love, loves impetuous rage,
> Be my true mistris still, not my feign'd page. . . .
> Fall ill or good, 'tis madness to have prov'd
> Dangers unurg'd; Feede on this flatterye,
> That absent lovers one in th'other bee.
> Dissemble nothing, not a boy, nor change
> Thy bodies habit, nor mindes; bee not strange
> To thy self onely; All will spye in thy face
> A blushing womanly discovering grace.[43]

'Dissembling', 'strangeness', 'change', are the sensual qualities of the 'feign'd page' whose demeanour inevitably reveals 'a blushing womanly discovering grace'. And to underscore the sexuality implicit in the suggestion – the *suggestiveness* of the proposal to cross-dress – he continues that, in any case, her male disguise would further threaten, not protect, her chastity:

> Men of France, changeable Camelions,
> Spittles of diseases, shops of fashions,
> Loves fuellers, and the rightest companie
> Of Players which upon the worlds stage bee,
> Will quickly knowe thee, 'and knowe thee; and alas
> Th' indifferent Italian, as wee passe
> His warm land, well content to thinke thee page,
> Will haunt thee, with such lust and hideous rage
> As Lots faire guests were vext.[44]

Frenchmen, whose court fashions reflect the decadence of theatre in costume which suggests cross-dressing,[45] will 'know her' as female, and seduce her – 'know her'. Italians, whose taste is in any case for young men (with the customary coy allusion to Biblical sodomy), will seduce her as an alluring boy. This poem was considered scandalous, and omitted from the 1633 edition of Donne's poems, appearing in 1635 under the title 'On his Mistress desire to be disguised and goe like a Page with him'. The woman's desire so to disguise herself is, of course, fictional and of its nature unfulfilled (as the delight of the girl reader of folk-tales of such disguise goes along with as yet submerged knowledge that she certainly never will be allowed such freedoms).[46] The man's enjoyment of such proposed demonstrations of devotion which sets the tone of the poem has the affirmative ring of patriarchal authority.

It is, I think, the association of the romance/saints' lives tradition of female virtue preserved through male dress with the current convention of theatre which allows Donne so clearly to articulate this explicitly titillating fantasy. Donne does, in fact, allude to the stage directly – 'the rightest companie / Of Players which upon the worlds stage bee'. The folk-tale, androgynously virtuous heroine – heroine turned female hero – becomes entangled with imputed *male* homosexuality (to which Donne also alludes directly). In *Arcadia*, Sir Philip Sidney exploits the same web of romantic / erotic possibilities linking traditional narrative with stage convention in his description of the 'amazon' Cleophila. Sidney's seventeen-year-old boy hero, Pyrocles, disguises himself as a warrior girl to pursue his (female) lover:

> His heyre, wch the younge men of *Greece* ware very longe, (accoumpting them moste beutyfull, that had· yt in fayrest quantity) lay uppon the uppermoste parte of his foreheade in Lockes, some curled, and some, as yt were forgotten: with suche a Careles care and wth suche an arte so hyding arte, that hee seemed hee would lay them for a Patern whether nature simply or nature helped by cunning bee the more excellent, the Rest wherof was drawne into a Coronet of golde wyers, and covered with fethers of dyvers Coloures, that yt was not unlike to a hellmett, suche a glittering shewe yt bare, and so bravely yt was helde up from the heade. Uppon his body hee ware a kynde of Dublett of skye coloured Satyn, so plated over with plates of Massy golde, that hee seemed armed in yt: His sleeves of the same in steade of plates, was covered wth purled Laçe, and suche was the nether parte of his garment, but that made so full of stuffe, and cutt after suche a fashyon, ye thoughe the lengthe fell under his anckles, yet in his goyng one mighte well perceyve the smalle of his Legg, wch with the foote, was covered wth a little short payre of Crimson vellvet buskyns, in some places open, as the auncyent maner was, to shew ye fayrenes of his skynn.[47]

The passage compounds the 'stage transvestism' polemic theme yet further, because the 'woman' Pyrocles disguises himself as is herself in *male* dress (the dress of the female warrior). Rainoldes drew particular attention (in the passage quoted earlier) to Juvenal's 'what modesty can you expect in a woman who wears a helmet' (*Satires* VI.252): Cleophila wears 'wanton' warrior's dress, whilst Pyrocles impudently shows the 'smalle of his Legg', and the 'fayrenes of his skynn' through his short boots, as provocative boy/girl. The description is, I think, deliberately evocative of the complex seductive themes of cross-dressing and undress batted to and fro in the stage pamphlets. Even Pyrocles' best friend and fellow prince, Musidorus, who helps him don his 'disguise' admits to being seduced by it:

> Well, (saide hee) sweete Cossen, since yow are framed of suche a Loving mettell, I pray yo* take heede of looking youre self in a glasse, leste *Narcissus* fortune falle unto yo*. For my parte, I promyse yo*, yf I were not fully resolved, never to submitt my hart to those fancyes, I were like ynoughe, while I dressed yow, to become a young *Pigmalion*.[48]

If we turn now to the female figures in Shakespeare's comedies, traditionally portrayed as healthily asexual heroines in Royal Shakespeare Company productions, we find them, I believe, strongly recalling the cross-dressing themes to which I have drawn attention. My contention is that these figures are sexually enticing *qua* transvestied boys, and that the plays encourage the audience to view them as such. The audience is invited to remark the 'pretty folly', the blush, the downcast shameful glance of the boy player whose 'woman's part' requires that he portray female qualities, but in *male* dress. The flavour of this 'unhealthy' interest is to be found in the stylised scene in *The Merchant of Venice* in which Jessica elopes with her lover Lorenzo:

> Jessica   I am glad 'tis night, you do not look on me,
> For I am much asham'd of my exchange;
> But love is blind, and lovers cannot see
> The pretty follies that themselves commit,
> For, if they could, Cupid himself would blush
> To see me thus transformed to a boy.
> Lorenzo   Descend, for you must be my torchbearer.
> Jessica   What! must I hold a candle to my shames?
> They in themselves, good sooth, are too too light.
> Why, 'tis an office of discovery, love,
> And I should be obscur'd.
> Lorenzo   So are you, sweet,
> Even in the lovely garnish of a boy.[49]

As it is also when the noble Portia herself describes how she will appear when she dons male dress to follow her husband secretly on his journey:

> Portia   When we are both accoutred like young men,
> I'll prove the prettier fellow of the two,

> And wear my dagger with the braver grace,
> And speak between the change of man and boy
> With a reed voice; and turn two mincing steps
> Into a manly stride; and speak of frays
> Like a fine bragging youth; and tell quaint lies,
> How honourable ladies sought my love,
> Which I denying, they fell sick and died –
> I could not do withal. Then I'll repent,
> And wish, for all that, that I had not kill'd them.
> And twenty of these puny lies I'll tell,
> That men shall swear I have discontinued school
> Above a twelvemonth.[50]

Are the 'mincing steps' Portia will turn into 'a manly stride' the
ambiguous stage manners of a 'womanish boy'?[51] When she
brags how she 'could not do withal', when ladies passionately
loved her, does she brag in her male persona, for which the ladies
fell (she had no inclination to take them up on their passion, or,
even, there were too many to cope with)? Or does she play on her
hidden female sex – she had no means of consummating such a
relationship?[52] Is Jessica coy because dressed as a boy her love for
Lorenzo is titillating (serving torchbearer, boy-lover), or because
she blushes to show her legs in breeches? In other words, the
double entendres of these speeches by blushing heroines (played
by boys) as they adopt male dress to follow their male lover are
both compatible with the heterosexual plot, and evocative of the
bisexual image of the 'wanton female boy'. When Julia, in *The
Two Gentlemen of Verona* prepares to adopt her male disguise,
she alludes directly to 'effeminacy' of boy's dress, and its seductive allure:

Lucetta	But in what habit will you go along?
Julia	Not like a woman, for I would prevent
	The loose encounters of lascivious men;
	Gentle Lucetta, fit me with such weeds
	As may beseem some well-reputed page.
Lucetta	Why then, your ladyship must cut your hair.
Julia	No girl; I'll knit it up in silken strings
	With twenty odd-conceited true-love knots –
	To be fantastic may become a youth
	Of greater time than I shall show to be.
Lucetta	What fashion, madam, shall I make your breeches?
Julia	That fits as well as 'Tell me, good my lord,
	What compass will you wear your farthingale'.
	Why ev'n what fashion thou best likes, Lucetta.

Lucetta   You must needs have them with a codpiece, madam.
Julia   Out, out, Lucetta, that will be ill-favour'd.
Lucetta   A round hose, madam, now's not worth a pin,
            Unless you have a codpiece to stick pins on.[53]

If Julia were really concerned to appear as a 'well-reputed page' to avoid the 'loose encounters of lascivious men', she would not purpose to adopt a hair-style 'knit up in silken strings / With twenty odd-conceited true-love knots': a style inveighed against as decadent and immoral by stage polemicists and dress reformers. Nor would she and Lucetta launch into a discussion of comparative breeches fashion which focuses on ornamental covering for the genitals – another favourite target for the moral indignation of contemporary pamphleteers.[54]

At the focus of attention in all these passages is the alluring 'beardless boy'. It does not matter that the coy seductiveness of the boy player is for plot purposes being appreciated by a woman (as in Viola's 'Make me a willow cabin at your gate' speech before Olivia in *Twelfth Night*,[55] or in Venus's uncontrolledly lascivious pursuit of Adonis in *Venus and Adonis*). 'Playing the woman's part' – male effeminacy – is an act for a male audience's appreciation. When the noble ladies of the drama dress their pages in women's dress in an idle moment, they draw attention to his availability as an object of *male* erotic attention:

Boy   It will get . . . me a perfect deale of ill will at the mansion you wot
            of, whose ladie is the argument of it: where now I am the
            welcom'st thing vnder a man that comes there.
Clerimont I thinke, and aboue a man too, if the truth were rack'd out of
            you.
Boy   No faith, I'll confesse before, sir. The gentlewomen play with
            me, and throw me o' the bed; and carry me in to my lady; and
            shee kisses me with her oil'd face; and puts a perruke o' my head;
            and askes me an' I will weare her gowne; and I say, no: and then
            she hits me a blow o' the eare, and calls me innocent, and lets me
            goe.[56]

The page confirms the lewd innuendo of his being 'the welcom'st thing vnder a man', even as he protests that he doesn't play sexual games with his mistress and her gentlewomen.

I think this must influence our reading of the dramatically powerful scenes in the drama in which cross-dressed girls appear (boy/girl/boy). At the height of the action in *The Two Gentlemen of Verona*, for instance, Julia, disguised as a boy, described her abandoned mistress (that is, in fact, Julia herself) to Silvia, now ardently pursued by Julia's fickle ex-lover:

Julia   I thank you, madam, that you tender her.
           Poor gentlewoman, my master wrongs her much.
Silvia   Dost thou know her?
Julia   Almost as well as I do know myself.
           To think upon her woes, I do protest
           That I have wept a hundred several times. . . .
Silvia   Is she not passing fair?
Julia   She hath been fairer, madam, than she is. . . .
Silvia   How tall was she?
Julia   About my stature; for at Pentecost,
           When all our pageants of delight were play'd,
           Our youth got me to play the woman's part,
           And I was trimm'd in Madam Julia's gown;
           Which served me as fit, by all men's judgments,
           As if the garment had been made for me;
           Therefore I know she is about my height.
           And at that time I made her weep agood,
           For I did play a lamentable part.
           Madam, 'twas Ariadne passioning
           For Theseus' perjury and unjust flight;
           Which I so lively acted with my tears
           That my poor mistress, moved therewithal,
           Wept bitterly; and would I might be dead
           If I in thought felt not her very sorrow.
Silvia   She is beholding to thee, gentle youth.
           Alas, poor lady, desolate and left!
           I weep myself, to think upon thy words.[57]

A recent critic has drawn particular attention to this scene in which 'Julia disguised as a page, invents for her rival . . . a story that describes her apparent male self playing "the woman's part" in the clothes of her real female self':[58]

> The layers insulating this story from reality enable [Julia] to reveal herself through her disguise, to express her deep grief at being abandoned, and to engender a sympathetic response from her onstage and offstage audience. . . . Julia, by playing male and female, actor and audience, herself and not herself, shares with Silvia grief at male betrayal and female abandonment.[59]

Everything that I have been saying suggests that we should be extremely wary of such a reading, which imputes peculiarly female insight to Julia, or to Silvia via Julia's masquerade. Julia is indeed, at this point in the play, 'herself and not herself'; but the play in this scene is largely on her *maleness*, as a means of projecting strong and theatrical feelings for the benefit of her 'onstage and offstage audience'. Silvia's exclamation of deep sympathy – 'Alas, poor lady, desolate and left!' – refers in the first instance to Ariadne's story, which stimulates and enhances a sense of 'grief' in general (as Lucrece's perusal of the tapestry of the weeping Hecuba underscores and generalises her despair in *The Rape of Lucrece*).[60] Both Julia then (supposedly) and Silvia now weep at the *proverbially* lamentable tale of Ariadne on Naxos. This is theatrical representation – not 'real' (female) feeling, as Hamlet is all too aware when he weeps at the player's 'lamentable' rendering of Aeneas' set speech recounting Hecuba's grief at the death of Priam, in *Hamlet*.[61]

Hamlet's reaction ('What's Hecuba to him or he to Hecuba, / That he should weep for her?') is that it is ironic that a mere player can weep real tears 'but in a fiction, in a dream of passion' (tears which in their turn stimulate Hamlet's own). Real grief is harder to face up to, to understand, to feel. So Julia, Silvia and their audience react with strong feelings of grief to a representation of pathos *with which they have nothing to do*. It is intrinsically 'pathetic', engendering pathos, stimulating grief. 'I weep myself to think upon thy words', says Silvia. The weeping is not *qua* woman, but *qua* audience, responding to a culturally familiar emblem of abandonment. The 'layers insulating this story from reality' reveal nothing about 'real' womanly feelings: on the contrary, they code 'admirable grief' in the stereotype representation of the 'weeping woman strong in suffering'.[62] The boy player armed with his arsenal of female characteristics and mannerisms mimes out the acceptable form of heroic womanhood prostrate with grief. The player's and 'Sebastian's' (alias Julia's) and Silvia's emotion is *womanish* because uncontrolled by 'manly' restraint.

Notes

1 J. Kott, 'Shakespeare's bitter Arcadia', in *Shakespeare Our Contemporary* (London, 1965, 1972 edn), pp. 191–236, does point to the importance of cross-dressing in the comedies, but not in a way which I find very useful. For an attempt to make more constructive critical use of the girl/boy disguise, see N. K. Hayles, 'Sexual disguise in "As You Like It" and "Twelfth Night"', *Shakespeare Survey*, 32 (1979), pp. 63–72. On acting

conventions in general in the period, see most recently A. Gurr, *The Shakespearean Stage 1574–1642* (Cambridge, 1980).

2   J. Rainoldes, *Th' Overthrow of Stage-Playes* (Middleburgh, 1599), p. 97. On the anti-stage polemic, especially its use of cross-dressing as a basic ground for attack, see K. Young, 'An Elizabethan defence of the stage', *Shakespeare Studies by Members of the Department of English of the University of Wisconsin* (Madison, 1916), pp. 103–24, and 'William Gager's defence of the academic stage', *Transactions of the Wisconsin Academy of Sciences, Arts and Letters* XVIII (1916), pp. 593–638; J. W. Binns, 'Women or transvestites on the Elizabethan stage? An Oxford controversy', *The Sixteenth-Century Journal*, V (1974), pp. 95–120; A. F. Kinney, *Markets of Bawdrie: The Dramatic Criticism of Stephen Gosson* (Salzburg, 1974).

3   Rainoldes, *op. cit.*, p. 97.

4   BL, Add. MS 11811, in H. Gardner (ed.), *The Metaphysical Poets* (Penguin, 1957). My thanks are due to Dr J. C. Barrell of King's College, Cambridge, who first drew my attention to this poem.

5   G. E. Bentley, *The Jacobean and Caroline Stage*, 7 vols (Oxford, 1941–68), I, 39.

6   Scolar Press Facsimile, 1969, p. 115.

7   See below, p. 148.

8   W. C. Hazlitt (ed.), *Poetical and Dramatic Works of Thomas Randolph*, 2 vols (London, 1875), II.540.

9   *Cymbeline* II.v.1–22.

10   ibid., II.v.22–8. Compare *As You Like It* III.ii.374–88.

11   C. R. S. Lenz, G. Greene and C. T. Neely (eds), *The Woman's Part: Feminist Criticism of Shakespeare* (Urbana, Chicago and London, 1981), Introduction, p. 14.

12   *Much Ado About Nothing* IV.i.58–60.

13   Letter from John Rainoldes to Thomas Thornton, 6 February 1592, in K. Young, 'An Elizabethan defence of the stage', note 13; on the detail of the controversy see J. W. Binns, *op. cit.*

14   Rainoldes, *op. cit.*, pp. 10–11.

15   See Binns, *op. cit.*, p. 102.

16   Loeb translation by H. E. Butler.

17   Aristotle, *Politics* II.ix.6. Loeb translation by H. Rackham.

18   Rainoldes, *op. cit.*, pp. 17–18.

19   See J. Duval, *Traité des Hermaphrodits, parties génitales, accouchemens des femmes et traitement qui est requis pour les relever en santé* (Rouen, 1612; reprint Paris, 1880).

20   Arthur Golding, *The XV Bookes of P. Ovidius Naso, entytuled Metamorphosis, translated out of Latin into English meeter* (1567), iv.426–60, in F. T. Prince (ed.), *The Poems of Shakespeare* (Arden, 1960), pp. 187–8.

21   M. Delcourt, *Hermaphroditea: recherches sur l'être double promoteur de la fertilité dans le monde classique* (Brussels, 1966), pp. 65–6 (my translation).

22   *Venus and Adonis* ll. 31–6.

23   Alanus de Insulis, *De planctu naturae*, Patrologia Latina 210, col. 431,

met. 1, transl. D. M. Moffat, *The Complaint of Alain de Lille* (New York, 1908), p. 3, in G. R. Crampton, *The Condition of Creatures* (New Haven and London, 1974), pp. 12–13.

24 *As You Like It* III.ii.374–81.

25 E. W. Gosse (ed.), *The Complete Works of Thomas Lodge*, 4 vols (New York, 1883; reissued New York, 1963), I,15.

26 *As You Like It*, Epilogue. On Lodge's source and *As You Like It*, see E. I. Berry, 'Rosalynde and Rosalind', *Shakespeare Quarterly*, 31 (1980), pp. 42–52.

27 R. Warwick Bond (ed.), *The Complete Works of John Lyly*, 3 vols (Oxford, 1902; reissued Oxford, 1967), II,419.

28 *Gallathea* I.i.59–91, ibid., II.433–4.

29 In P. H. Kocher, *Christopher Marlowe: A Study of his Thought, Learning and Character* (Chapel Hill, 1946), pp. 34–5.

30 I.i.1–45; H. J. Oliver (ed.), *Dido Queen of Carthage and The Massacre at Paris* (Revels, 1968).

31 I.i.51. Shakespeare uses male homosexual love to contribute to an atmosphere of distorted sexuality in *Troilus and Cressida*.

32 R. Gill (ed.), *The Plays of Christopher Marlowe* (Oxford, 1971), I.i.50–70.

33 See C. L. Barber, *Shakespeare's Festive Comedy: A Study of Dramatic Form and its Relation to Social Custom* (Princeton, 1959).

34 I.ii.46–54.

35 I.iv.327–32.

36 J. D. Jump (ed.), *Doctor Faustus* (Revels, 1962; 1973 edn), sc. VI, ll. 116–21.

37 I.iv.145.

38 See below, p. 187.

39 A. B. Grosart (ed.), *The Life and Complete Works in Prose and Verse of Robert Greene, MA*, 15 vols (New York, 1964 reissue), V,213–14.

40 See below, p. 187.

41 Retold by A. Lurie, *Clever Gretchen and other Forgotten Folktales* (London, 1980), p. 28. See also the title story in M. Hong Kingston, *The Woman Warrior: Memoirs of a Girlhood among Ghosts* (1975; London, 1977), a traditional Chinese tale about a girl trained as an outstanding (male) warrior. Hong Kingston makes it the theme of her novel that there is *no* match whatsoever between real Chinese attitudes towards girl children and the female heroism of the woman warrior. Both tales share the theme of service as vassal to a lord, which cannot be done by a daughter.

42 In J. M. Lothian and T. W. Craik (eds), *Twelfth Night* (Arden, 1975), p. 177.

43 H. Gardner (ed.), *The Elegies and The Songs and Sonnets* (Oxford, 1965), pp. 23–4.

44 *ibid.*, ll. 33–41.

45 See below, p. 155.

46 See Hong Kingston, *op. cit.*, p. 26: 'I had forgotten this chant that was once mine, given me by my mother, who may not have known its power to

remind. She said I would grow up a wife and slave, but she taught me the song of the warrior woman, Fa Mu Lan.'

47 A. Feuillerat (ed.), *The Prose Works of Sir Philip Sidney* (Cambridge, 1912; reprinted 1970), IV,23. In this reworking of the passage in the original *Old Arcadia* Sidney makes more explicitly provocative the details of 'her' dress (I,75–6).

48 ibid., IV,24.

49 *The Merchant of Venice* II.vi. 34–45.

50 III.v.63–76.

51 For explicit reference to the 'reed voice' of the boy player, see *Hamlet* II.ii.416.

52 'Withal' has just this ambiguity in the period: it has the sense both of 'therewith' and 'moreover', 'in addition': 'I couldn't do anything with it' (I couldn't perform), and 'I couldn't cope with it'.

53 *The Two Gentlemen of Verona* II.vii. 39–56.

54 See below, p. 148.

55 I.v.250.

56 Ben Jonson, *Epicoene, or The Silent Woman*, I.i.6–18, in C. H. Herford and P. Simpson (eds), *Works* (Oxford, 1937), V,165.

57 IV.iv.136–71.

58 Lenz, Greene and Neely, *The Woman's Part*, p. 13.

59 ibid.

60 See below, p. 192.

61 *Hamlet* II.ii.513.

62 See below, p. 181.

'She openeth her mouth with wisdom': The Double Bind of Renaissance Education and Reformed Religion

In the opening scene of Thomas Heywood's *A Woman Killed with Kindness* (1602), the Lady Anne is introduced in meticulous detail as embodying three key attributes for the virtuous woman: Christian modesty, intelligence with education, and partnership within her (extremely recent) marriage:

Sir Charles Mountford   Master Frankford,
You are a happy man, sir; and much joy
Succeed your marriage mirth, you have a wife
So qualify'd and with such ornaments
Both of the mind and body. First, her birth
Is noble, and her education such
As might become the daughter of a prince.
Her own tongue speaks all tongues, and her own hand
Can teach all strings to speak in their best grace,
From the shrill treble, to the hoarsest bass.
. . .

Sir Francis Acton A perfect wife already, meek and patient.
How strangely the word 'husband' fits your mouth,
Not marry'd three hours since, sister. 'Tis good;
You that begin betimes thus, must needs prove
Pliant and duteous in your husband's love.
Godamercies, brother, wrought her to it already?
'Sweet husband', and a curtsey the first day.
. . .

Sir Charles This lady is no clog, as many are;
She doth become you like a well-made suit
In which the tailor hath us'd all his art,
Not like a thick coat of unseason'd frieze,
Forc'd on your back in summer; she's no chain
To tie your neck and curb you to the yoke,
But she's a chain of gold to adorn your neck.
You both adorn each other, and your hands
Methinks are matches. There's equality

> In this fair combination; you are both scholars,
> Both young, both being descended nobly.
> There's music in this sympathy, it carries
> Consort and expectation of much joy.[1]

Anne Frankford is 'pliant and duteous in [her] husband's love', she is educated 'as might become the daughter of a prince', fluent in languages, gifted in music, and she is her husband's equal partner, 'both scholars, both young, both being descended nobly'. What more could Frankford ask for? For these, as we have been told fairly regularly recently, are precisely the gifts which the Renaissance offered women for the first time, and which gave women a freedom and a voice they had hitherto never had.[2]

But Anne Frankford is *not* a virtuous wife. Or rather, before she dies virtuously, chastened and grief-stricken, at the end of the play, she betrays her husband in a gratuitously sensual relationship with his friend and guest, Wendoll. She becomes 'a shame' for womanhood, 'though once an ornament' (sc. xiii), whose baser nature in spite of initial reluctance overwhelms the veneer of fashionable aptitudes for which she was earlier prized. True womanhood (the base kind) will out.

True womanhood is mastered not in 'equality' and 'fair combination', the resolution of the play seems to suggest, but by letting her know who's boss. Having discovered her shameful behaviour, Frankford behaves as benevolent despot: he does not kill her on the spot, nor even denounce her openly; instead he denies her access to himself and to her children, and banishes her to a dower house on his estate (widow before her time). There she dies of grief and starvation (having vowed never to eat again as a penance), reunited, moments before her death, with her magnanimous and benevolent husband.

In the present chapter I want to look at the triad of 'liberating' possibilities for women: Protestantism, humanist education, marital partnership. And I draw the reader's attention to Heywood's version because I think it conveys rather elegantly the 'double bind' that these involve. As long as woman uses her natural intelligence to set off the man's abilities with her own grasp on religion, learning, household management, she is his supreme ornament, 'a chain of gold to adorn [his] neck'. But the minute she shows signs of independence (inevitably represented on stage as adultery and sexual rapaciousness) those gifts become responsible for her downfall: they masked her 'normal' baseness, they provided the means of her acting of her own free will. Because this is the case, we shall always, I suggest, find two distinct types of source material when as historians we try to research topics associated with the 'emancipation' of women. On the one hand we are likely to find generous and confident extension of opportunities for education (secular and religious) and for partnership (outside and inside the home) from those who take it for granted that the women they address themselves to will observe due moderation in their pursuit of these goals. Authors like Erasmus and Vives, who have in mind a readership of leisured and prosperous noblewomen, are delighted to suggest that the daughters of the nobility should share the new cultural treasures first extended to their brothers. But on the other hand, those who already feel the oppressive presence of a 'new order', 'the world turned upside down' – the moralist and social satirist – are almost inevitably going to seize on unfamiliar opportunities for women as yet another example of the misguided attitudes of the times. For authors like Stubbes and Knox, zealously religious women, and stridently opinionated women svmbolise the negative outcome of too much indulgence of the weaker sex, which in turn confirms a general breakdown of 'law and order'.

If we confine our attention to texts of the former kind we shall arrive at the conclusion that the early modern period was indeed a 'paradise for women'. If we confine our attention to texts of the latter kind we shall conclude that women were more oppressed during this period than at any time before or since. Neither view is accurate, although each has its firm following amongst contemporary historians.[3] A more constructive approach, I suggest, depends on our facing up to the inevitable equivocations which attend even the most liberal patriarchal discussion of the appropriate place of women in religion, education and the home.

Suppose we start with the issue of equality or partnership within marriage. A number of clerics and moralists do stress the desirability of intelligent give-and-take between man and woman within marriage (like Sir Charles Mountford in *A Woman Killed with Kindness*). Such give-and-take, however, is premised on what is universally regarded (except in satirical pamphlets to which I shall return later) as a self-evident natural inferiority of the female of the species. The standard 'scientific' account of this inferiority in the period is still that which is found in Aristotle, the standard authority on natural scientific 'fact' throughout the seventeenth century:

> In all genera in which the distinction of male and female is found, Nature makes a similar differentiation in the mental characteristics of the sexes. This differentiation is the most obvious in the case of human kind and in that of the larger animals and viviparous quadrupeds. . . . The female is less spirited than the male, . . . softer in disposition, more mischievous, less simple, more impulsive, and more attentive to the nurture of the young. . . . Woman is more compassionate than man, more easily moved to tears, at the same time more jealous, more querulous, more apt to scold and strike. She is, further-more, more prone to despondency and less hopeful than the man, more void of shame or self-respect, more false of speech, more deceptive, and of more retentive memory. She is also more wakeful, more shrinking, more difficult to rouse to action, and requires a smaller quantity of nutriment.[4]

A compassionate and thoughtful approach to woman's place in marriage therefore incorporates some measured recognition of the woman's need to be guided by her husband, or in other words, a need for the willing submission of the wife to her husband's authority:

> Woman, insofar as she is a wife, is the glory of man, that is his glorious image, as I said above: because God formed woman, that is Eve, from man, and in man's likeness, so that she might represent man as a copy of him, and be as it were his image. But woman is not in the full sense of the word the image of man, if we talk of image in the sense of mind and intellect, by which woman like man is endowed with a rational soul, intellect, will, memory and freedom, and can acquire, just as a man, all wisdom, grace and glory. For woman is equal to man in possessing a rational soul, and both, that is woman and man, are made in the image of God. But she is the image of man in a restrictive and analogical sense; because woman was made from man, after man, inferior to him and in his likeness. It is for this reason that St Paul does not say explicitly 'woman is the image of man', but rather 'woman is the glory of man'; because without doubt, as Alfonso Salmeron rightly pointed out, woman is an excellent ornament of man since she is granted to man not only to help him to procreate children, and administer the family, but also in possession and, as it were, in dominion, over which man may exercise his jurisdiction and authority. For the authority of man extends not only to inanimate things and brute beasts, but also to reasonable creatures, that is, women and wives.[5]

As Christopher Hill writes, exonerating Milton from the charge of inveterate misogyny:

Posterity has remembered 'He for God only, she for God in him.' On the basis of this line, taken out of context, the poet has been blamed for failing to rise above his age in this one respect, despite all the others in which he did rise above it. Posterity has forgotten too that the line is only a poetical version of St Paul's 'wives submit yourselves unto your husbands as unto the Lord'; 'the husband is the head of the wife even as Christ is the head of the church.' Ephesians 5:22–3. Given Milton's assumptions, it is difficult to see how he could have rejected St Paul's clear and explicit statements. What Milton says about the subordination of women is strictly Biblical, backed up in the *De Doctrina Christiana* by an impressive array of texts.⁶

Biblical authority was the mainstay of reformed Christianity. The 'willingness' of the wife's acceptance in good part of submission, obedience and silence,⁷ is derived from texts like the Hebrew alphabet catalogue of wifely virtues in Proverbs 31.10–29, much cited in the Renaissance, but unfamiliar enough now to deserve quoting in full:

Who can find a virtuous woman? for her price is far above rubies.
The heart of her husband doth safely trust in her, so that he shall have no need of spoil.
She will do him good and not evil all the days of her life.
She seeketh wool, and flax, and worketh willingly with her hands.
She is like the merchants' ships; she bringeth her food from afar.
She riseth also while it is yet night, and giveth meat to her household, and a portion to her maidens.
She considereth a field, and buyeth it: with the fruit of her hands she planteth a vineyard.
She girdeth her loins with strength, and strengtheneth her arms.
She perceiveth that her merchandise is good: her candle goeth not out by night.
She layeth her hands to the spindle, and her hands hold the distaff.
She stretcheth out her hand to the poor; yea, she reacheth forth her hands to the needy.
She is not afraid of the snow for her household: for all her household are clothed with scarlet.
She maketh herself coverings of tapestry; her clothing is silk and purple.
Her husband is known in the gates, when he sitteth among the elders of the land.
She maketh fine linen, and selleth it; and delivereth girdles unto the merchant.
Strength and honour are her clothing; and she shall rejoice in time to come.
She openeth her mouth with wisdom; and in her tongue is the law of kindness.
She looketh well to the ways of her household, and eateth not the bread of idleness.

> Her children arise up, and call her blessed; her husband also, and he praiseth
> her.
> Many daughters have done virtuously, but thou excellest them all.[8]

Both the tone and the content make it clear that the household's harmony is to depend upon the gracious acceptance on the part of the wife of her serving role in the family: supporting staff without independent authority.

A number of recent feminist historians have advanced the view that humanitarian amelioration of the position of the wife within the traditional household brought about by the Reformation did give to women some freedom which they had not hitherto had:

> For Protestant women, marriage was the acceptable option [to entering a convent]. The married Protestant woman controlled her own destiny within the limits of her household, just as the nun might within the confines of her convent. What the Protestants had done was shift the status of the wife within the family. This becomes apparent in the writings of Puritan theologians, although we have already seen that marriage was dignified from the earliest days of Protestantism because of the new attitudes towards celibacy and sexuality the reformers expressed. Various Puritan theologians, already writing systematically on the subject of marriage during the reign of Elizabeth I, certainly viewed the wife as subordinate to the husband. The marriage relationship itself, however, was one of mutual aid, comfort, and sustaining companionship. Other treatises refer to the single essential division in the family as between the 'governors' (which includes husband and wife jointly) and 'those that must be ruled' (children and servants). English Protestant women in particular had a reputation for living with great freedom within marriage.[9]

It is, however, quite possible to read this new 'responsibility' of the Protestant wife within the marriage bond in a different way. As long as the wife was a passive object of a commercial transaction in marriage, the subsequent state of the household was in a strong sense none of her business. The wife performed a number of clearly allotted tasks (including reproduction), and would be better or worse off depending on whether she became the wife of a good- or ill-natured husband (assuming she performed her tasks satisfactorily). But the quality of the relationship lay only minimally within her control. The 'freedom of conscience' which the reformed Church gave the wife gave her the added burden of taking a share in the responsibility for how the marriage turned out. At the same time, her acknowledgedly subordinate role gave her no real means of controlling the state of affairs.[10] The absence of any actual means of altering her condition, however piously her entitlement to such alteration was affirmed, comes clearly through in modern authorities' accounts of Puritan emancipation like Dusinberre's influential one:

> If women were spiritually equal to men the questions about their subjection would have, at least, to be rephrased, and this is exactly what the Puritans set themselves to do in their sermons and domestic conduct books. If they arrived at traditional conclusions it was by way of new enquiries and new attitudes. . . . The Puritans did not repudiate the authority of the husband, but they qualified it. The picture of the uncompromising Puritan patriarch presiding over his family ignores the extent to which Puritans encouraged women to dispute his dominion. For the Puritans the only justification for a wife's submission was a diplomatic one that mutual comfort – to them the chief end of marriage – required it. For the latter-day female saint this is a highly dubious and dangerous philosophy, but the change of direction which it recorded in male thinking about women made other changes possible because it released women from the strait-jacket of theology. If the criterion of good was domestic harmony, the conditions for achieving it might admit of infinite variety. Adam's rights over an erring wife allowed no such flexibility.[11]

The 'ifs' and 'buts' in this account reveal quite clearly the double bind in which the author finds herself. Justifications for subjugation altered towards sophisticated mutual consent theories, but the actuality of the woman's role in the household remained, as far as one can discover, unchanged. Instead, it sounds suspiciously as if (in common with sophisticated moderates' views on such relationships in all periods) the Protestants maintained that moderation in marital relations made the task of authoritative control of wives simpler. The homilist in 'The homily on matrimony', introduced as compulsory reading in English churches by Elizabeth I's government in 1562,[12] has the following advice for husbands:

> The husband should be the leader and author of love, in cherishing and increasing concord: which then shall take place, if he will use moderation, and not tyranny, and if he yield something to the woman. For the woman is a weak creature not endued with like strength and constancy of mind; therefore they be the sooner disquieted, and they be the more prone to all weak affections and dispositions of the mind, more than men be; and lighter they be, and more vain in their phantasies and opinions.[13]

As for the remedies against unsatisfactory arrangements available to the wife: in 1619, William Whately published a tract on
marriage entitled *A Bride-Bush: or a direction for married
persons*, which advanced the view that marriage was automatically dissolved if either party wilfully deserted the other, or
committed adultery. As a result, the Court of High Commission
summoned Whately before it, and he solemnly recanted in later
editions, and included a full retraction of his original view in the
preface to his second tract on marriage, published in 1624, *A
Care-Cloth: or a* TREATISE *of the cumbers and troubles of
marriage*.[14] Since the original *Bride-Bush* consisted in very large
part in advice to women dutifully and obediently to perform a
large number of tasks so as to ameliorate family life, the retraction effectively withdrew her one means of redress if her
exemplary behaviour should none the less result in 'chidings,
brawlings, tauntings, repentings, bitter cursings, and fightings',
which the homilist maintained were characteristic of the majority
of marriages.[15]

Shakespeare's *The Comedy of Errors* (which Dusinberre takes
as central evidence in her section on 'Women and authority' to
show that women gained freedom within marriage during the
late-sixteenth and seventeenth centuries) wittily ironises the
consequences of the wife's maximised obligations and minimal
redress. Adriana is married to one of the Antipholus twins and is
unaware of the existence of the other, so that when (as a result of
series of 'errors') the two become involved in her domestic life,
she faces husbandly schizophrenia: one minute Antipholus is her
accustomed husband – cheating her and treating her shabbily –
the next he does not recognise her as his wife at all, and makes
passionate advances to her sister Luciana. All of this Adriana is
obliged to participate in as passive 'victim'. At no point does she
deliberately oppose her husband's behaviour (and on several
occasions she imputes it to her own shortcomings as a wife). And
when she *accidently* locks out her husband for the night (having
locked in the 'wrong' twin, and retired to her quarters to try in her
wifely capacity to revive his flagging interest in her) he feels
entitled to resort to the strongest measures against her. He
promptly retires to a house of ill-repute, bestows a costly present
intended for his wife on his whore, and ultimately threatens to
horsewhip Adriana. The audience's reaction to Adriana's prot-

estations at her ill-treatment can only, I think, be hilarity: it is all so appalling, so much like a travesty of ordinary domestic relations that the speeches become set pieces for a male audience's amusement:

> *Adriana*   Ay, ay, Antipholus, look strange and frown.
> Some other mistress hath they sweet aspects;
> I am not Adriana, nor thy wife,
> The time was once when thou unurg'd wouldst vow
> That never words were music to thine ear,
> That never object pleasing in thine eye,
> That never touch well welcome to thy hand,
> That never meat sweet-savour'd in thy taste,
> Unless I spake, or look'd, or touch'd, or carv'd to thee.
> How comes it now, my husband, O, how comes it,
> That thou art then estranged from thyself?
> Thyself I call it, being strange to me,
> That, undividable, incorporate,
> Am better than thy dear self's better part.
> Ah, do not tear away thyself from me;
> For know, my love, as easy mayst thou fall
> A drop of water in the breaking gulf,
> And take unmingled thence that drop again
> Without addition or diminishing,
> As take from me thyself, and not me too.[16]

Adriana's husband is in fact estranged from her; does, in fact, look more kindly on his mistress than on her; does tear himself from her. But the man to whom this speech is addressed is not in fact her husband. And what follows underscores the heavy irony that, because Adriana so dutifully pursues matrimonial accord in the face of all her 'husband's' negative efforts, she finds herself currently, unbeknownst to herself but to the amusement of the audience, hotly pursuing an adulterous relationship:

> *Adriana*   How dearly would it touch thee to the quick,
> Shouldst thou but hear I were licentious,
> And that this body, consecrate to thee,
> By ruffian lust should be contaminate!
> Wouldst thou not spit at me and spurn at me,
> And hurl the name of husband in my face,
> And tear the stain'd skin off my harlot-brow,
> And from my false hand cut the wedding-ring,
> And break it with a deep-divorcing vow?
> I know thou canst, and therefore see thou do it.
> I am possess'd with an adulterate blot;
> My blood is mingled with the crime of lust;

> For if we two be one, and thou play false,
> I do digest the poison of thy flesh,
> Being strumpeted by thy contagion.
> Keep then fair league and truce with thy true bed;
> I live dis-stain'd, thou undishonoured.[1]

Subsequently the non-husband Antipholus's attentions to Adriana's sister Luciana produce a similar ambiguity of response, this time ironically underlining the acceptableness of a double standard applied to male and female marital fidelity; Luciana admonishes Antipholus for his behaviour:

> Luciana   And may it be that you have quite forgot
> A husband's office? Shall, Antipholus,
> Even in the spring of love, thy love-springs rot?
> Shall love, in building, grow so ruinous?
> If you did wed my sister for her wealth,
> Then for her wealth's sake use her with more kindness;
> Or, if you like elsewhere, do it by stealth;
> Muffle your false love with some show of blindness;
> Let not my sister read it in your eye;
> Be not thy tongue thy own shame's orator;
> Look sweet, speak fair, become disloyalty;
> Apparel vice like virtue's harbinger;
> Bear a fair presence, though your heart be tainted;
> Teach sin the carriage of a holy saint;
> Be secret-false.[18]

In fact, Antipholus is here being upright in the face of immense provocation (Adriana would have had him seduce her *qua* husband in the previous scene). And now Luciana upbraids him in terms of matrimonial apologetics: deceive your wife if you must, but do it decently, covertly. Antipholus's open courting of her is in fact honesty; his refusal of aggressive sexual advance on the part of Adriana positively heroic.

The only redress the wife has against entirely customary behaviour on her husband's part is to resort to the customary appeals for decorum. Any *action* she takes results in (comic) indecorousness on her own part. And this, I think, captures fairly accurately the actual (and actually far from comic) helplessness of the wife in a liberalised marriage which laid strong emphasis on dialogue between partners, but continued (as we shall see in chapter 4) to treat articulateness in women as unseemly and unreliable. Liberal theory encourages the partner-wife to speak her mind; illiberal tradition, on the look out for signs of female disruptiveness, reduces her to a silence which renders her more powerless than ever.

In Webster's *The White Devil*, the loyal Isabella, whose husband Bracciano has just privately renounced her (and technically divorced her) in favour of his mistress Vittoria, publicly pretends that it is she who has renounced her husband:

Francisco	Are you foolish?
	Come dry your tears, – is this a modest course,
	To better what is nought, to rail and weep?
	Grow to a reconcilement, or by heaven,
	I'll ne'er more deal between you.
Isabella	Sir you shall not,
	No though Vittoria upon that condition
	Would become honest.
Francisco	Was your husband loud,
	Since we departed?
Isabella	By my life sir no, –
	. . .
	O that I were a man, or that I had power
	To execute my apprehended wishes,
	I would whip some with scorpions.
Francisco	What? turn'd Fury?
Isabella	To dig the strumpet's eyes out, ler her lie
	Some twenty months a-dying, to cut off
	Her nose and lips, pull out her rotten teeth,
	Preserve her flesh like mummia, for trophies
	Of my just anger: hell to my affliction
	Is mere snow-water: . . .
	Henceforth I'll never lie with you, by this,
	This wedding-ring. . . .
Francisco	Now by my birth you are a foolish, mad,
	And jealous woman.[19]

John Russell Brown, commenting on this passage has the following to say about Isabella:

Because she appears as a defenceless woman speaking [earlier] in a submissive tone, and because [Bracciano] is openly angry, scornful, and brutal, the natural tendency is to side with Isabella. But on a closer, or more sensitive, view, it is impossible to side with either. There is perhaps a further subtlety: Isabella suggests laying the blame for their divorce on her 'supposed jealousy' and promises to deceive the others into believing this by playing her part with 'a piteous and rent heart', yet when she does put the blame on herself, she does it with such abandoned hatred towards Vittoria and in a manner so calculated to infuriate Bracciano (who must now, of course, say nothing) that we may be tempted to think she is indeed that which she seems, 'a foolish, mad, And jealous woman', perhaps deceiving herself.[20]

Isabella is blameworthy, as Brown detects, *because she utters at all*, and despite the fact that it is absurd for the audience to attach to her any blame whatsoever, in a chain of events in which she is entirely passive victim. It is not 'a modest course', however she has been provoked. When it comes to Vittoria's own turn, in her trial scene, she understands clearly that by seeking articulately to defend herself she condemns herself – to speak out of turn (that is, at all) is to be guilty:

> Vittoria   Instruct me some good horse-leech to speak treason,
> For since you cannot take my life for deeds,
> Take it for words, – O woman's poor revenge
> Which dwells but in the tongue.[21]

Marriage is an equal partnership, but some partners are more equal than others. All too easily, an *equal* share in household decisions could be interpreted as female licence – the licence of the scold, the shrew, the woman on top, an ever-present threat of 'the world turned upside down'.[22] And since, as I have suggested, the idealised notion of 'partnership in mutuality' was not supported by legal rights, the practical outcome for women in general was probably a *diminished* ability to influence their own lives.

If more civilised theoretical attitudes towards marriage had complicated consequences for women, so did the general reforms of Protestantism. One of the criticisms regularly levelled at Protestantism by its Catholic opponents was indeed that it proved peculiarly attractive to women – the suggestion that the Protestant cause was peculiarly well suited to the weak will and feeble intellect of women was calculated to discredit it.[23] Here again the problem of our assessment of the actual impact of Protestantism on the average woman's self-awareness and opportunities lies with the partisanship of the evidence. Protestant reformers stress the democratic impact of religious change: *even* women and the low-born will have access to the text of Scripture; *even* they will read and understand, and contribute to their own salvation. Meanwhile, opponents of reform stress the disruptive, and potentially uncontrollable consequences of allowing women their head in matters in which they have traditionally been guided by their male pastors and spouses: 'scare' stories of women throwing off the shackles of domestic constraint because of their commitment to Protestantism are hard to disentangle from biographical accounts of courageous individual women who followed their beliefs into considered action. In both types of account, women figure talismanically, for social change – in the first case as a negative concomitant of reformed religion; in the second as a positive one. In a later chapter I shall suggest that pro- and anti-woman pamphlets figure prominently in the literature of social reform and social satire in the period through a displacing of change in general on to women in particular.[24]

Within the framework of Protestantism, the woman's freedom to think and act for herself is carefully contained within a freshly romanticised picture of the family, which takes us back to the 'marriage' question. The family became, on the Protestant view, a little kingdom in its own right, ruled benevolently by the father (privy to divine purpose), supported by maternal solicitude.[25] Discipline, self-control, obedience and duty were the watchwords of this little community, and the woman's active part in educating, disciplining and supporting her family hardly seems suggestive of 'liberation' in our modern sense.

In some respects, the Reformation actually removed some of the traditional possibilities for women's independent thought and action. Whilst women could participate in services, and were encouraged to read the Scriptures, those who encouraged them insisted on woman's essential purity and control on the Pauline and Old Testament model as a pre-emptive strike against accusations of encouraging the unworthy. That essential purity was what justified including women with men as qualified to receive Christ's message:

> You say that women who want to read the Bible are just libertines? I say you call them lewd merely because they won't consent to your seduction. You say it's permitted to women to read Boccaccio's *Flamette* or Ovid's *Art of Love* . . . which teach them to be adulterers, and yet you'll send a woman who's reading a Bible to the flames. You say it's enough for a woman's salvation for her to do her housework, sew and spin? . . . Of what use then are Christ's promises to her? You'll put spiders in Paradise, for they know how to spin very well.[26]

By observing a code of conduct which confirmed her seriousness, obedience and modesty, a woman could, within Protestantism, debate the Scriptures with men, and put her religious awareness into practice in her godly and god-fearing home. In both spheres the conditions of her assimilation were an acceptance of a willing second place. Even then her conduct could be effortlessly condemned as 'monstrous' and 'against nature' in invectives which had centuries of misogynistic stereotypes of the active woman to draw on. And of course, Protestant preachers were themselves first amongst those to resort to exactly the same stereotypes when chastising the ungodly conduct of women in the opposite (Catholic or High Anglican) camps: much of the most vigorously misogynistic writing of the period comes from the pens of low church Protestant preachers, most notoriously John Knox's *First Blast of the Trumpet against the Monstrous regiment of Women* (1558), against Mary Tudor.[27]

Two direct consequences of Protestant reform had the accidental effect of disadvantaging women and women's thought. The abolition of the convents removed a sphere of separatist, independent activity for women, in which during the Middle Ages individual women has risen to intellectual prominence unhampered by family obligations. The family was now the only support system for women, few of whom were in a position to support themselves. And the abolition of saint worship, as Natalie Davis has pointed out, removed a moral support from women which went unexpectedly deep:

> The loss of the saints affected men and women unequally. Reformed prayer could no longer be addressed to a woman, whereas the masculine identity of the Father and Son was left intact. It may seem anachronistic to raise the matter of sexual identity in religious images during the Reformation, but it is not. Soon afterward, the Catholic poet Marie le Jars de Gournay, friend and editor of Montaigne, was to argue in her *Equality of the Sexes* that Jesus' incarnation as a male was no special honor to the male sex but a mere historical convenience; given the patriarchal malice of the Jews, a female savior would never have been accepted. But if one were going to emphasize the sex of Jesus, then it was all the more important to stress the perfection of Mary and her role in the conception of our Lord. So if the removal from Holy Mother Church cut off certain forms of religious affect for men, for women the consequences for their identities went even deeper. Now during their hours of childbirth – a 'combat,' Calvin described it, 'a horrible torment' – they called no more on the Virgin and said no prayers to Saint Margaret. Rather, as Calvin advised, they groaned and sighed to the Lord and he received these groans as a sign of their obedience.[28]

Men and women joined together in the crowds which zealously

smashed statues of the saints; male and female saints were abolished together. But the consequences for women were more telling, since religious iconoclasm removed an area of representation in which female figures really did stand shoulder to shoulder with male ones, and even offered alternative role models.

I have left until last that area of progress which has most often led feminists nostalgically to invoke the Renaissance as the golden age of emancipation for women: education. Protestantism may have encouraged women, and then in practice withdrawn much of that encouragement (individual spirited women who became dissident preachers were denigrated and pilloried by the very communities which had encouraged their freedom of thought and action).[29] Humanism and humanist education both encouraged them in theory, and commended them on their practice. The letters and treatises of male humanists are liberally scattered with tributes to individual cultivated and educated women.[30] Once again, I am afraid, we need to exercise a measure of caution in grasping at these tributes as proof of a genuine area of liberation, where even four centuries ago women could develop fully, freely and unself-consciously their intellectual gifts. For this returns us to Lady Anne Frankford, the woman 'killed with kindness'.

Education, in the early modern period, was only available to high-ranking women; and education for these women was regarded as an ornament – an adornment along with beauty and manners, needlepoint and music. Lady Anne's noble birth, and the ornamental appropriateness of her learning ('a chain of gold to adorn [her husband's] neck') are ideologically linked. Cultivation is a luxury of the idle (and like needlework it keeps the fingers of the idle rich women busy); as they produced fine tapestry and embroidery, so they might produce elegant translation and occasional literary treatises.[31]

Humanism – the new learning – is of its essence non-vocational; a programme of study based on the literature of antiquity designed to produce an eloquent and cultivated individual equipped with the urbanity and civility necessary for full social participation in the higher echelons of civic life.[32] The fact that it came, for a period, to be the programme favoured by the establishments of a number of major European powers as the preferred 'liberal' introduction to statecraft and government should not mask from us the fact that of its nature it is a programme for the leisured.[33] Indeed, this latter fact is part of a conventional strategy on the part of a ruling élite to preserve the higher ranks of administration for those from among its own numbers.[34]

It is not, therefore, surprising that with humanism it became acceptable for the first time since a comparable programme dominated antique education in a similar fashion, for women from the ruling classes to be educated to a level equivalent to that of men.[35] The 'learned lady', often alluded to as a symptom of incipient emancipation,[36] is a natural consequence of a gentrified educational movement set resolutely against clerkly competence.[37] William Wotton reflected aptly on humanistic studies in the sixteenth century:

> Men fancied that everything could be done by it, and they were charmed by the Eloquence of its Professors. . . . It was so very modish that the Fair Sex seemed to believe that *Greek* and *Latin* added to their charms; and *Plato* and *Aristotle* untranslated, were frequent ornaments of their closets. One would think by the Effects that it was a proper Way of Educating them, since there are no Accounts in History of so many truly great Women in any one Age, as there are to be found between the years MD and MDC.[38]

'Charm' and 'femininity' are of the essence of humanistic studies: small wonder that they were considered a suitable pastime for the noble-women of the Tudor Royal House and their companions. But precisely the characteristics of humanism which opened its pursuit to women made it unsuitable as a means of consciousness-raising. In fact, one is tempted to conclude exactly the opposite: that humanist education conveniently distracted able women from any studies which might have led them to notice that change was opening up possibilities for emancipation in social and political fields. Elegant Latin and Greek, the ability to compose verse and *extempore* orations, were accomplishments to be valued in the drawing-room, whilst unlikely to lead to political or radical involvement. It is, indeed, striking that Greek was much encouraged for women, whilst it remained useless for civic affairs, which were conducted in Latin.[39] And the *Lisle Letters*, which provide a fine insight into an average well-to-do and well-connected family in the early decades of the sixteenth century in England, show clearly the tacit but careful difference in attitude which remained between educating sons and educating daughters, even within humanism. Daughters are sent to French households where they learn French, to read and write, music and needlework.[40] Son James, however, was sent at ten to the prestigious College of Navarre in Paris, to learn something more substantial.[41]

When the educationalist Roger Ascham characterised the education of his pupil Queen Elizabeth I and her outstanding ability, he stressed above all the 'chastening' effect of her accomplishment on her personality and ability:

> She had me as her tutor in Greek and Latin for two years. . . . She talks French and Italian as well as English: she has often talked to me readily and well in Latin, and moderately so in Greek. When she writes Greek and Latin, nothing is more beautiful than her hand-writing. She is as much delighted with music as she is skilful in the art. . . . She reads with me almost all Cicero, and great parts of Titus Livius; for she drew all her knowledge of Latin from those two authors. She used to give the morning of the day to the Greek Testament, and afterwards read select orations of Isocrates and the tragedies of Sophocles. For I thought that from those sources she might gain purity of style, and her mind derive instruction that would be of value to her to meet every contingency of life. To these I added Saint Cyprian and Melanchthon's common places, &c., as best suited, after the Holy Scriptures to teach her the foundations of religion, together with elegant language and sound doctrine. Whatever she reads she at once perceives any word that has a doubtful or curious meaning. She cannot endure those foolish imitators of Erasmus who have tied up the Latin tongue in those wretched fetters of proverbs. She likes a style that grows out of the subject; chaste because it is suitable, and beautiful because it is clear. She very much admires modest metaphors, and comparisons of contraries well put together and contrasting felicitously with one another.[42]

'Purity', 'chasteness', 'modesty' (albeit of language) are qualities which the young queen has learnt to recognise as a result of her humanistic training.[43] Docility and obedience are also qualities which humanistic educators associated with their schooling.[44] Small wonder that Thomas More was prepared strongly to support the education of his daughters (and the women of England of a suitable class in general) in the interests of piety, and keeping them out of mischief.[45] As a sixteenth-century tombstone to a virtuous and educated lady put it:

> Latine and Spanishe, and also Italian,
> She spake, writ, and read, with perfect vtterance;
> And for the English she the Garland wan,

> In Dame Prudence Schoole, by Graces purueyance,
> Which cloathed her with Vertues, from naked Ignorance;
> Reading the Scriptures, to judge Light from Darke,
> Directing her faith to Christ, the onely Marke.[46]

Education, like spinning and needlepoint, would keep women from the idleness which might lead them astray (lead them to challenge their customary roles, for instance); it would make them pious and suitable companions for their husbands, and mothers for their children.[47] Dusinberre points out with approval:

> Significantly More's tribute to Catherine of Aragon stresses her womanly qualities. . . . 'She it is who could vanquish the ancient Sabine women in devotion, and in dignity the holy, half-divine heroines of Greece. She could equal the unselfish love of Alcestis or in her unfailing judgment, outdo Tanaquil. In her expression, in her countenance, there is a remarkable beauty uniquely appropriate for one so great and good. Cornelia, that famous mother, would not yield to her in eloquence; Penelope, in loyalty to a husband.'[48]

This is More's verdict on a lady whose learning he upheld as a paradigm for all English women – she surpassed all notable ancient stereotypes of feminine obedience, loyalty and honour.[49] More's tribute bodes ill for emancipation.[50]

There is a further possible implication of the extension of humanistic education to women which invites comment: the close relationship between the growing political impotence of the courtier, and the rise of voguish humanism, particularly in England. By the sixteenth century, humanist studies in England in particular were closely associated with the appropriate training of the courtier.[51] The courtier in the courts of Europe became the latter-day supporter of feudal order and centralised government; but his actual role became increasingly parasitic, and the lack of any real function for him or her is reflected in increased decadence in court dress, increased stylisation in court behaviour, elaborate ceremonial and formalised leisure activities.[52] To leave court was to risk your family's losing its place in the precarious noble pecking-order; to stay was to be condemned to weeks and months of 'waiting', on and for the monarch. Elizabeth I encouraged large-scale court attendance because she thought it kept her nobility out of mischief: they could not

be fomenting rebellion in the provinces if they were playing
flirting games with her at court.[53]

Castiglione's early sixteenth-century handbook of humanistic
studies for the nobility, *The Courtier* was resurrected in Elizabeth's reign in Thomas Hoby's translation, and became the Bible
of aspiring courtiers throughout England. The advantage of such
a manual lay in the fact that it established even a male courtier's
value entirely in terms of his manners and social accomplishments. The ability to dispute elegantly on the finer features of the
Latin language: skill in drawing-room accomplishments at the
feet of a noble lady (the supposed convener of the colloquium of
courtiers and scholars in Castiglione's work is Elizabeth Gon-
zaga, an Italian female patron and paragon of all female virtue):[54]
poetic ability, as a natural gift: these are the marks of the true
courtier. Financial and political acumen or professional training
are apparently of no consequence in the parlour-game atmosphere of the Ferrara Court.[55]

Significantly, this nostalgically fictional version of early sixteenth-century court life (already obsolete by the time Castiglione wrote in 1528) corresponds to an actual loss in real power.
As Joan Kelly-Gadol writes: '*The Courtier* created a mannered
way of life that could give to a dependent nobility a sense of
self-sufficiency, of inner power and control, which they had lost
in a real economic and political sense.'[56] Kelly-Gadol argues that
the downgrading of the courtier resulted in a corresponding loss
of status for the lady – who in feudal terms had held a measure of
power, both within the kinship structure, and as a part of the
secular cultural fiction of the 'courtly love' tradition. Both dis-
appeared with the age of humanism:

> As the state overrode aristocratic power, the lady suffered a double loss.
> Deprived of the possibility of independent power that the combined interests
> of kinship and feudalism guaranteed some women in the Middle Ages, and
> that the states of early modern Europe would preserve in part, the Italian
> noblewoman in particular entered a relation of almost universal dependence
> upon her family and her husband. And she experienced this dependency at
> the same time as she lost her commanding position with respect to the secular
> culture of her society.[57]

I suggest that we can take this argument a stage further. Kelly-
Gadol maintains that 'the accommodation of the sixteenth- and
seventeenth-century courtier to the ways and dress of women in

no way bespeaks a greater parity between then'.[58] Since she is arguing that women were deliberately relegated to a position yet more dependent than their now dependent menfolk (even riding and military skills being carefully removed from women's courtly education as improperly functional, whilst it figured in a decorative form for the male courtier), this is a fair point. Nevertheless, there is, I think, a strong point to be taken from the elaborate decorativeness of all court dress, manners and behaviour in our period. That is that decorativeness is a signal of role loss. That it should be a feature of male court behaviour of the period (much referred to in moralising pamphlets as we shall see later) suggests that dependency is a characteristic of both male and female courtiership of our period. The Elizabethan court lady is cultivated, accomplished (in decorative skills like fine needlepoint and keyboard instruments), elaborately ornamented (in costumes which defy sense and the laws of gravity)[59] *because* she has no active social role. She is object not subject in the game of court politics. In this context 'education' is not a means of liberation, it is a stigma of social redundancy.

It would not do to overstate the case: individual noble-women achieved standards of proficiency in the specialist skills of humanism – the ancient languages, poetry, translation.[60] Some took extremely courageous decisions to refuse their traditional careers as wives and mothers, and retire instead into voluntary celibacy to enable them to continue to pursue their scholarly studies. From their male intellectual colleagues these women earned the tribute of being 'beyond their sex', 'like men', honorary members of the male community. But it is these very individuals who provide us most strikingly with our evidence of the permanently precarious 'honour' of such (deviant) achievement. One and the same set of abilities and activities can appear in startlingly different lights depending on the ideology and vested interest of the beholder. In the case of female zealots of the religious sects, the incompatibility of accounts is easy to predict – Protestants will, within limits, sanctify female members of their particular sects, Catholics will vilify them and vice versa.[61] In the case of female scholars and intellectuals, the tendency to vilify them as 'monstrous', 'unnatural', and (inevitably) sexually rapacious, may appear more surprising. But it serves to remind us that it is a matter of considerable patriarchal importance for social stability to celebrate brilliant exceptions to the female 'rule' only reluctantly, and then as exceptions.

Isotta Nogarola of Verona was a humanist of distinction.[62] She was of noble birth, of a distinguished family, all of whose members (male and female) gained reputations for education and scholarship. She wrote numerous Latin letters, corresponding with major male humanists like Guarino and Ermolao Barbaro, and was the author of a celebrated disputation on the relative sinfulness of Eve and Adam. Unlike her sister Ginevra (a promising Latin poet), she did not marry but persisted in her scholarly pursuits. Lauro Querini wrote of her:

> The greatest praise is justly bestowed upon you, illustrious Isotta, because you have overcome, as one might say, your own nature. For with singular application you have pursued that true virtue which is essentially male (*virorum propria est*), and that not just in an ordinary fashion, as with most men, but as befits the most complete and perfect wisdom men attain to.[63]

Here is the highest accolade – to overcome woman's essential nature, to become *other* than woman. For her opponents, those who deplored any activity in woman inconsistent with her traditional domestic role, that otherness was readily translated into the otherness of sexual deviancy:

> She who has acquired for herself such praise for her eloquence behaves in ways utterly inconsistent with so much erudition and such a high opinion of herself: although I have long believed that saying of numerous wise men, 'the woman of fluent speech (*eloquentem*) is never chaste, and this can be supported by the example of the great number of most learned women'. . . . And lest you condone even in the slightest degree this exceedingly loathsome and obscene misconduct, let me explain that before she made her body generally available for uninterrupted intercourse she had first submitted to, and indeed earnestly desired, that the seal of her virginity should be broken by none other than her brother, to make yet tighter her relationship with him. By God ('who does not mingle the heavens with the earth, nor the seas with the heavens')! when that woman, whose most filthy lust knows no bounds, dares to boast of her abilities in the finest literary studies.[64]

Here we are again with the transformation of articulateness into promiscuousness: 'the woman of fluent speech is never chaste' is a worthy epigram to head *A Woman Killed With Kindness*.

Ben Jonson's *Epicoene or The Silent Woman* (1609) contrasts the ideal of 'the woman who holds her tongue' of the title, with the learned woman – the archetypal strumpet:

True-wit   Why, is it not arriu'd there yet, the newes? [There is] a new
             foundation, sir, here i' the towne, of ladies, that call themselues
             the Collegiates, an order between courtiers, and country-
             madames, that liue from their husbands; and giue entertainement
             to all the *Wits*, and *Braueries* o' the time, as they call 'hem: crie
             downe, or vp, what they like, or dislike in a braine, or a fashion,
             with most masculine, or rather hermaphroditicall authoritie: and
             euery day, gaine to their colledge some new probationer.[65]

Once again, since silence = virtue in woman, learning/articulate-
ness = vice: only find a woman who does not speak at all, and you
are guaranteed a virtuous wife.[66] A recent historian has summed
up the achievement of female humanist scholars as follows:

> [The learned woman of the Renaissance] received no degrees. She wrote no
> truly great works. She exerted no great influence on emerging trends in the
> history of ideas. She was probably unhappy. But she was perhaps the earliest
> figure of the type of the learned woman who is still with us. She was educated
> and excelled in the highest tradition of learning available to male contempor-
> aries – not in needlework, not in graceful conversation, not in tinkling
> accomplishments, but in the language and literature that were the vehicles of
> the most profound thoughts the age produced. . . . For the phenomenon of
> the learned woman, whose learning destroyed the integrity of her sexual
> identity, [men] fashioned a fitting image: that of the armed maiden, a fusion
> of the icons of Athena, the chaste goddess of wisdom, and of the Amazons,
> fierce warriors ruthless to men. . . . These images from antiquity were
> invested with fresh meaning when they were jointly applied to the learned
> woman: they expressed the relation men perceived between wisdom in
> women and preternatural aggression. Learned women fascinated learned
> men, and men applauded, *of course*, their retreat to quiet studies apart from
> male society. There, in solitude, they were both magnificent and chained:
> fierce goddesses in book-lined cells. Thus confined, it is no wonder they won
> no battles.[67]

Portia, in *The Merchant of Venice*, neatly solving a knotty legal
problem, Helena, in *All's Well That Ends Well*, curing the King of
France, partake of this chaste goddess/fierce warrior quality
which celebrates and contains female achievement, and which is
ultimately found wanting alongside the richer qualities of 'fulfilled' womanhood – wifehood and motherhood.

I have been arguing that in spite of the wider range of opportunities which became available to (some) women during the
Renaissance and Reformation, attitudes towards women did not
perceptibly change – may in fact have become somewhat hard-
ened as individual women challenged traditional roles. Where
does this leave us with two major passages from Shakespeare,

cherished by those who like to maintain that Shakespeare enter-
tains a modestly enlightened view of 'woman's place' and 'the
woman question' in general: Katherina's (Kate's) final speech in
support of wifely deference at the close of *The Taming of the
Shrew*, and Portia's abdication of her hereditary independence to
Bassanio in *The Merchant of Venice?* Of the former, J. C. Bean
has written recently:

> Kate's final speech in *The Shrew*, then, in its use of political analogies and its
> emphasis on woman's warmth and beauty rather than on her abject sinful-
> ness, is not a rehearsal of old, medieval ideas about wives, but of relatively
> contemporary ideas growing out of humanist reforms. Male tyranny, which
> characterizes earlier shrew-taming stories, gives way here to a nontyrannical
> hierarchy informed by mutual affection.[68]

And Bean goes on to cite Meredith in support of the view that this
kind of good-humoured comic use of willing female submission
indicates incipient emancipation in Shakespeare's England:

> Where [women] have no social freedom, comedy is absent; where they are
> household drudges, the form of comedy is primitive; where they are tolerably
> independent, but uncultivated, exciting melodrama takes its place, and a
> sentimental version of them. . . . But where women are on the road to an
> equal footing with men, in attainment and in liberty – in what they have won
> for themselves, and what has been granted them by a fair civilization – there,
> and only waiting to be transplanted from life to the stage, or the novel, or the
> poem, pure comedy flourished.[69]

But the 'celebration of partnership in mutuality' is extremely
hard to find in Kate's speech; it is the critic who imputes a
celebratory tone to Kate's utterance at all.[70] What is in fact
striking here is the entire absence of any locating tone (an absence
which might equally be noted in equivalent speeches by female
characters from Adriana in *The Comedy of Errors* to Desdemona
in *Othello*, which affirm conventional views of wifely 'obedience', 'serving', 'duty', 'silence', and so on). It is not clear that we
can safely relate the speech to the predicament at all. This indeed
confuses the critic, and allows conflicting and contradictory
readings based on identical cultural evidence drawn from treatises and social history. Depending on how we take her tone, Kate
is seriously tamed, is ironic at Petruchio's expense, has learned
comradeship and harmonious coexistence, or will remain a
shrew till her death. 'Dutiful' Kate first obediently removes her
'cap' and treads on it on her husband's orders (thus winning him

his wager), and then, as a gloss on this 'duty' orates as follows:

> A woman mov'd is like a fountain troubled –
> Muddy, ill-seeming, thick, bereft of beauty;
> And while it is so, none so dry or thirsty
> Will deign to sip or touch one drop of it.
> Thy husband is thy lord, thy life, thy keeper,
> Thy head, thy sovereign; one who cares for thee,
> And for thy maintenance commits his body
> To painful labour both by sea and land,
> To watch the night in storms, the day in cold,
> Whilst thou liest warm at home, secure and safe;
> And craves no other tribute at thy hands
> But love, fair looks, and true obedience –
> Too little payment for so great a debt.[71]

Fine ringing words, but ones which bear no relation to the preceding action. As Bianca expostulates when Kate ruins her cap: 'Fie! what a foolish duty call you this?'[72] Duty is an abstract: it never correlates with the unreasonable demands of individual petulant (or bloody-minded) husbands. And it is by no means the case that Kate is obliged in Christian humility to serve her breadwinner husband: he is a fortune-hunting rascal, supported by *her* fine dowry. If obedience correlates with financial support, then it is Petruchio who should kneel to Kate. As Luciana reminds Antipholus in *The Comedy of Errors*: 'If you did wed my sister for her wealth, Then for her wealth's sake use her with more kindness.'[73] Portia supports the same empty fiction that husbands are of their essence economically superior to their (extremely wealthy) wives, when she abdicates her rank and status in favour of Bassanio. The speech is in fact more directly of interest than Kate's, since it attempts actually to distort the perceived circumstance (the impoverished Bassanio fortune-hunting the hand of the wealthy lady by means of folkloristic solving of a riddle) into a 'dutiful' marital relationship:

> You see me, Lord Bassanio, where I stand,
> Such as I am. Though for myself alone
> I would not be ambitious in my wish
> To wish myself much better, yet for you
> I would be trebled twenty times myself,
> A thousand times more fair, ten thousand times more rich,
> That only to stand high in your account
> I might in virtues, beauties, livings, friends,

Exceed account. But the full sum of me
Is sum of something which, to term in gross,
Is an unlesson'd girl, unschool'd, unpractis'd;
Happy in this, she is not yet so old
But she may learn; happier than this,
She is not bred so dull but she can learn;
Happiest of all is that her gentle spirit
Commits itself to yours to be directed,
As from her lord, her governor, her king.
Myself and what is mine to you and yours
Is now converted. But now I was the lord
Of this fair mansion, master of my servants,
Queen o'er myself; and even now, but now,
This house, these servants, and this same myself,
Are yours – my lord's.⁴

Here is a financial balance sheet, like Kate's 'Too little payment
for so great a debt'. And in the same way, the 'accounting'
conducted simply will not balance. Portia converts her hard
financial currency (the means of her dominion over the action
prior to this moment) into 'virtues, beauties, livings, friends'.
Meanwhile the 'full sum of her' (her putative marital worth in the
moral sphere) is fraught with disadvantages ('unlesson'd girl,
unschool'd, unpractis'd') – all of which subsequently turn out to
be fictions when Portia pleads as an accomplished advocate later
in the play. However, she engineers these disadvantages into total
capitulation: Bassanio can claim a legitimate 'taming' of the
independent woman, despite lack of means or real claim, because
Portia has rhetorically contrived it.

If these speeches reflect in any way the underlying social
realities, it is in precisely this verbal uneasiness about where the
moral centre of the balance of power is actually located in the
household. Does 'duty' mean notional moral subservience (unre-
lated to fiscal and class constraints), or is it in fact the solution of a
complicated financial balance sheet? Both Portia's and Kate's
speeches prevaricate on this issue. The patriarchy can hardly
afford to admit the elaborate double standard that is being
applied.

In 1587 the usually scurrilous Robert Greene published a
sanctimonious treatise entitled, *Penelope's Web: Wherein a
christall myrror of faeminine perfection represents to the view of
euery one those vertues and graces, which more curiously
beautifies the mynd of women, then eyther sumptuous Apparell,*

*or Iewels of inestimable valew: the one buying fame with honour,
the other breeding a kynd of delight, but with repentance,*[75] in
which he has the chaste Penelope argue at length (as she unravels
her tapestry of a night) that:

> As a looking glasse or Christall though most curiously set in Ebonie, serueth
> to small purpose if it doth not liuely represent the proportion and lineaments
> of the face inspicient, so a woman, though rich and beautiful, deserueth smal
> prayse or fauour, if the course of her life be not directed after her husbands
> compasse. And as ye Mathematicall lines which Geometricians doe figure in
> their carrecters, haue no motion of themselues, but in the bodyes wherein
> they are placed, so ought a wife to haue no proper or peculiar passion or
> affection, vnlesse framed after the speciall disposition of her husband: For, to
> crosse him with contraries as to frowne when he setleth him selfe to mirth, or
> amidst his melancholie to shewe her selfe passing merrie, discouereth either a
> fond or froward will, opposite to that honorable vertue of Obedience.[76]

On successive nights, Penelope embroiders a picture of the virtuous wife (decorated with fictional tales to provide exemplary
embellishment) as obedient, chaste and silent. Coming from one
of the great rogues of the Elizabethan period, the reader must find
it all a bit 'rich'. Why should these noble and well-endowed ladies
'buy' fame with honour, when they could in fact 'buy' security
and independence by straight financial barter? That, I think, is
the point. Greene panders to a patriarchal desire to 'keep women
in their place' which appears to be the more vehement for its
failure to correlate with the actual economic circumstances of the
small and select group of noble-women to whom the tract is
notionally addressed (Greene dedicates his treatise to the 'cour-
teous and courtly ladies of England'). The distinct sense we get of
whistling in the dark is supported, I think, by evidence in other
pamphlets on wifely duty directed at the upper echelons of
society. William Whately's *A Bride-Bush*[77] insists that it is a
wife's duty to cohabit with her husband, and to remain faithful
to him (both in her social behaviour and sexually): the noble-
woman of independent means never had, and probably never
would, play the game according to these rules. But from the early
decades of the sixteenth century – with the demise of the feudal
order which had partially protected women of the nobility from
such pressures[78] – educational treatises, pamphlets on manners,
spiritual tracts, sermons and literature all conspire to try to turn
the wishful thinking of the male community into a propaganda
reality.

Notes

1 R. W. van Fossen (ed.), *A Woman Killed with Kindness* (Revels, 1961), scene i.12–70.

2 This case has been argued most recently and vigorously by J. Dusinberre, *Shakespeare and the Nature of Women* (London, 1975). Social historians are generally significantly less optimistic than literary critics on this issue. Christopher Hill comments bluntly, with reference to Milton's views on women: 'To criticize Milton because he stated a theory of male superiority is like criticizing him because he did not advocate votes or equal pay for women. No one, to my knowledge, in the seventeenth century claimed that women were wholly equal to men, just as no one, not even Levellers, seriously proposed to give them the vote', *Milton and the English Revolution* (London, 1977), p. 118. See also L. Stone, *The Family, Sex and Marriage in England 1500–1800* (London, 1977) and *The Crisis of the Aristocracy 1558–1641* (Oxford, 1965), both *passim*. Stone is always realistic about actual advances in women's status, although recent social historians have begun to query some of his specific conclusions. See A. Macfarlane, *The Origins of English Individualism* (Oxford, 1978); P. Laslett, *The World we have Lost* (Cambridge, 1965); P. Laslett (ed.), *Household and Family in Past Time* (Cambridge, 1972). I am not clear myself why feminist social historians and critics are so eager to see emerging emancipation in the seventeenth century, and especially to read liberation into concessions which they would readily recognise as trivial in their own day.

3 For the first view, see in particular Dusinberre, *op. cit.*, *passim*. Her most extravagant claims run as follows: 'The cause of women's rights is the poor relation of democracy. Wherever and whenever men raise a voice for freedom from tyranny in the state, that inconspicuous figure becomes articulate too, shouting against the tyranny of men both in the home and outside it. The Elizabethan and Jacobean periods bred the conditions of a feminist movement; the breakdown of old ideas and forms in religion, in politics, in the structure of society: the beginning of a new economy; and the spirit of independence which the Puritans fostered in their followers not only in religion, but in their attitude to the ruling classes. . . . The spirit of unrest which moves men to recognise their rights as individual citizens, infects their women', pp. 80–1. The pessimistic view is taken by a number of recent social historians, including G. R. Quaiffe, *Wanton Wenches and Wayward Wives: Peasants and Illicit Sex in Early Seventeenth-Century England* (London, 1979). This useful work is unfortunately quite relentless in unconsciously pinning the blame for all the extensive and persisting sexual harassment and misdemeanour of the period squarely on women themselves (who are 'wanton' and 'wayward', whilst the male protagonists are unjudged). Macfarlane, *op. cit.*, supports the view that nothing much changed, certainly in peasant communities, and also the view that 'middle-class values' did not seep very far down the social scale.

4 In I. Maclean, *The Renaissance Notion of Woman* (Cambridge, 1980), p. 42. Aristotle, *Historia animalium* IX.1.

5 Cornelius a Lapide, *In omnes divi Pauli epistolas commentaria* (Paris,

1638), pp. 284–5, in Maclean, *op. cit.*, p. 11. See also Hill, *op. cit.*, p. 119.
6 Hill, *op. cit.*, p. 117.
7 See below, p. 106.
8 One reason for giving this alphabet in full is that its categories recur regularly in Renaissance euologies of famous women. (Eulogies traditionally are built patchwork fashion out of conventional terms of praise.) There is also a vigorous pamphlet literature of anti-woman inverted alphabets which parody the Proverbs alphabet of praise.
9 S. Marshall Wyntjes, 'Women in the Reformation era', in R. Bridenthal and C. Koonz (eds), *Becoming Visible: Women in European History* (Boston, 1977), pp. 165–91, 186.
10 Except perhaps with her tongue: see the discussion of shrews below, p. 115. M. Wolf, talking about the traditional role of Chinese women, suggests that shrewishness and acute verbal aggressiveness on the part of wives are parts of a system which tyrannically circumscribes possibilities for female action to alleviate her subordinate position. See M. Wolf, 'Chinese women: old skills in a new context', in M. Zimbalist Rosaldo and L. Lamphere (eds), *Woman, Culture, and Society* (Stanford, 1974, pp. 157–72.
11 Dusinberre, *op. cit.*, pp. 82–3. The confident tone in which writers like Dusinberre talk about 'what went on' in the Renaissance household is extremely misleading. Recent work has shown that we have very little evidence to link what actually happened in the home with theoretical and abstract discussions in handbooks. Macfarlane recently suggests that we are not even sure what the average age of marriage was for the period (very young or comparatively mature). It makes a considerable difference for making sound judgements of the type of household in existence which is the case. See Macfarlane, *op. cit.*, pp. 27–8, 155–9.
12 See D. M. Stenton, *The English Woman in History* (1957; reprint New York, 1977), p. 104.
13 *Certain Sermons or Homilies appointed to be read in Churches* (Oxford, 1844 edn), pp. 446–58, in Stenton, *op. cit.*, p. 105.
14 Stenton, *op. cit.*, p. 107.
15 ibid., p. 105. Milton, who advocated divorce on liberal grounds, also interestingly drew the charge that *women* thus gained too much freedom: 'all his arguments . . . prove as effectually that the wife may sue for divorce from her husband upon the same grounds', *An Answer to a Book Intituled The Doctrine and Discipline of Divorce* (1644), p. 13, in Hill, *op. cit.*, p. 120.
16 *The Comedy of Errors* II.ii.109–28. 'meat' and 'carv'd to thee' are crude puns on sexual intercourse.
17 ibid., II.ii.129–45. There seems to be an implicit (male joke) pun in the last line, suggesting that whilst Adriana is 'stained' as long as her husband is unfaithful, she is 'disdained' when he returns home honourably.
18 ibid., III.ii.1–15.
19 J. Russell Brown (ed.), *The White Devil* (Revels, 1960), II.i.229–65.
20 ibid., p. lii.
21 ibid., III.ii.281–4.

22 See below, chapter 4.
23 See N. Z. Davis, 'City women and religious change', in *Society and Culture in Early Modern France* (London, 1975), pp. 65–95, 65.
24 See below, chapter 5.
25 See, for instance, M. Walzer, *The Revolution of the Saints: A Study in the Origins of Radical Politics* (Cambridge, Mass., 1965), pp. 190–3.
26 In Davis, *op. cit.*, p. 78.
27 See K. M. Rogers, *The Troublesome Helpmate: A History of Misogyny in Literature* (Seattle, 1966; 1973 edn), pp. 135–59.
28 Davis, *op. cit.*, p. 88.
29 See, e.g., Hill, *op. cit.*, pp. 135–6.
30 See P. H. Labalme (ed.), *Beyond their Sex: Learned Women of the European Past* (New York, 1980), *passim*.
31 For a guide to Renaissance publications by learned women see P. Gartenberg and N. Thames Whittemore, 'A checklist of English women in print 1475–1640', *Bulletin of Bibliography*, 34 (1977), pp. 1–13; M. Reynolds, *The Learned Lady in England 1650–1760* (Boston, 1920); G. F. Waller (ed.), *'The Triumph of Death' and other Unpublished and Uncollected Poems by Mary Sidney, Countess of Pembroke* (Salzburg, 1977); P. Hogrefe, *Women in Action in Tudor England* (Pennsylvania, 1979); Labalme, *op. cit.*
32 J. E. Seigel, '"Civic humanism" or Ciceronian Rhetoric?', *Past and Present*, 34 (1966), pp. 3–48; A. T. Grafton and L. Jardine, 'Humanism and the school of Guarino: a problem of evaluation', *Past and Present*, 96 (1982), pp. 51–80; R. R. Bolgar, *The Classical Heritage and its Beneficiaries* (Cambridge, 1954).
33 See particularly Grafton and Jardine, *op. cit.*
34 See L. Martines, *The Social World of the Florentine Humanists 1390–1460* (Princeton, 1963); P. Bourdieu, 'Systems of education and systems of thought', in E. Hopper (ed.), *Readings in the Theory of Educational Systems* (London, 1971), pp. 157–83.
35 On the comparable situation in antiquity see S. F. Bonner, *Education in Ancient Rome* (London, 1977); Bolgar, *op. cit.*
36 See e.g. Stenton, *op. cit.*, p. 120.
37 On the achievement of female humanists, see P. H. Labalme (ed.), *op. cit.*
38 *Reflections upon Ancient and Modern Learning* (2nd edn London, 1697), p. 412, in Stenton, *op. cit.*, p. 125.
39 Juvenal, *Satires* VI, comments disparagingly on the social affectation of Roman ladies speaking Greek in an earlier period of fashionable female learning.
40 M. St Clare Byrne (ed.), *The Lisle Letters*, 6 vols (Chicago and London, 1981), III, letters 570–627.
41 ibid., III, letters 551–69; IV, letters 1042–85.
42 Letter from Ascham to Sturm, in T. W. Baldwin, *William Shakspere's small Latine and lesse Greeke*, 2 vols (Urbana, 1944), I, 259. For similar comment on Elizabeth's education see J. E. Neale, *Queen Elizabeth* (London, 1934), pp. 20–6.
43 Even the Puritan Lucy Hutchinson remarked with approval that Queen

Elizabeth was to be praised for 'her submission to her masculine and wise councillors', in Hill, *op. cit.*, pp. 118–19.

44 See Grafton and Jardine, *op. cit.*

45 Dusinberre, *op. cit.*, p. 204; Stenton, *op. cit.*, p. 120.

46 Tombstone of Elizabeth Lucar, died 29 October 1537, from Stow's *Survey of London* (1598; 1618 edn), p. 416, in Stenton, p. 124.

47 Dusinberre, *op. cit.*, pp. 207–8. In More's treatment of women's education, as in that of other humanist contemporaries, learning is linked with spinning and sewing (as in the Proverbs alphabet of female virtues) as idleness-avoiding pursuits.

48 Dusinberre, *op. cit.*, p. 210.

49 For similar comment on Dusinberre's use of this passage on Catherine of Aragon, see M. Andresen-Thom, 'Thinking about women and their prosperous art: a reply to Juliet Dusinberre's *Shakespeare and the Nature of Women*', *Shakespeare Studies*, 11 (1978), pp. 259–76.

50 Both Erasmus and More are remarkably consistent in mentioning education of women in the same breath as the traditional female pursuits for avoiding idleness: spinning and sewing. See, e.g. J. O'Faolain and L. Martines (eds), *Not in God's Image: Women in History* (London, 1979), p. 194 (Erasmus, *Christiani matrimonii institutio*): 'The distaff and spindle are in truth the tools of all women and suitable for avoiding idleness. . . . Even people of wealth and birth train their daughters to weave tapestries or silken cloths . . . it would be better if they taught them to study, for study busies the whole soul. . . . It is not only a weapon against idleness but also a means of impressing the best precepts upon a girl's mind and of leading her to virtue.'

51 See L. Jardine, 'Humanism and the sixteenth-century Cambridge Arts course', *History of Education*, 4 (1975), pp. 16–31; 'Humanism and dialectic in sixteenth-century Cambridge: a preliminary investigation', in R. R. Bolgar (ed.), *Classical Influences on European Culture, AD 1500–1700* (Cambridge, 1976), pp. 141–54; M. H. Curtis, *Oxford and Cambridge in Transition 1558–1642* (Oxford, 1959); J. K. McConica, *English Humanists and Reformation Politics* (Oxford, 1965).

52 See, for instance, F. A. Yates, *Astraea: the Imperial Theme in the Sixteenth Century* (London, 1975); S. Anglo, *Spectacle, Pageantry, and Early Tudor Policy* (Oxford, 1969).

53 See Neale, *op. cit.*

54 For a vivid picture of the learned patronage of another Italian noble woman, Eleanora of Aragon, see W. L. Gundersheimer, 'Women, learning, and power: Eleanora of Aragon and the Court of Ferrara', in Labalme, *op. cit.*, pp. 43–65.

55 For female courtiers there were real educational parlour-games which served the same purpose. See M. I. Ringhieri, *Cento Givochi liberali, et d'ingegno* (Bologna, 1551).

56 J. Kelly-Gadol, 'Did women have a Renaissance?', in Bridenthal and Koonz (eds), *op. cit.*, pp. 137–64, 157.

57 ibid., p. 159.

58 ibid. Wives of male courtiers did not necessarily come to court at all.

59 See below, chapter 5.
60 See Labalme (ed.), *op. cit.*, *passim*. On the strictly comparable individual voices and achievements of women in religion in the Renaissance period, see S. Marshall Wyntjes, 'Women in the Reformation era', in Bridenthal and Koonz, *op. cit.*, pp. 165–91; M. U. Chrisman, 'Women and the Reformation in Strasbourg 1490–1530', *Archiv für Reformationsgeschichte*, 63 (1972); R. Bainton, *Women of the Reformation in Germany and Italy* (Minneapolis, 1971). What is not clear is how much these individual opportunities are correlated with economic possibilities for women. Some women did play significant mercantile roles in the early modern period, and women were manual workers throughout the period from sheer economic necessity. See K. Casey, 'The Cheshire Cat: reconstructing the experience of medieval woman', in B. A. Carroll (ed.), *Liberating Women's History: Theoretical and Critical Essays* (Urbana, 1976), pp. 224–49; O'Faolain and Martines (eds), *op. cit.*, pp. 167–78. This was in fact a period of transition for women from part of the manual labourforce into serving domestic (in the course of which she may have lost her individual public voice). See Macfarlane, *op. cit.*
61 On the comparability of achievement on the part of women in religion in the period, whether they were Catholic or Protestant, see Davis, *op. cit.*
62 See P. O. Kristeller, 'Learned women of early modern Italy: humanists and university scholars', in Labalme (ed.), *op. cit.*, pp. 91–116, 96–7.
63 In M. L. King, 'Book-lined cells: women and humanism in the early Italian Renaissance', in Labalme (ed.), *op. cit.*, pp. 66–90, 89, my translation.
64 In King, *op. cit.*, p. 90, my translation.
65 C. H. Herford and P. Simpson (eds), *Works* V, I.i.73–81.
66 See below, chapter 4.
67 King, *op. cit.*, pp. 80, 79.
68 'Comic structure and the humanizing of Kate in *The Taming of the Shrew*', in C. R. S. Lenz, G. Greene and C. T. Neely (eds), *The Woman's Part: Feminist Criticism of Shakespeare* (Urbana, 1980), pp. 65–78, 70.
69 ibid., p. 76.
70 ibid., p. 77. See, however, the view advanced by C. L. Barber that Shakespearean comedy is celebratory of cherished and deep-rooted values in society; see *Shakespeare's Festive Comedy* (Princeton, 1959).
71 *The Taming of the Shrew* V.ii.142–54.
72 But see below on dress codes, p. 154.
73 *The Comedy of Errors* III.ii.5–6.
74 *The Merchant of Venice* III.ii.149–72.
75 A. B. Grosart (ed.), *The Life and Complete Works in Prose and Verse of Robert Greene, MA*, 15 vols (New York, 1964 reissue), V, 139–234.
76 ibid., pp. 163–4.
77 See above, p. 44.
78 See Kelly-Gadol, *op. cit.*

3

'I am Duchess of Malfi still': Wealth, Inheritance and the Spectre of Strong Women

In the last chapter I traced the absence, in the early modern period, of emancipation of women through marital instruction and humanist learning. Where, then, do the strong female characters who wheeler-deal their way through Jacobean drama in particular come from? How are they related to their real-life sisters who were, I have argued, increasingly constrained by an ideology of duty and obedience which removed from them the most elementary possibilities for rebellion against traditional serving roles?

Let us begin by trying to identify some of the features of female characterisation which lead the critics to refer to them as 'strong', and as admirable in their strength. Passion, sensuality, courage, cunning, ambition, are some of the attributes associated with female heroes like Bianca in Middleton's *Women Beware Women*, Beatrice-Joanna in Middleton and Rowley's *The Changeling*, Vittoria in Webster's *The White Devil* and his Duchess of Malfi. These characteristics go to make up such compelling stage characters that they seduce each generation of audiences into wishing them to represent genuine force and spirited independence as part of a consistent and believable heroic persona. It is in the interests of such 'believableness' that critics are led to assert the correspondence between such 'strong women' and emancipated possibilities for individual women of the period.[1] A recent critic writes: 'One of John Webster's most original contributions to English tragedy consisted in his examination of the characteristics which combine to produce a convincing tragic heroine.'[2] But as she pursues this 'convincingness' it emerges that the critic sees this in a very particular sense; the 'convincing tragic heroine' is plausibly (and, the suggestion is, realistically) threatening to men:

> While providing a convincing answer to the question, 'What did this woman do to merit death?', the tragedy which successfully presents a sympathetic tragic heroine must also be concerned with the question, 'Can this woman be trusted?' It is not a matter of one woman being able to trust another . . . but it is a matter of whether one man or many men can trust one particular woman.[3]

'Can this woman be trusted?' is a peculiarly patriarchal question to ask, and indeed, our critic acknowledges this:

> In Webster's major tragedies this point is emphasised by the strange situation of his heroines. Both Vittoria and the Duchess of Malfi move in exclusively masculine worlds; both appear to be cut off from contact with other women; both are virtually isolated from the friendship or companionship of women of their own rank.[4]

The female hero moves in an exclusively masculine stage world, in which it is the task of the male characters to 'read' her. Is she what she appears? 'Look to' t: be not cunning: / For they whose faces do belie their hearts / Are witches, ere they arrive at twenty years – / Ay: and give the devil suck.'[5] Shakespeare's 'strong' women find themselves in a similarly male world: Gertrude in *Hamlet* (and her reflection in Ophelia), Desdemona in *Othello* (more manipulated than manipulating), Cleopatra.

So when the critic tells us that the Jacobean dramatist shows peculiar insight into female character, and even into female psychology, we should pause for a moment. What he or she means is that a convincing portrayal of female psychology is given *from a distinctively male viewpoint* (even if this is not actually made explicit by the critic). Another female critic (who is presumably content that 'psychological insight' into female character be male insight) writes:

> Middleton's capacity for tragedy is inseparable from his other supreme gift, his discernment of the minds of women; in this no dramatist of the period except Shakespeare is his equal at once for variety and for penetration [sic].[6]

The strength of the female protagonist is as seen through male eyes.

It is seen through male eyes, and as such is dramatically compelling. But the female character traits to which the critics give such enthusiastic support are almost without exception morally reprehensible: cunning, duplicity, sexual rapaciousness, 'changeableness', being other than they seem, untrustworthiness and general secretiveness. In *The Duchess of Malfi*, the first entrance of the Duchess is in an atmosphere fraught with explicitly offensive sexual innuendo in which she is implicated, and which controls our assessment of her character:

Ferdinand	You are a widow:
	You know already what man is; and therefore
	Let not youth, high promotion, eloquence –
Cardinal	No, nor anything without the addition, honour,
	Sway your high blood.
Ferdinand	Marry! they are most luxurious [lustful]
	Will wed twice.
	. . .
Duchess	Will you hear me?
	I'll never marry: –
Cardinal	So most widows say:
	But commonly that motion lasts no longer
	Than the turning of an hour-glass – the funeral sermon
	And it, end both together.¯

A handful of speeches later, the sexual innuendo comes to a climax, and the Duchess reveals the accuracy of her brothers' accusations (confirming their dark travesty of female lasciviousness and 'doubleness') simultaneously:

Ferdinand	You are my sister –
	This was my father's poinard: do you see?
	I'd be loth to see 't rusty, 'cause 'twas his: –
	A visor and a mask are whispering-rooms
	That were ne'er built for goodness: fare ye well: –
	And women like that part which, like the lamprey,
	Hath ne'er a bone in't.
Duchess	Fie sir!
Ferdinand	Nay,
	I mean the tongue: variety of courtship; –
	What cannot a neat knave with a smooth tale
	Make a woman believe? Farewell lusty widow. [Exit.]
Duchess	Shall this move me? If all my royal kindred
	Lay in my way unto this marriage,
	I'd make them my low footsteps.⁸

The picture of stereotype female virtue painted in advance of her appearance by the Duchess's infatuated servant (and subsequent husband) Antonio cannot make up for the impact of this initial encounter.⁹ The Duchess's 'luxuriousness' (lustfulness) drives her powerfully into secret marriage and flagrant flouting of her brothers' wishes, just as Gertrude's sexuality in *Hamlet* drives her into her dead husband's brother's bed. Hamlet perceives his mother's 'strength' in the same terms as Ferdinand and the Cardinal do their sister's:

> *Hamlet*   That it should come to this!
> But two months dead! nay, not so much, not two.
> So excellent a king that was to this
> Hyperion to a satyr; so loving to my mother,
> That he might not beteem the winds of heaven
> Visit her face too roughly. Heaven and earth!
> Must I remember? Why, she would hang on him
> As if increase of appetite had grown
> By what it fed on; and yet, within a month –
> Let me not think on't. Frailty, thy name is woman! –
> A little month, or ere those shoes were old
> With which she followed my poor father's body,
> Like Niobe, all tears – why she, even she –
> O God! a beast that wants discourse of reason
> Would have mourn'd longer – married with my uncle,
> My father's brother; but no more like my father
> Than I to Hercules. Within a month,
> Ere yet the salt of most unrighteous tears
> Had left the flushing of her galled eyes,
> She married. O, most wicked speed, to post
> With such dexterity to incestuous sheets!¹⁰

Lower in her sexual drive than 'a beast that wants discourse of reason', the Duchess of Malfi, like Hamlet's mother, steps out of the path of duty and marries for lust. Thereafter she remains heroically determined to follow through the consequences of her initial base action, until she comes to resigned acceptance of the inevitable downfall:

> *Ferdinand* How doth our sister duchess bear herself
>   In her imprisonment?
> *Bosola*   Nobly; I'll describe her:
>   She's sad, as one long us'd to 't; and she seems
>   Rather to welcome the end of misery
>   Than shun it; – a behaviour so noble
>   As gives a majesty to adversity;
>   You may discern the shape of loveliness
>   More perfect in her tears, than in her smiles.¹¹

'Majesty' in the female hero is here at its most reassuring and admirable when associated with patient suffering: Griselda; the Virgin Mary, mother and true spouse of Christ; Hecuba.¹² A 'convincing' representation of the developing psychology of the female hero is apparently the conversion of lascivious waywardness into emblematic chaste resignation.[13]

It is the male characters who perceive free choice on the part of the female character as an inevitable sign of irrational lust, and as the inevitable prelude to disorder and disaster. The critics acknowledge as much when they draw attention to the discrepancy between the obsessive insistence on the parts of both Ferdinand and Hamlet on the sexual motivation of the Duchess of Malfi's supposed desire to remarry (subsequently confirmed), and Gertrude's remarriage within two months to her dead husband's brother.[14] But that male interpretation of female action must colour the audience's own response: only men surround the Duchess; the audience can do little more than accept their version of her behaviour and motives. Hamlet manipulates his authority in defining by description the actions of the play's female characters when he taunts Ophelia (whilst secretly observed by her father and Claudius). Ophelia has been instructed by the two concealed onlookers to return to Hamlet his gifts – a sign of a betrothal broken off[15] – so that they may observe Hamlet's reactions. Hamlet proceeds to demonstrate that interpretation of Ophelia's actions towards himself is entirely dependent on his male description of them. (We are already aware that her actions at this moment are entirely determined by the two concealed male onlookers):

Ophelia	My lord, I have remembrances of yours
	That I have longed long to re-deliver.
	I pray you now receive them.
Hamlet	No, not I;
	I never gave you aught.
Ophelia	My honour'd lord, you know right well you did,
	And with them words of so sweet breath compos'd
	As made the things more rich; their perfume lost,
	Take these again; for to the noble mind
	Rich gifts wax poor when givers prove unkind.
	There, my lord.
Hamlet	Ha, ha! Are you honest?
Ophelia	My Lord?
Hamlet	Are you fair?
Ophelia	What means your lordship?
Hamlet	That if you be honest and fair, your honesty should admit no discourse to your beauty.

Ophelia	Could beauty, my lord, have better commerce than with honesty?
Hamlet	Ay, truly; for the power of beauty will sooner transform honesty from what it is to a bawd than the force of honesty can translate beauty into his likeness. This was sometime a paradox, but now the time gives it proof. I did love you once.
Ophelia	Indeed, my lord, you made me believe so.
Hamlet	You should not have believ'd me; for virtue cannot so innoculate our old stock but we shall relish of it. I loved you not.
Ophelia	I was the more deceived.[16]

Ophelia is honest (chaste) or a bawd (a whore) depending on how Hamlet now chooses to describe his own behaviour towards her. If he loved her, declared that love to her, and she accepted his gifts and embraces, then she is chaste.[17] If he never loved her, but attempted to seduce her only, then *she* is lewd and lascivious, because *Hamlet* trifled with her. Either way she should 'get [her] to a nunnery' – 'nunnery', as all modern editions of the play hasten to tell the reader, meant both a convent and a brothel in Elizabethan colloquial expression.[18]

The impulsive offer of love by a woman is most likely to be a sign of unreliableness and untrustworthiness if the male characters are allowed the final say in 'reading' that offer. Such a view is only a more sophisticated version of the one aired by Julia in *The Two Gentlemen of Verona*:

> What fool is she, that knows I am a maid
> And would not force the letter to my view!
> Since maids, in modesty, say 'No' to that
> Which they would have the profferer construe 'Ay'.[19]

Virgins who say 'no' mean 'yes'; those who say 'yes' once are likely to prove insatiable. The man who fails to recognise this is accordingly, in the drama, a dupe. At the beginning of Middleton's *Women Beware Women* the gullible Leantio boasts to his mother of the unfailing love of the heiress with whom he has eloped, while his mother warns anxiously of possible downfall:

Mother	What ableness have you to do her right then
	In maintenance fitting her birth and virtues?
	Which ev'ry woman of necessity looks for,
	And most to go above it; not confined
	By their conditions, virtues, bloods, or births,
	But flowing to affections, wills, and humours. . . .
Leantio	I pray do not you teach her to rebel
	When she's in a good way to obedience;

> To rise with other women in commotion
> Against their husbands, for six gowns a year,
> And so maintain their cause when they're once up,
> In all things else that require cost enough.
> They are all of 'em a kind of spirits soon raised,
> But not so soon laid, Mother. As for example,
> A woman's belly is got up in a trice –
> A simple charge ere it be laid down again.
> So even in all their quarrels, and their courses.
> And I'm a proud man, I hear nothing of 'em,
> They're very still, I thank my happiness,
> And sound asleep; pray let not your tongue wake 'em.
> If you can but rest quiet, she's contented
> With all conditions that my fortunes bring her to:
> To keep close as a wife that loves her husband;
> To go after the rate of my ability,
> Not the licentious swinge of her own will,
> Like some of her old school-fellows.[20]

In fact predictably (in dramatic terms), Bianca his wife *is* seduced by wealth and licentiousness (even though she is not herself responsible for seeking the occasion of it). And Leantio's speech already tells us why: in men's eyes, woman *is* 'affections', 'wills', 'humours', 'a kind of spirits soon raised' (easily sensually stimulated), 'a woman's belly is got up in a trice' (the passive construction emphasises the irrelevance of the woman's assent in seduction; she is complicit all the same).[21] It is Leantio's folly which blinds him to the fact that his wife is like all other women: having followed the desires of the sense in marrying him impetuously, she has displayed her permanent unreliability, sensuality and changeableness. When Othello leaves the court in triumph with his wife Desdemona, having convinced the hearing that she married him 'for love' although against her father's wishes, her father warns: 'Look to her, Moor, if thou hast eyes to see: / She has deceiv'd her father, and may thee.'[22] When Beatrice-Joanna, in *The Changeling* takes the decision to follow her sensual desire and marry Alsemero by disposing of her husband-to-be, she is already embarked on the course which will lead to her obsessive sexual involvement with De Flores:

> De Flores   if a woman
>   Fly from one point, from him she makes a husband,
>   She spreads and mounts then like arithmetic,
>   One, ten, a hundred, a thousand, ten thousand,
>   Proves in time sutler to an army royal. . . .

> Methinks I feel her in mine arms already,
> Her wanton fingers combing out this beard,
> And being pleased, praising this bad face.
> Hunger and pleasure, they'll commend sometimes
> Slovenly dishes, and feed heartily on 'em,
> Nay, which is stranger, refuse daintier for 'em.[23]

If we miss this patriarchal assumption in the drama we are bound to be bemused by subsequent developments. In *Othello*, Desdemona has amply demonstrated her driving sensuality by marrying for love without parental consent, and by marrying a black – whose superior sexuality was as strong a Renaissance fiction as it remains today: 'An old black ram / Is tupping [fucking] your white ewe', Iago tells Desdemona's father, and that remains a relevant view of Desdemona throughout the play.[24]

So it is not at all surprising to find that at the climax of the play, as the about-to-become-victim Desdemona prepares for bed, she reminds the audience once more of her sensual drive. This she does by commenting favourably on a man other than her husband (as De Flores observed, women who follow the lusts of the flesh do so indiscriminately). Editors and producers of the play anxiously try to explain away this passage, which flaws the 'innocence' which a modern audience looks for in Desdemona. But the sensual remains one of her defining qualities:

Desdemona	He says he will return incontinent.
	He hath commanded me to go to bed,
	And bade me to dismiss you.
	. . .
Emilia	Shall I fetch your night-gown?
Desdemona	No, unpin me here.
	This Lodovico is a proper man.
Emilia	A very handsome man.
Desdemona	He speaks well.
Emilia	I know a lady in Venice would have walk'd barefoot to Palestine for a touch of his nether lip.[25]

Such careful intrusions into the drama in order to remind the audience of the sensual strain in the central female character should, I think, alert us to the guilt which adheres to such characters. In the eyes of the Jacobean audience they are above all culpable, and their strength – the ways in which they direct the action, scheme and orchestrate, evade the consequences of their spontaneous decisions, and ultimately face resolutely the final outcome – needs to be seen in this context. Over the years critics have tended to attempt complicated exonerations of the female heroes of the Jacobean drama, to make them 'innocent' of the sexual slur. Let us instead try to specify rather more carefully the nature of that guilt. It is clearly to be found, I suggest, in a play like *The Duchess of Malfi*.

The acknowledged source for Webster's *The Duchess of Malfi* is William Painter's *The Palace of Pleasure* (1567), an extremely popular compendium of lively tales of domestic and Court life, drawn from ancient and Italian traditions.[26] A number of sources for plays by Shakespeare are to be found within the same collection. The twenty-third 'nouel' is entitled 'The Duchesse of Malfi, the Infortunate marriage of a Gentleman, called Antonio Bologna, with the Duchesse of Malfi, and the pitifull death of them bothe'.[27] The moral message of this novella is unequivocal from the opening paragraphs of the tale:

> Wherefore it behoueth the Noble, and such as haue charge of Common wealth, to liue an honest lyfe, and beare their port vpryght, that none haue cause to take ill example vpon dyscourse of their deedes and naughtie life. And aboue all, that modestie ought to be kept by women, whome as their race, Noble birth, authoritie and name, maketh them more famous, euen so their vertue, honestie, chastitie, and continencie more praiseworthy. And behoueful it is, that like as they wishe to be honoured aboue all other, so their life do make them worthy of that honour, without disgracing their name by deede or woorde, or blemishing that brightnesse which may commende the same. I greatly feare that all the Princely factes, the exploits and conquests done by the *Babylonian* Queene *Semyramis*, neuer were recommended with such praise, as hir vice had shame in records by those which left remembrance of ancient acts.[28] Thus I say, bicause a woman being as it were the Image of sweetenesse, curtesie and shamefastnesse, so soone as she steppeth out of the right tracte, and leaueth the smel of hir duetie and modestie, bisides the denigration of hir honor, thrusteth hir self into infinite troubles and causeth the ruine of such which should be honored and praised, if womens allurement solicited them not to follie.[29]

The litany of conventional cautions against 'dishonest' behaviour sets the tone of the story. 'Woman being as it were the Image of sweetenesse, curtesie and shamefastnesse' has no means of escape: any single act which does not square with this emblem of passive and dutiful behaviour condemns the individual as 'fallen' from the pedestal. An entire glorious military career is blotted out when Semiramis seduces her own son.

In the dramatic version of *The Duchess of Malfi*, active sexuality codes for female breach of decorum. As Marina Warner has ably shown, absence of sexuality early became a defining virtue of Mary, the ultimate icon of female virtue.[30] Mary, the second Eve, compensated for and atoned for Eve's concupiscence through her intact virginity even in motherhood:

> Through the virgin birth Mary conquered the post-Eden natural law that man and woman couple in lust to produce children. Chaste, she escaped the debt of Adam and Eve. . . . In the *City of God*, written 413–26, Augustine noted that Adam and Eve, after they had eaten the forbidden fruit, covered their genitals, not their hands or mouths, which had done the deed. From this he reasoned that the knowledge they had acquired was of an inner force, which he called *epithymia* (concupiscence). It affects all areas of life, he wrote, but particularly the sexual act, which cannot be performed without passion. In the involuntary impulse of desire, which cannot be quelled by the will, Augustine perceived the penalty of Adam's sin.[31]

Female sexuality (personified in Mary Magdalene, the anti-type of Mary, mother of Christ) negates all those attributes which bring women closer to the ideal model. It does not matter how a woman uses her sexuality; that she is sexually aware brands her as Eve/Magdalene as opposed to Mary: 'In her myth, Mary Magdalene sins because she is not chaste, and not for any other reason that might be considered more grave.'[32]

In the moment of disobeying her brothers and remarrying (remarrying a social inferior to emphasise the contrast between 'lust' and 'duty') the Duchess of Malfi asserts her sexual self. In so doing she is metamorphosed from ideal mirror of virtue ('Let all sweet ladies break their flatt'ring glasses, / And dress themselves in her') into lascivious whore. It is not merely that her brothers see her as such; the dominant strain in the subsequent representation of her is such. And we have to ask ourselves what it is about that knowing step she takes which is sufficient of a shock to the social system to warrant such ritualised condemnation. From the moment of her assertion of sexual independence, the Duchess moves with dignity but inexorably towards a ritual chastisement worthy of a flagrant breach of public order. Thereafter her strength lies in her fortitude in the face of a doom she has brought upon herself.

Yet the initial stand taken by the Duchess remains a strong move, despite the fact that success was never a real possibility, the threat to patriarchal order never an actual one. I want now to suggest that there was an area of early modern society in which apparently, although not actually, women had become frighteningly strong and independent, and one which maps plausibly on to the dominant preoccupations of the drama. This was the area of inheritance of property, and Land Law.

The sixteenth century in England was a period of major and far-reaching change in inheritance practice. Unfortunately these changes are masked from the student of literature by blanket references, whenever some comment on customary inheritance is called for, to a ubiquitous law of primogeniture (inheritance of the entire estate by the eldest male heir). Immediately he has introduced his bastard son, Edmund, to Kent in *King Lear*, Gloucester specifies his family position:

> But I have a son, sir, by order of law, some year elder than this, who yet is no dearer in my account. Though this knave came something saucily to the world before he was sent for, yet was his mother fair.[33]

This, we are told, is to establish that Edgar is Gloucester's legitimate heir as well as his legitimate son, since either way he is older than Edmund. Lear himself, meanwhile, divides his kingdom by 'partible' inheritance (equal division) among his daughters, in the absence of a male heir. Certainly by the sixteenth century this was the ideal state of affairs, as codified in English Land Law;[34] but as recent historians, and historians of Land Law themselves are quick to point out, inheritance practice consisted in modifying or evading the most stringent requirements of lineal inheritance as codified, because of possible disastrous consequences this could in practice have in fragmenting individual estates.[35]

Under English law all land is held in tenancy, either from a noble landlord, or ultimately from the Crown. The type of tenure (the nature of the tenancy) determines the manner in which the land can be disposed of. Although it appears to us self-evident that the individual in possession of land has the right to pass it on to his[36] natural heirs, land tenure meant that it was ultimately a matter between the lord of whom the land was held and any possible inheritor, not the tenant currently holding the land.

The great English landowners held their lands of the sovereign in return for direct services to the Crown: provision of knights for the sovereign's armies and household, or services in lieu of knight-service. All other land was held in 'socage': in return for a nominal or real rent (in money or in kind). Further down the social scale land was usually held as 'copy-hold' tenure: a notional contract existed between the major tenant of the land and his subordinate tenant. Copyhold tenants were at the mercy of their landlord to uphold their sub-tenancy.

The passing down of land from generation to generation was therefore a matter for concern not simply for the family in residence on the land, but also for the technical landlord. It was in the interests of the landlord that the land be kept in intact parcels – passed down from tenant father to eldest son, say. But for the tenant himself, this primary desire to keep landholdings intact was to be set against his inevitable desire to settle each of his children comfortably. Much of the complexity of actual Land Law practice derives from attempts to square these two competing sets of requirements in deciding on inheritance.

The passing of land out of the control of the incumbent tenant and his immediate family is termed 'alienation'. A good deal of English Land Law is concerned with avoiding possibilities of accidental alienation of land (for instance, if an heir dies without issue, or if an heir's widow remarries). For this purpose a number of conditions might be imposed on inheritance: if the inheriting son dies without issue, the inheritance reverts to the next-of-kin of the father from whom he inherited (rather than being alienated to his wife's family). If there are no sons to inherit, and the holding is divided amongst the daughters of a marriage, the land reverts intact to the male heir in the next generation. If a surviving widow who has retained a portion of her dead husband's lands dies (though not normally if she remarries) that portion reverts to the next-of-kin on her husband's side.[37]

Landlords (and the Crown) were opposed entirely to alienation of land since it dispersed holdings. And since landlords were inevitably the more powerful body, 'inalienable rights' dominated the inheritance scene. Tenants, on the other hand, frequently pressed for alienation, which would enable them, for instance, to sell estates when in financial need (which tenants increasingly were during the economic upheavals of the sixteenth century). Where a will was made in accordance with inalienable provisions, it required a special parliamentary Bill to overturn it. As the century wore on, growing numbers of such Bills appear in the records as Elizabeth's ministers played the inheritance stakes to maximise the wealth and landholdings of a small, select group of nobles.[38]

Against the rules for preserving landholdings intact are another group to uphold the interests of dependent individuals. On the death of her husband, a widow normally retained one-third of all his estate for her use during her lifetime – her 'dower'.[39] Correspondingly, if a wife with landholdings of her own died, her husband had 'curtesy' – use of her lands until his own death, provided that there was a child of the marriage who had been heard to cry (that is, who had survived at least a short time after birth). Daughters who were not to inherit were cus-tomarily allocated cash dowries, and sometimes dowries in land (or a house), which they retained for their own use within the marriage, and which reverted to their own families in case of their death before their husband's. Alternatively, the daughter could pass her dowry monies by will to her children. Younger sons who were not to inherit main tenancy lands were also 'endowed' with cash or subsidiary lands, whose subsequent ownership was in their own hands.

A landlord's rights extended to the families of tenants in their capacity as heirs. If the tenant died while his heir was a minor, his landlord acquired the heir as ward until his or her majority (twenty-one for a son, sixteen for a single daughter, fourteen for a married daughter). He was then responsible for the keep and education of the ward, but in return could sell the wardship to another landlord, and could also sell the marriage of the ward, provided he did not marry the ward downwards in the social class structure – termed 'disparagement'.[40] In Shakespeare's *Henry VI Part I*, the breaking of Henry's betrothal in order to marry the politically preferable Margaret is justified ironically in terms of disparagement. 'A poor earl's daughter' is not a fit match for Henry: Margaret's father is 'King of Naples and Jerusalem', so she is a fit match for the royal ward (although in fact, of course, 'King of Naples and Jerusalem' is meaningless, and her father an impoverished nobody).[41]

Such possibilities should warn us that attitudes towards family and children in noble households liable to have their small children seized into wardship are likely to have been different from our modern notions of 'natural' emotional bonds within the family. Noble babies were usually put out to live with a wet-nurse from birth until the age of two or three (and infant mortality amongst babies of all classes was appallingly high), and were generally sent to serve in the household of an appropriate patron from seven; they might be married by fourteen.[42] Children in such households were investments in a lineal future for the family, and thus had a public identity from birth, and a place in the power structure. As such they were less suitable objects of intense, possessive affection of the kind dubbed 'maternal' in our own day, than the publicly invisible offspring of our modern nuclear family.[43] When Hermione, in *The Winter's Tale*, dispatches her young son with the impatient words, 'Take the boy to you; he so troubles me, / 'Tis past enduring',[44] any comment on her lack of maternal solicitude is a modern one. Juliet's mother, in *Romeo and Juliet*, cannot remember exactly how old her daughter is; it is left to the nurse who raised her to be precise.[45]

It was not only the direct male heir who was likely to be raised away from the parental hearth, given the high mortality rate amongst children. The mother mourning the death of her firstborn was likely to find her grief compounded by the seizure of the next child in line to the estate, as substitute ward. Here is a single example of the summary requisitioning of offspring in this way:

> To Mabel late the wife of Roger Torpell. She must well remember that the king gave the custody of the lands and heirs of the said Roger de Torpell, with the marriage of the heirs, to R. bishop of Chichester, the chancellor, during the minority of the heirs, whereof because William the elder son and heir, had died, the king commands her, as she loves herself and her goods, not to eloign Acelota, sister and next heir of the said William, whom the chancellor committed to her ward to nurse, but to deliver her to the messenger of the said bishop bearing the letters with letters of the bishop testifying that he is his messenger.[46]

In the society which produced a letter like this, the mother's 'duty' towards her children is defined in terms of the patriarchal linear descent: she is custodian of the carriers of the line. In our own society, by contrast, the mother in the nuclear family is defined purely as rearer of her children (with no evident purpose beyond the immediate family group); the children are her badge of office, to be 'worn' as evidence in themselves of her wifely role. Summing up the feudal situation Sue Sheridan Walker writes: 'Among major feudatories, it was rare for the child heir to be left in the care of the mother.'[47] *All's Well That Ends Well* opens with the death of the Count of Rousillon, an event which is immediately associated with the departure of his son to the court of the King of France as ward:

> Countess　In delivering my son from me, I bury a second husband.
> Bertram　And I in going, madam, weep o'er my father's death anew; but I must attend his Majesty's command, to whom I am now in ward, evermore in subjection.[48]

In *The Duchess of Malfi*, pathos is engendered by the intimate detail of the Duchess's concern for her children by Antonio, even *in extremis*:

> Duchess　　　　　　　　　　　Farewell Cariola:
> In my last will I have not much to give;
> A many hungry guests have fed upon me,
> Thine will be a poor reversion.
> Cariola　　　　　　　　　　　I will die with her.
> Duchess　I pray thee, look thou giv'st my little boy
> Some syrup for his cold, and let the girl
> Say her prayers, ere she sleep.[49]

But it is as woman deprived of her hereditary rights that she has become stereotyped nurturing motherhood. As hereditary Duchess, in Act III, she dispatches her eldest son with his father:

> Duchess　　　　　　　　　　　I suspect some ambush:
> Therefore by all my love (Antonio), I do conjure you
> To take your eldest son, and fly towards Milan:
> Let us not venture all this poor remainder
> In one unlucky bottom.[50]

While, even more strikingly, in Painter's source story the Duchess's devotion to her firstborn, son and heir to the Duke of Amalfi, is entirely characterised in terms of her assiduous care for his inheritance:

> I have liued and gouerned my self in such wise in my widow state, and there is no man so hard and seuere of iudgement, that can blason reproche of me in that which appertaineth to the honesty and reputation of such a Ladie as I am, bearing my port so right, as my conscience yeldeth no remorse, supposing that no man hath wherewith to bite and accuse me. Touching the order of the goods of the Duke my sonne, I have vsed them with such diligence and discretion, as bisides the dettes which I haue discharged sithens the death of my Lord, I haue purchased a goodly Manor in *Calabria*, and haue annexed the same to the Dukedom of his heire: and at this day doe not owe one pennie

to any creditor that lent mony to the Duke, which he toke vp to furnish the charges in the warres, which he sustained in the seruice of the Kings our soueraine Lords in the late warres for the kingdome of *Naples*. I haue as I suppose by this meanes stopped the slaunderous mouth, and giuen cause vnto my sonne, during his life to accompt himself bound vnto his mother.[51]

To us these are the cold words of a calculating power politician; to Painter they are the appropriate evidence for the Duchess's enduring concern with and commitment to her son and heir.

As these remarks are meant to make clear, *family*, particularly for the nobly born, means first and foremost in the sixteenth and seventeenth centuries the continuing kinship relations down the generations, within which the individual family group played an extremely small part. Where the demands of the two clashed it would almost inevitably be the case (the more so the more powerful and wealthy the line) that the requirements of lineage and inheritance overrode those of personal love and affection. This was particularly the case for remarriage of widows: in spite of the Church's emphasis on the chastity of widows, who should remain true to the loving memory of the man they married with God's blessing,[52] the widows of wealthy men were married off again with quite undignified haste where those responsible for them considered it financially advantageous to the line to do so. When Sir Horatio Palavicino died in 1600 he had left his lands in trust to a consortium which included Sir William Cornwallis and Sir Robert Cecil, to be administered in the interests of his eldest son Henry and his heirs, and failing them, the second son Toby and his heirs. Horatio's widow was to have the use of the substantial estate during her lifetime, provided she remained chaste and single. However, Lady Anne was far too desirable a catch (left as she was to administer a very substantial estate) to be allowed to mourn her dead husband for long. Exactly a year after his death (the very first day after the end of her official period of mourning) she was pressed into marriage with Oliver Cromwell of Hinchinbrook, a political ally of Sir Robert Cecil, whose fortunes were at an extremely low ebb. Cecil wrote to Lady Anne recommending the marriage to Cromwell in the strongest possible terms, and turned a complete blind eye to the fact that Sir Horatio's will explicitly barred her from continuing to administer his estate if she remarried:

. . . although it is far from my purpose to persuade you to change your present condition, because marriages are made in heaven and never prosper better than when they proceed from free and mutual election, yet having understood that this gentleman, Mr. Oliver Cromwell, hath disposed his heart to seek you and deserve you not only by true affection but by offer and performance of all such conditions as may be consonant to the will of the dead and the desire of those that live, whose chiefest care must appear to be the hindering of all courses which may prove to the prejudice of his children whose memory and trust we cannot forget.[53]

The two competing sets of values are clearly apparent in this letter: on the one hand Cecil acknowledges the Church's view that 'marriages are made in heaven'; on the other, Cromwell is a husband strongly to be recommended because he offers 'performance of all such conditions as may be consonant to the will of the dead' – language which all too evidently has to do with succession and administration of lands and monies.[54] In the event, Cecil and Cromwell did all they could to wrest the Palavicino inheritance from the grasp of the rightful heirs by astute marriages and parliamentary Bills.[55]

Nowhere was the collision between two sets of attitudes more apparent than in the role played by women within the inheritance and lineal picture. It has been pointed out recently that early modern European custom differs strikingly from most other agricultural societies in preferring female heirs to distant male heirs where inheritance cannot pass directly through an obvious male heir:

If one looks in a broad comparative way at systems of agricultural production, one of the significant features of European societies, as indeed of the major states of Asia, is the fact that the property from some kind of conjugal estate devolves on both men and women. . . . One implication is that even when a certain type of property (such as land) is restricted to males, women are nevertheless seen as residual heirs in preference to more distant males. This diverging system of devolution is in stark contrast to most of traditional Africa where, if a man did not have a male heir, then a search would be made among the male children of his brothers. . . . Virtually everywhere the rule existed that property descended from males to males and from females to females. . . . Where women receive land, the basic means of production, either as a dowry or as part of their inheritance (that is, even when they have brothers), the social implications are greater because its ownership is drastically reorganized at every generation. Land changes hands between the sexes at every marriage or death, and large quantities of land may come under the direct or indirect control of women.[56]

It is, that is to say, a built-in feature of the European inheritance system that women are potentially powerful, albeit within a basically patrilinear system – they intrude and intervene where necessary to amend the simple law of male inheritance, either as subsidiary heirs, or in marriage settlements. In the sixteenth century, entailed land (land for which a strict sequence of inheritance was legally specified) either passed in *tail male* (from eldest son to eldest son) or in *tail general* (to the eldest child of either sex). Increasingly in the latter half of the sixteenth century and the early part of the seventeenth, families made efforts to convert *tail male* into *tail general* to avoid alienation of lands outside the immediate family to distant male relatives. A number of factors contributed to this change of strategy away from strict male succession to one involving daughters as direct heirs; the most obvious was the dearth of male heirs amongst the nobility:

> The decisive factors were firstly ill-balanced diet, tight-corseting, lack of fresh air and exercise, liability to infection, all of which seriously impaired female health and encouraged miscarriages and still-births; secondly, the high adult mortality rate, which meant that only about a half of all marriages were completed (i.e. lasted throughout the whole fertile period of women); thirdly, the fact that . . . female fertility in the seventeenth century ended very early, at about 41. As a result the recorded evidence shows that 19 per cent of first marriages among the nobility between 1540 and 1660 were childless and no less than 29 per cent produced no male children. These figures are undoubtedly exaggerated by failure to record some children who died in infancy, but since only two noble children out of three survived their fifteenth year at this period they are an optimistic estimate of the proportion of first marriages which produced an adult male of marriageable age to carry on the line.[57]

In addition, severe economic pressures on noble fortunes led families to draw in the net of kinship to keep lands within the immediate family. The abolition of convents with the Reformation meant a significant increase in the number of daughters for whom marriage portions (usually in cash) had to be provided, often by mortgaging estate lands, which in turn produced a strong incentive to hold lands intact.[58] Furthermore, the period represents a peak in a combination of drains on resources which included dower obligations (lifetime financial support of widows), sometimes to three women left without husband on a single estate, grants to younger sons in lieu of land prospects, and general debts in cash due to heavy court expenditure.[59] Small wonder that Theseus, in *A Midsummer Night's Dream* should use the lifespan of the dowager widow as a vivid image for the slow passing of time:

> But, O, methinks, how slow
> This old moon wanes! She lingers my desires,
> Like to a step-dame or a dowager,
> Long withering out a young man's revenue.[60]

Female heirs provided a solution to the dissipation of intact estates; the estate could pass to the eldest daughter in the absence of a son, rather than being divided by partible inheritance amongst all the surviving children. Female heirs and well-dowered widows also offered the possibility of accumulating land holdings, and therefore power:

> Family after family rose up in the world by the simple device of piling estate upon estate by judicious choice of brides. It was generally appreciated that two or three gentry rolled into one, or an aristocratic coheiress and a gentleman combined, were the financial equivalent of a baron. In the circumstances of the day, such entrepreneural activity usually resulted in the granting of a title.[61]

In Sir John Davies' 'Contention between a Wife, a Widowe, and a Maide for Precedence at an Offringe', peformed before Queen Elizabeth in December 1602, the wife taunts the widow: 'Goe widow, make some younger brother rich, / And then take thought and dye, and all is well.'[62] In their concern over the absence of male heirs, and over the damage being done to their estates by strict entailment and traditional patterns of inheritance, heads of household increasingly turned their attention to the settlements on daughters and on younger sons. Traditionally these took the form of 'portions' allocated in place of land inheritance (a girl with a portion automatically dropped out of the family inheritance stakes), at the time at which the younger children left home. Strategically, heads of household concentrated on these settlements to compensate for erosion of the main estates: if a well-dowried daughter could attract a good husband, or a younger son make a match with a wealthy heiress or widow, that might more than compensate for the outlay on the portion. Particularly important for the bargaining power of dowries was the fact that the daughter's cash dowry was available to the father of the bridegroom to pay off his debts in ready money.[63]

Portions for younger sons and marriageable daughters increase dramatically during the Elizabethan and Jacobean period.[64] 'Dowry inflation' was considered the curse of the period, decried by clergy and lawyers:

> The excesses of our time in giving great Dowries is growen to such a height, that it impoverisheth oftentimes the Parents; it seemeth a point worthy the consideration whether it were not expedient that the Parliament should limit the quantity of Dowries according to the State and Condition of every Man; which no doubt would greatly ease the Nobility and Gentry.[65]

The effectiveness of the strategy as a lure is evidenced by the fact that some sumptuary legislation (legislation controlling richness of dress according to rank and status)[66] aligned the permitted richness of dress for a woman with the size of her marriage portion. In Thomas Heywood's *A Woman Killed with Kindness* the shifting fortunes of Mountford are directly reflected on stage by the dress his sister wears:

> *Enter* SIR CHARLES, *gentlemanlike, and his Sister, gentlewomanlike.*
> Susan   Brother, why have you trick'd me like a bride?
>   Bought me this gay attire, these ornaments?
>   Forget you our estate, our poverty?[67]

Here the woman's dress defines her power as a magnet to attract wealth on behalf of the paternal line. 'Dotal inflation was – in the eyes of fathers – the curse of early modern Europe', writes one recent historian.[68]

The prominent position occupied by female heirs in all this discussion of the complicated tactical manoeuvring surrounding inheritance is in striking contrast to the ideology of modesty and dutiful submissiveness which I discussed in the last chapter. This fact is, of course, somewhat ironic. It was certainly not in the minds of lawyers and landowners preoccupied with patrilinear succession that their women might be involved as other than means to a patriarchal end. But it does turn out to be the case, as recent studies of the European family confirm, that female nobles and gentry are obtrusive during the period in their importance as carriers of inheritance. Stanley Chojnacki has drawn attention to a similarly striking discrepancy between patriarchal ideology and the actual effectiveness of women as operators within the economic system in Renaissance Venice. On the one hand 'the general concept that Venetians had of women' is appropriately captured by the following.

Neither works of imagination, nor high intellectual attainments, nor flights of poetry adorn the figure of woman in Venice's earlier epoch. Modest, domestic [*casalinga*], she is swept up in the great whirlwind of life; and she appears to us only in her weaknesses, or in the splendor of her beauty, or in the context of one of the high offices of her mission – her children, her family.[69]

On the other, Chojnacki concludes that in actual fact:

In view of the larger estates that they now possessed by reason of their larger dowries, and in view of the always-present possibility that the plague might suddenly snatch them away, these Venetian patrician wives took occasion to write several wills in the course of their adult lifetimes. The fact that they did so, taking pains to determine for themselves the destiny of their estates instead of letting the statutory regulations take effect, indicates that women had a clear sense of their legal prerogatives and their economic significance, and were determined to exercise them on behalf of the kin that they felt most responsibility for or sympathy with – and without regard for lineage. . . . Women's economic substance increased – largely a result of dowry inflation – and . . . their determination to keep control of this enlarged wealth also increased. The general impression that this configuration of women's position conveys is that they had the means of producing a pretty sizable impact on society.[70]

As 'carriers', as transmittors of wealth and power, women produce 'a pretty sizable impact'. Female idiosyncracy may be stifled amongst a mass of womanly 'duties' in the home – it cannot be controlled in the writing of wills. In *The Duchess of Malfi* it is not irrelevant that the Duchess 'wilfully' declares her passion for Antonio under cover of writing her will.

Not that this gives individual women power over their own lives; and this is really the point at issue. They are technically strong (strong enough to have some 'economic leverage', and to cause patriarchal anxiety), but actually they remain in thrall.[71] In Middleton's *Women Beware Women*, the amply-dowered Isabella bewails her lack of personal choice of a marriage partner, whilst at the same time affirming her importance in the inheritance stakes:

Isabella   Oh the heart-breakings
Of miserable maids, where love's enforced!
The best condition is but bad enough:
When women have their choices, commonly
They do but buy their thraldoms, and bring great portions
To men to keep 'em in subjection –
As if a fearful prisoner should bribe

> The keeper to be good to him, yet lies in still,
> And glad of a good usage, a good look sometimes.
> By 'r Lady, no misery surmounts a woman's:
> Men buy their slaves, but women buy their masters.[72]

At the beginning of *Cymbeline*, the flouting by Imogen and Posthumus of a financially-advantageous arranged marriage results in imprisonment and banishment of the partners respectively. Juliet, in *Romeo and Juliet*, may carry a handsome fortune as her father's sole heir, but she is powerless to oppose his choice of a partner to optimise the financial effectiveness of that fortune. When she claims free choice her father rants at her:

> Day, night, hour, tide, time, work, play,
> Alone, in company, still my care hath been
> To have her match'd; and having now provided
> A gentleman of noble parentage,
> Of fair demesnes, youthful, and nobly train'd,
> Stuff'd, as they say, with honourable parts,
> Proportion'd as one's thought would wish a man –
> And then to have a wretched puling fool,
> A whining mammet, in her fortune's tender,
> To answer 'I'll not wed, I cannot love,
> I am too young, I pray you pardon me!'
> But, an you will not wed, I'll pardon you.
> Graze where you will, you shall not house with me.[73]

The declamatory tone of the last two speeches quoted suggests that acknowledging publicly the absolute rights of parents over their daughters was a commonplace. And indeed, a wealth of contemporary social documentation on alliances confirms the actual powerlessness of girls in their marriage arrangements:[74] one of the Earl of Surrey's sisters was reduced to petitioning Henry VIII when her husband persisted in treating her lands as if they were his own, whilst neglecting her for her wet-nurse; dowager widows were remarried in games of pure power-politics; wives were set aside in favour of more advantageous ones.[75]

Yet in *Women Beware Women* it is in fact the female characters who, whilst formally protesting their ineffectualness, weakness and submissiveness to men, wheeler-deal their way through adultery, murder and incest. The alliance of the heart which Isabella in *Women Beware Women* would prefer to arranged marriage with a wealthy ward is an incestuous relationship with her uncle (even if she is duped into believing him no uncle at all): the female drive towards independent choice leads to sexual licence. The shift from passivity to bravura activity is accompanied by a marked moral decline, apparent in her subsequent disparaging reference to the indignity of being 'marketed' as an heiress:

> *Isabella* (aside)   But that I have th' advantage of the fool [the ward],
> As much as woman's heart can wish and joy at,
> What an infernal torment 'twere to be
> Thus bought and sold, and turned and pried into; when alas
> The worst bit is too good for him! And the comfort is
> 'Has but a cater's place on't, and provides
> All for another's table.[6]

With comparable bravado, the Duchess of Malfi resolutely identifies her elevated fiscal position (as young widow to a large estate, and heiress in her own right) with her actual entitlement to act exactly as she chooses:

> *Duchess*   The misery of us that are born great –
> We are forc'd to woo, because none dare woo us:
> . . .
>   sir, be confident –
> What is't distracts you? This is flesh, and blood, sir;
> 'Tis not the figure cut in alabaster
> Kneels at my husband's tomb. Awake, awake, man!
> I do here put off all vain ceremony,
> And only do appear to you a young widow
> That claims you for her husband, and like a widow,
> I use but half a blush in't.

In both cases, I suggest, we are witness to the acting out of a taboo. As the loyal Cariola comments on the Duchess's behaviour: 'Whether the spirit of greatness or of woman / Reign most in her, I know not, but it shows / A fearful madness.'[8] The Duchess acts out her remarriage and its consequences as if her forcefulness as royal heir, dowager of the Dukedom of Amalfi, carrier of a substantial dowry in moveable goods (which she and Antonio take legitimately with them when they flee together), gave her real power to determine her own behaviour. In this she is proved pathetically wrong. In a passage which modern producers prefer to omit as tedious, the patriarchy's retaliation for her behaviour is spelt out:

2nd Pilgrim	They are banish'd.
1st Pilgrim	But I would ask what power hath this state
	Of Ancona to determine of a free prince?
2nd Pilgrim	They are a free state sir, and her brother show'd
	How that the Pope, fore-hearing of her looseness,
	Hath seiz'd into th' protection of the church
	The dukedom, which she held as dowager.⁻ʸ

The Duchess has lost her princely immunity through forfeiture of her dower – the forfeiture being because she proved herself 'loose' by marrying without her brothers' consent 'so mean a person' as Antonio (who himself has his own lands confiscated for his 'felony').⁸⁰ From this moment she is not, despite her own protests to the contrary, 'Duchess of Malfi, still':

Duchess	Am I not thy duchess?
Bosola	Thou art some great woman, sure, for riot begins to sit on thy forehead, clad in gray hairs, twenty years sooner than on a merry milkmaid's. Thou sleepest worse than if a mouse should be forced to take up her lodging in a cat's ear: a little infant that breeds its teeth, should it lie with thee, would cry out, as if thou wert the more unquiet bedfellow.
Duchess	I am Duchess of Malfi still.
Bosola	That makes thy sleep so broken.⁸¹

Proved pathetically wrong in her belief in emancipation through hereditary strength, the Duchess is reduced to the safe composite stereotype of penitent whore, Virgin majestic in grief, serving mother, and patient and true turtle-dove mourning her one love. Strength of purpose is eroded into strength of character in adversity. The duchess acts out on stage her inheritance-power (her 'economic leverage'), which in real life had little help to offer the individual woman. In real life the verdict on spirited independent behaviour was a foregone conclusion. Painter sums it up as follows:

Beholde here (O ye foolish louers) a Glasse of your lightnesse, and ye women, the course of your fonde behauior. ... Shall I be of the opinion that a householde seruaunt ought to sollicite, nay rather suborne the daughter of his Lord without punishment, or that a vile and abiect person dare to mount vpon a Princes bed? No no, pollicie requireth order in all, and eche wight ought to be matched according to their qualitie, without making a pastime of it to couer our follies, and know not of what force loue and desteny be, except the same be resisted. A goodly thing it is to loue, but where reason loseth his place, loue is without his effect, and the sequele rage and madnesse.⁸²

In Webster's play, the spectre of real female strength implicit in the inheritance structure is ritually exorcised. Headstrong, emancipated female lover is chastened into figurative resignation.[83]

In *Hamlet*, I suggest, Hamlet's horror at his mother Gertrude's remarriage calls into play this same suppressed fear of female interference in patrilinear inheritance. For Gertrude has, by her remarriage, effectively cut off Hamlet from his hereditary entitlement. Like Ferdinand in *The Duchess of Malfi*, Hamlet insists on attributing the choice of marriage partner which 'alienates' him from his inheritance solely to female lust – rampant sexuality is the dramatic representation of independent choice on woman's part. Gertrude is dowager queen during Hamlet's minority; in *tail male* the kingdom passes to Hamlet. But if Hamlet remains unmarried and childless (and Claudius terminates a possible betrothal to Ophelia), then Claudius (his father's brother) and *his* offspring are next in line of succession to the throne of Denmark. The combination of Gertrude's dowager rights and Claudius's own means that any child of their union will displace Hamlet. Even if this is only a subsidiary theme of the play, it must, I think, add substance to Hamlet's obsessive preoccupation with Gertrude's *sexual* relations with Claudius, on which so many critics have commented. In the first place, as I have said, female sexuality regularly represents woman's uncontrollable interference with inheritance (as in *The Duchess of Malfi*). In addition, copulation inevitably implies reproduction, in the absence of contraception,[84] and it is Gertrude's active copulation with Claudius which absorbs Hamlet (over and above the 'wantonness' of the remarriage itself). Copulation between Gertrude (Hamlet's mother) and Claudius (Hamlet's paternal uncle) therefore means a new heir, who will oust Hamlet from his place as 'son':

> King (Claudius) But now, my cousin Hamlet, and my son –
> Hamlet (Aside) A little more than kin, and less than kind.
> King How is it that the clouds still hang on you?
> Hamlet Not so, my lord; I am too much in the sun [son].[85]

Hamlet is too much his father's son, too little his uncle's, despite Claudius's formal use of the term: more than mere 'kin' (cousin), but less than 'kind', Claudius's own flesh and blood. The threat of an alternative heir provides a concrete focus of indignation for Hamlet's psychological distaste and revulsion at the union – a focus a modern audience is almost bound to miss. And as in the case of the Duchess of Malfi, it provides a convenient means of making Gertrude guilty, independently of any conscious intention on her part. Whether she has knowingly or unwittingly been draw into Claudius's plot, she is guilty by virtue of her power to disrupt the patriarchal power structure *in spite of* her actual passivity.

Coda: hic mulier: Female bogey

Since the daies of *Adam* women were neuer so Masculine; Masculine in their genders and whole generations, from the Mother, to the youngest daughter; Masculine in Number, from one to multitudes; Masculine in Case, euen from the head to the foot; Masculine in Moode, from bold speech, to impudent action; and Masculine in Tense: for (without redress) they were, are, and will be still most Masculine, most mankinde, and most monstrous.[86]

As I suggested earlier, moralists and satirists were quick to convert an uneasy sense that women (like younger sons, the low born, and traditional servant groups) were acting with greater freedom, into a potent symbol of general disorder. With growing frequency in the early modern period the faintest possibility of female effectiveness spills over into outright horror and abuse of 'monstrous' womanhood – the not-woman. And when it does so it finds ready and waiting a wealth of ancient and medieval commonplaces of female monstrosity: Juvenal, Martial, Ovid and Seneca amongst the ancients; the witty 'role reversal' figures of ballad and folk-tale amongst the more recent possibilities.[87] Incantatory excoriation of the 'not-woman', like that of the pamphleteer above, belongs to a long tradition which includes women who murder or emasculate men, like Judith and Delilah, and those who mutilate themselves to deny their sex, like the Amazon who cuts off her right breast so that she can draw a bow without hindrance.[88]

The drama of the early modern period is full of set-piece denunciations of the 'not-woman' in her many forms. Jonson's *Epicoene* and Marston's *Insatiate Countess* (1613) could provide endless examples; Webster's *The Duchess of Malfi*, *The White Devil* and *The Devil's Law-Case* whilst less thoroughgoingly misogynistic, provide equally typical ones. A safe dramatic starting-point for what is evidently a popular form of declamatory speech is the denunciation of the woman of easy virtue:

> Farewell, thou private strumpet, worse than common!
> Man were on earth an angel but for woman.
> That sevenfold branch of hell from them doth grow,
> Pride, lust, and murder, they raise from below,
> With all their fellow-sins. Women are made
> Of blood, without souls: when their beauties fade,
> And their lust's past, avarice or bawdry
> Makes them still loved; then they buy venery,
> Bribing damnation, and hire brothel-slaves:
> Shame's their executors, infamy their graves.
> Your painting will wipe off, which art did hide,
> And show your ugly shape in spite of pride.[89]

'Painting', and the intrinsic corruption and putrefaction of the female flesh which it conceals is another stock theme:

Bosola	You come from painting now?
Old Lady	From what?
Bosola	Why, from your scurvy face-physic – to behold thee not painted inclines somewhat near a miracle: these, in thy face here, were deep ruts and foul sloughs the last progress. There was a lady in France, that having had the smallpox, flayed the skin off her face to make it more level; and whereas before she looked like a nutmeg-grater, after she resembled an abortive hedgehog.
Old Lady	Do you call this painting?
Bosola	No, no, but careening of an old morphewed lady, to make her disembogue again – there's rough-cast to your plastic.
Old Lady	It seems you are well acquainted with my closet.
Bosola	One would suspect it for a shop of witchcraft, to find in it the fat of serpents, spawn of snakes, Jews' spittle, and their young children's ordure – and all these for the face: I would sooner eat a dead pigeon, taken from the soles of the feet of one sick of the plague, than kiss one of you fasting. Here are two of you, whose sin of your youth is the very patrimony of the physician, makes him renew his footcloth with the spring and change his high-prized courtezan with the fall of the leaf: I do wonder you do not loathe yourselves.[90]

It is this steady misogynistic tradition which is involved at moments when female figures like Lady Macbeth are represented as 'not-woman' at the peak of dramatic tension before committing 'unwomanly' acts – generally murder. She is 'Masculine in (her) gender', 'most mankinde, and most monstrous':

> *Lady Macbeth*   Come you spirits
> That tend on mortal thoughts, unsex me here;
> And fill me, from the crown to the toe, top-full
> Of direst cruelty. Make thick my blood,
> Stop up th' access and passage to remorse,
> That no compunctious visitings of nature
> Shake my fell purpose nor keep peace between
> Th' effect and it. Come to my woman's breasts,
> And take my milk for gall, you murd'ring ministers,
> Wherever in your sightless substances
> You wait on nature's mischief. Come, thick night,
> And pall thee in the dunnest smoke of hell,
> That my keen knife see not the wound it makes,
> Nor heaven peep through the blanket of the dark
> To cry 'Hold, hold'."[1]

In neo-Latin Senecan tragedy of the same period, written for and performed by the students of Oxford and Cambridge, such travesties of monstrous womanhood are found in abundance – after all, these performances catered for an exclusively male audience. When William Gager added a number of scenes to Seneca's *Hippolytus* for an Oxford student production, he included an extravagant diatribe against women in general which goes far beyond what is appropriate in the context of Phaedra's behaviour:

> O blanda vox, turpisque lenonum fides!
> O faeminarum semper impurum genus!
> Molle, et cruentum; frigidum, et mundum cremans;
> Vile, et superbum; debile, et quantum potens?
> Timidum, et rebelle; mobile, et constans malo;
> Stolidum, et dolosum; pertinax, brutum, impudens,
> Procax, avarum, perfidum, ingratum, impium.
> Immensa mundi, et generis humani parens
> Natura, quin nos arborum potius modo
> Tellure nasci sponte voluisti editos,
> Quam serere stirpe surculos tali novos?
> Cur faemina uti, tanta voluisti artifex?
> Draconis antrum potius, et tigris libet
> Subire, et ursae turpis, et diram prius
> Sedem leaenae, et si vel his gravior fera est;
> Nostro scelestam quam toro uxorem pati. . . .
> Quin noxiorem faeminam fugitis, viri?

> Effugite iuvenes, o viri, lenes viri,
> Nimiumque faciles! miseret, et vestri pudet;
> In messe serpens, anguis in gremio latet.
> Totam mariti mulier evertit domum,
> Stirpemque totam persequitur, odio viri.
> Quis faeminarum multiplex narret scelus?
> Non tota tellus charta si, et caelum forent,
> Et omnis atramentum aqua, et fluvio, et mari,
> Lignum omne calami, quisque scribendi artifex,
> Nequita vel sic faeminea queat exprimi.

[O voice which is seductive, and the disgraceful faith of bawds! O race of women always impure! Soft, and bloody; cold, and yet consuming the Universe with fire; vile, and proud; weak, yet how powerful? Timid, and rebellious; volatile, and constant in evil; obtuse, and full of guile; pertinacious, unreasonable, shameless, wanton, greedy, treacherous, ungrateful, and impious. O Nature, mighty parent of the Universe and of the human race, why did you not rather wish us to be born from the earth, after the manner of trees, spontaneously, than to plant fresh grafts from such a stock? Why did you, who are such a creator, wish to make use of woman? I would rather enter the lair of a dragon, and of a tiger, and of a dreadful bear, rather enter the awful den of a lioness, or of any animal fiercer than these, than allow a wicked wife in my bed. . . . Why, O men, do you not flee woman, who is more harmful? Flee, young men, O men, O gentle men, who are too compliant. I have pity on you, and I am ashamed of you. The serpent lurks in the harvest, the snake in one's bosom. Woman overturns the whole household of her husband, and through hate of her husband, persecutes his whole stock. Who can tell of the manifold crimes of woman? If all the earth and all the sky were paper, and all the water in both river and sea were ink, and if every piece of wood were a pen, and every person skilled in writing, the wickedness of woman could not even thus be expressed.][92]

Female anti-heroes in these plays regularly compare themselves with touchstones of classical not-womanhood like Medea (who murdered her own children to avenge herself on their father, Jason, and who persuaded the daughters of Pelias to murder, dismember and boil their own father) – and find her less monstrous than themselves. In William Alabaster's *Roxana* (c. 1592), the female anti-hero Atossa boasts:

> Haec dicta Medeae date; haud superbiat
> Cristaque tollat propter antiquum scelus:
> Atossa maius hoc dedit, maius dabit.

[Bear these words to Medea: let her not be proud, let her not preen herself on her ancient crime; Atossa has committed a greater one, and will commit a greater.][93]

Atossa has tortured her husband's mistress, Roxana, in a chamber decorated with pictures of Medea dividing the limbs of her brother (another of her heinous crimes), and of Thyestes eating his own children. She has then forced her to kill her own children, and has served their bodies to her husband at a banquet. All this is guaranteed to make the hair of a male audience stand on end in pleasurable terror.

Tamora in *Titus Andronicus*, and Lady Macbeth in *Macbeth* belong to this same tradition, which is careless of verisimilitude in the interests of the *frisson* of horror to be derived from such representations of threatening womanhood. On stage the male protagonist is galvanised into horrified action, as Macbeth is by his wife:

> *Macbeth*   I dare do all that may become a man;
>   Who dares do more is none.
> *Lady Macbeth*   What beast was 't then
>   That made you break this enterprise to me?
>   When you durst do it, then you were a man;
>   And to be more than what you were, you would
>   Be so much more the man. . . .
>   I have given suck, and know
>   How tender 'tis to love the babe that milks me –
>   I would, while it was smiling in my face,
>   Have pluck'd my nipple from his boneless gums,
>   And dash'd the brains out, had I so sworn
>   As you have done to this.[94]

Tamora's sons are likewise goaded on to rape and mutilation by their mother:

> *Tamora*   Hadst thou in person ne'er offended me,
>   Even for his sake am I pitiless.
>   Remember, boys, I pour'd forth tears in vain
>   To save your brother from the sacrifice;
>   But fierce Andronicus would not relent.
>   Therefore away with her, and use her as you will;
>   The worse to her the better lov'd of me.[95]

Off stage, the male member of the audience recognises the representation of perennially threatening woman (perennial source of horror) . . . and recognises equally its absurd excessiveness. No woman of *his* will ever get thus out of hand, and hence the representation is equally a source of delight.

These surreally-threatening female figures in the drama thus, I suggest, carry a good deal less actual dramatic weight (despite the seriously unsettling misogyny they encapsulate) than the 'strong' women I have discussed in the body of the present chapter. Like the female stereotypes of modern advertising they are (we are told) not really intended seriously, they are too much in excess, even of the strongest patriarchal perception of 'woman's place'. Lady Macbeth is a nightmare; the Duchess of Malfi is an insidiously subversive force to be reckoned with. And that distinction is reflected in the way in which the 'nightmare' figure can be nonchalantly dispatched in the dramatic action ('She should have died hereafter'), whereas the 'strong' woman must be systematically taught the error of her ways.

Notes

1 See recently, for instance, M. C. Bradbrook, *John Webster: Citizen and Dramatist* (London, 1980).

2 E. M. Brennan (ed.), *The Devil's Law-Case* (New Mermaid, 1975), p. xvi.

3 ibid., p. xvii.

4 ibid.

5 J. Russell Brown (ed.), *The Duchess of Malfi* (Revels, 1964), I.i.308–11. Compare Freud's question, 'Was will das Weib?': 'The great question that has never been answered and which I have not yet been able to answer, despite my thirty years of research into the feminine soul, is "What does a woman want?",' in E. Jones, *Sigmund Freud: Life and Works* (London, 1955), II,468.

6 U. Ellis-Fermor, *The Jacobean Drama* (London, 1936), p. 149. In critical editions of the plays of this period admiration for the individual dramatist's female characterisation has become almost obligatory.

7 I.i.293–304.

8 I.i.330–43.

9 'I'll case the picture up . . . All her particular worth grows to this sum: / She stains the time past, lights the time to come' (I.i.207–9).

10 *Hamlet* I.ii.137–57.

11 *The Duchess of Malfi* IV.i.1–8.

12 See below, p. 181; see also M. Warner, *Alone of All Her Sex: The Myth and the Cult of the Virgin Mary* (London, 1978), pp. 81–210.

13 Obviously, individual critics show more insight than I am here able to attribute them. My aim here is to redress a particular imbalance.

14 See, for example, T. S. Eliot, 'Hamlet' (1919), in *Selected Essays* (London, 1932; 1976 edn), pp. 141–6: 'Hamlet is up against the difficulty that his disgust is occasioned by his mother, but that his mother is not an adequate equivalent for it; his disgust envelops and exceeds her' (p. 145).

15 See H. Swinburne, *A Treatise of Spousals* (London, 1686; written c. 1620), p. 229.
16 *Hamlet* III.i.93–120.
17 Swinburne tells us that kisses are acceptable behaviour during a courtship where a spousal is anticipated.
18 The ambiguity of Ophelia's position is increased by her social status: Polonius has encouraged a possible marriage upwards. In *Troilus and Cressida* V.ii, three male eavesdroppers provide relentlessly patriarchal commentary on what might (at the outset of the scene at any rate) be merely dutiful behaviour towards Diomedes on Cressida's part (Cressida is Diomedes' ward).
19 I.ii.53–6. Female characters in the drama may themselves, of course, quite appropriately articulate the male view of their behaviour, since they are permanently subject to male 'reading'.
20 J. R. Mulryne (ed.), *Women Beware Women* (Revels, 1975), I.i.65–93.
21 Pregnancy is considered the inevitable outcome of willing or unwilling intercourse. Swinburne explains that a marriage is 'consummated' (converted from a spousal *de futuro* into a binding promise) if the woman either sleeps willingly with her betrothed or is raped by him.
22 *Othello* I.iii.292–3.
23 N. W. Bawcutt, *The Changeling* (Revels, 1958), II.ii.60–152.
24 For this universal fantasy, see e.g. R. F. Burton (ed.), *The Book of the Thousand Nights and a Night*, 17 vols (London, 1885), opening tale, the story of King Shahryar and his brother, I,6. The fantasy includes the assumption that sexual prowess transforms hideousness (blackness) to beauty in the woman's eyes. In *Titus Andronicus*, the monstrous Tamora cuckolds her emperor with the blackamoor Aaron – and is betrayed by the birth of a black child.
25 *Othello* IV.iii.11–38. For a sensitive treatment of this scene see S. N. Garner, 'Shakespeare's Desdemona', *Shakespeare Studies*, IX (1976), pp. 233–52.
26 A number of these didactic cautionary tales (which were immensely popular) recount the horrors which inevitably befall women who flout convention or abandon their traditionally submissive roles.
27 Reprinted in the Revels, *The Duchess of Malfi*, pp. 175–209.
28 See Boccaccio, *De claris mulieribus* (c.1359), transl. G. A. Guarino (New Brunswick, 1963), p. 6: 'But with one wicked sin this woman [Semiramis] stained all these accomplishments worthy of perpetual memory, which are not only praiseworthy for a woman but would be marvelous even for a vigorous man. It is believed that this unhappy woman, constantly burning with carnal desire, gave herself to many men.'
29 ibid., pp. 176–7.
30 M. Warner, *op. cit.*
31 ibid., pp. 52–4.
32 ibid., p. 235.
33 *King Lear* I.i.17–20.
34 See J. Thirsk, 'The European debate on customs of inheritance, 1500–1700', in J. Goody, J. Thirsk and E. P Thompson (eds), *Family and*

Inheritance: Rural Society in Western Europe, 1200–1800 (Cambridge, 1976), pp. 177–91.

35 For a lucid account of the history of English Land Law and its modifications in practice and precedent, see A. W. B. Simpson, *An Introduction to the History of the Land Law* (Oxford, 1961). I am grateful to Mr Peter Glazebrook and Professor Glanville Williams for their advise on the history of the Land Law. On inheritance practice as opposed to codified law, see A. Macfarlane, *The Origins of English Individualism* (Oxford, 1978); M. Spufford, *Contrasting Communities: English Villagers in the Sixteenth and Seventeenth Centuries* (Cambridge, 1974).

36 I use the pronoun 'he' in this synopsis of sixteenth-century Land Law, since in the context of the Land Law a female heir is merely a stand-in for an absent male heir (that is the theory, at least).

37 A further strategy, which becomes increasingly common during the period, involves the husband renouncing tenancy of part of his estate on marriage, and taking it on again as joint tenant with his wife (who then retained her tenancy in the event of her husband's death). This practice is termed 'jointure'.

38 See e.g. Sir Hugh Palavicino below, p. 83.

39 The terms 'dower' and 'dowry' though quite distinct, are regularly confused in popular parlance. This may be because both single out women for special provision in Land Law. See for example, P. S. Clarkson and C. T. Warren, *The Law of Property in Shakespeare* (Baltimore, 1942). There is a single term (step-mother) for both step-mother and mother-in-law in this period, perhaps for the same reason. In *The Taming of the Shrew*, II.i, Baptista, who has already promised Bianca a handsome dowry, haggles with her suitors over the dower *they* must provide.

40 See Chaucer, 'The Clerk's Tale', in F. N. Robinson (ed.), *The Works of Geoffrey Chaucer* (Oxford, 1970 edn), p. 111: 'For evere he deemed, sith that it bigan, / That whan the lord fulfild hadde his corage, / Hym wolde thynke it were a disparage / To his estaat so lowe for t' alighte' (IV.906–9).

41 On the Land Law in Shakespeare see Clarkson and Warren, *op. cit.*

42 See L. Stone, *The Crisis of the Aristocracy 1558–1641* (Oxford, 1965); *The Family, Sex and Marriage in England 1500–1800* (London, 1977).

43 See S. Sheridan Walker, 'Widow and ward: the feudal law of child custody in medieval England', in S. M. Stuard (ed.), *Women in Medieval Society* (University of Pennsylvania Press, 1976), pp. 159–72. Parental affection had at least to be restrained by likelihood of loss. For a classical precedent much emulated in Renaissance letters of consolation, see Plutarch, 'A letter of consolation to his wife on the death of an infant daughter', in R. Warner (ed.), *Moral Essays* (Penguin, 1971), pp. 176–85.

44 *The Winter's Tale* I.ii.1.

45 Stone gives this example, *The Family, Sex and Marriage, op. cit.*, p. 106.

46 In Sheridan Walker, *op. cit.*, p. 160.

47 ibid., p. 166.

48 *All's Well That Ends Well* I.i.1–5.

49 *The Duchess of Malfi*, IV.ii.199–205.

50 ibid., III.v.56–60.

51 Reprinted in the Revels *The Duchess of Malfi*, pp. 185–6.
52 See e.g. Jerome, Letter 54 (to Furia), in H. Wace and P. Schaff (eds), *St. Jerome: Letters and Select Works* (Oxford, 1893).
53 L. Stone, *An Elizabethan: Sir Horatio Palavicino* (Oxford, 1956), pp. 289–99.
54 See G. Duby, *Medieval Marriage: Two Models from Twelfth-Century France*, transl. E. Forster (Baltimore, 1978) for the vocabulary of morals versus fiscal alliance.
55 Stone, *The Family, Sex and Marriage*.
56 J. Goody, 'Inheritance, property and women: some comparative considerations', in Goody, Thirsk and Thompson, *op. cit.*, pp. 10–36, 10.
57 Stone, *The Crisis of the Aristocracy*, *op. cit.*, pp. 167–8.
58 See Stone, *The Family, Sex and Marriage*, *op. cit.*, p. 43: 'With the abolition of nunneries . . . the marriage market was flooded with girls who had hitherto been consigned to nunneries, but who now had to be married off, at considerable cost, to their social equals.'
59 For a general discussion of 'strategies' developed in social systems for optimising family prospects through inheritance and dowry rules, see P. Bourdieu, 'Les stratégies matrimoniales dans le système de reproduction', *Annales Economiques, Sociales et Culturelles*, 27 (1972), pp. 1105–27.
60 *A Midsummer Night's Dream* I.i.3–6.
61 Stone, *The Crisis of the Aristocracy*, *op. cit.*, p. 192.
62 R. Krueger (ed.), *The Poems of Sir John Davies* (Oxford, 1975), p. 220.
63 See J. P. Cooper, 'Patterns of inheritance and settlement by great landowners from the fifteenth to the eighteenth centuries' in Goody, Thirsk and Thompson, *op. cit.*, pp. 192–305.
64 See Cooper, *op. cit.*, by contrast with what Stone says.
65 In Cooper, *op. cit.*, p. 222.
66 See below, p. 142.
67 The diary of the contemporary theatre manager Philip Henslowe includes the following entry: 'pd vnto Thomas hewode the 5 of febreary 1602 for a womones gowne of blacke velluett for the playe of a womon kylld wth kyndnes some of vj[li]13'.' This expensive gentlewoman's gown would be appropriate to Susan here, though perhaps black is a bit sombre for marriage. See Revels edition, p. xvi.
68 D. O. Hughes, 'From brideprice to dowry in Mediterranean Europe', *Journal of Family History* (1978), pp. 262–96. I am most grateful to Diane Hughes for first making me aware of the importance of dowry practice in the early modern period.
69 S. Chojnacki, 'Patrician women in early Renaissance Venice', *Studies in the Renaissance*, XXI (1974), pp. 176–203, 176.
70 ibid., pp. 197–8.
71 For a striking confirmation of the discrepancy between technical and actual power, see E. W. Ives, '"Agaynst taking awaye of women": the inception and operation of the Abduction Act of 1487', in E. W. Ives, R. J. Knecht and J. J. Scarisbrick (eds), *Wealth and Power in Tudor England* (London, 1978), pp. 21–44.
72 *Women Beware Women* I.ii.166–76.

73 *Romeo and Juliet* III.v.177–89. See also *A Midsummer Night's Dream* for an equivalent attack on Hermia by her father.

74 See Stone, *The Family, Sex and Marriage*, pp. 180–3, 187–9. Sons were, of course, correspondingly powerless, but at least had the option of supporting mistresses to make up for unwelcome marriage partners.

75 See Strong, *The Cult of Elizabeth*, p. 107 for some complex widow-bargaining involving Dorothy Unton; for ruthless playing off of children's prospects see ibid., pp. 25–8 (the Russells). In the course of plotting a fitting match for her son Thomas to the suddenly widowed Margaret Dakins, Lady Russell suggested someone 'help to steal her away [abduct her].' See Ives, *op. cit.*

76 *Women Beware Women* III.iv.33–9.

77 *The Duchess of Malfi* I.i.441–59.

78 I.i.504–6.

79 III.iv.27–33.

80 See Henry III's statute for France, limiting widows' free use of their dower lands. J. O'Faolain and L. Martines (eds), *Not In God's Image: Women in History* (London, 1979) p. 233.

81 IV.ii.134–43.

82 Revels edition, pp. 192–3.

83 For a telling analogous real-life case, in which a wealthy widow of twenty-five was forcibly abducted by the landowner of the adjacent territory and pressed into a marriage to consolidate their lands, see the case of Margaret Kebell (1502). Margaret spent years and a small fortune contesting the marriage, with minimal success. See the gripping account of the story in E. W. Ives, *op. cit.*, pp. 31–44.

84 See below, p. 130.

85 *Hamlet* I.ii.64–7.

86 *Hic Mulier: or the Man-Woman* (London, 1620; reprint 1973), fo.A3ʳ.

87 See K. M. Rogers, *The Troublesome Helpmate: A History of Misogyny in Literature* (Seattle, 1966; 1973 edn); L. de Bruyn, *Woman and the Devil in Sixteenth-Century Literature* (Wiltshire, 1979).

88 See M. Warner, *Joan of Arc: The Image of Female Heroism* (London, 1981), p. 204. On 'bad' women in general in the drama of this period see A. J. C. Ingram, 'Changing attitudes to "bad" women in Elizabethan and Jacobean Drama' (unpublished Cambridge PhD dissertation, 1978).

89 Marston, *The Insatiate Countess*, in Rogers, *op. cit.*, p. 125.

90 *The Duchess of Malfi* II.i.21–44.

91 *Macbeth* I.v.38–51.

92 Addition to Act II, scene iii. Reprinted in full in J. W. Binns, 'William Gager's additions to Seneca's *Hippolytus*', *Studies in the Renaissance*, XVII (1970), pp. 153–91, 174–7 (Binns' translation).

93 In J. W. Binns, 'Seneca and neo-Latin tragedy in England', in C. D. N. Costa (ed.), *Seneca* (London, 1974), pp. 205–34, 214.

94 *Macbeth* I.vii.46–58.

95 *Titus Andronicus* II.iii.161–7.

4

Shrewd or Shrewish? When the Disorderly Woman has her Head

The scolding woman traditionally represents the irrational and uncontrollable in even the best-ordered male life. Socrates' wife, so the story goes, was a scold who made her philosopher husband's life a misery:

> Xanthippe, the wife of the philosopher Socrates, is said to have been ill-tempered and quarrelsome to a degree, with a constant flood of feminine tantrums and annoyances day and night. Alcibiades, amazed at this outrageous conduct of hers towards her husband, asked Socrates what earthly reason he had for not showing so shrewish a woman to the door. 'Because,' replied Socrates, 'it is by enduring such a person at home that I accustom and train myself to bear more easily away from home the impudence and injustice of other persons.'[1]

Even men of supreme intellect are not above the humdrum trials and tribulations of everyday domestic life – that is, the scolding wife. Open any classical reference book and you will find under Xanthippe the entry: 'Wife of Socrates allegedly a shrew' or 'a notable scold'.[2] Xanthippe empties a chamber pot on Socrates' head; Phyllis rides Aristotle round the room on all fours, naked and bridled. Renaissance scholars from Richard Hooker to Francis Bacon are credited with scolding wives. Society seems to find it irresistible to characterise the 'unworldliness' of the male intellectual and academic in terms of his failure to control the women in his life.[3]

In literature, from folk-tale to romance, shrews are always women, though philologically they may properly be male,[4] and they exercise a bewitching effect on the men who are subjected to their tongue's lash.[5] Indeed, the fate of such ill-natured wives as did inevitably exist (there were of course some real ones) was not uncommonly to be accused of witchcraft: an Essex witchcraft trial record of 1591 records of Thomas Sare's wife that she has been 'a very Skoulding and disquiet woman among her neighbours'. The record goes on to instruct that she 'confess' (elsewhere in the same records we find entries: 'a witch: to confess'). Other indictments refer to 'a witch and scolder (to confess for scolding)'; 'a slanderer' and 'called the wife of James Bean a witch and fought with another woman'; 'develishe of her tongue'; 'a scold, slanderer, and resorted to cunning men for help'.[6]

I choose the shrew or scold for this chapter in order to explore for this single case the complicated relationship between traditional representations of the disruptive woman with a quick tongue and even the most plausibly lively of female characters in the drama: Beatrice in *Much Ado About Nothing*, Kate in *The Taming of the Shrew*, Desdemona sparring with Iago in *Othello*, Helena equivocating on virginity in *All's Well That Ends Well*. For unlike the chaste and steadfast virgin, or the silent and obedient spouse (to whom I shall return in a later chapter), the scold/shrew appeals to our twentieth-century notions of alert and emancipated womanhood to a degree which makes us reluctant to acknowledge them as in any way ciphers: these must be the racy women who roamed Elizabethan England, which contemporary male observers pronounced 'the Paradice of Women'.[7]

Greek and Roman comedy and satire, Eastern legend, medieval estates literature, and Biblical iconography (Eve back-chatting the serpent; Noah's wife)[8] all contain representations of garrulous, determined and ingenious women.[9] And there is a disturbing consensus amongst these varied sources as to the unacceptable, emasculating, and yet curiously seductive nature of such female attributes. If the definition of the virtuous wife is as chaste, obedient, dutiful and silent, then the definition of the wife without virtue is as lusty, headstrong and talkative. These qualities make her both provocative and threatening. Woman's moist humours, which make her lascivious, also loosen her tongue.[10] The tongue is symbol of *impudence*, that is, immodesty, to be carefully covered by the teeth (so gentlewomen are advised).[11] Wherever one turns to in the catalogue of classical tags which bolster the new Renaissance confidence in itself with comforting corroborating attitudes from antiquity, the female tongue is coupled with the ever-present threat of female dominion in the home:

The bed that holds a wife is never free from wrangling and mutual bicker-
ings; no sleep is to be got there! It is there that she sets upon her husband,
more savage than a tigress that has lost her cubs.[12]

The threat of the shrew/scold is more familiar (and the dread it
evokes closer to home) than that of the 'mannish' woman, the
woman who apes male dress and postures. The threat of the scold
is local and *domestic*; that of the Amazon/virago is generalised
'rejection of her sex', a strangeness which travesties nature. The
scold is a disturbingly persuasive possibility; the man-woman, an
outsider and a sensationalised freak.[13] Joan of Arc belongs to the
latter class; according to Edward Hall's *The Vnion of the Two
Noble and Illustre Famelies of Lancastre and Yorke* (1548), she
was 'a rampe of suche boldnesse, that she would course horses
and ride theim to water, and do thynges, that other yong
maidens, both abhorred & wer ashamed to do'.[14] And he asks
rhetorically:

Where was her shamefastnes, when she daily and nightly, was conuersant
with comen souldiors, and men of warre, emongest whom, is small honestie,
lesse vertue, and shamefastnesse, least of all exercised or vsed? Where was
her womanly pitie, when she takyng to her, the harte of a cruell beaste, slewe,
man, woman, and childe, where she might haue the vpper hand? Where was
her womanly behauor, when she cladde her self in a mannes clothyng, and
was conuersant with euery losell [good for nothing], geuyng occasion to all
men to iudge, and speake euill of her, and her doynges.[15]

While Holinshed, in his *Chronicles* (1577; emended edition
1586/7) expresses the same decisively condemnatory view of
Joan's behaviour as against nature:

In which for her pranks so uncouth and suspicious, the lord regent . . . caused
hir life and beleefe, after order of law, to be inquired upon and examined.
Wherein found though a virgin, yet first, shamefullie rejecting hir sex
abominablie in acts and apparell, to have counterfeit mankind, and then, all
damnablie faithlesse, to be a pernicious instrument to hostilitie and bloud-
shed in divelish witchcraft and sorcerie, sentence accordinglie was pronounced against hir.[16]

The female warrior is 'though a virgin, yet . . . shamefullie
rejecting hir sex':

The Amazons, with their two most famous queens, Hippolyta and Penthe-
silea, were Diana's chief votaries, their cult celebrated in particular at
Ephesus, site of one of Diana's greatest temples. They lived by her example,

spurning men, tracking game, rejoicing in battle, inverting biology and flouting nature.[17]

The French, requiring a positive image of Joan as their national hero, converted her into a more acceptably iconic 'ideal androgyne'.

By contrast, the woman with a sharp tongue breaks the social order: she is strictly disorderly. Discordant, disruptive, unruly, she threatens to sabotage the domestic harmony which depends upon her general submissiveness. William Whately devotes three long paragraphs of his *Bride-Bush* to specifying the ways in which a wife's speech must be guided by assumptions of obedience, humility and dependence:

> First, in speeches and gestures vnto him. These must carry the stampe of feare vpon them, and not be cutted, sharpe, sullen, passionate, teechie; but meeke, quiet, submissiue, which may shew that she considers who herselfe is, and to whom she speakes. The wiues tongue towards her husband must bee neither keene, nor loose, nor countenance neither swelling nor deriding: her behauiour not flinging, not puffing, not discontented; but sauouring of all lowlinesse and quietnesse of affection. Looke what kinde of words or behauiour thou wouldst dislike from thy seruant or childe, those must thou not giue to thine husband: for thou art equally commanded to be subiect.[18]

After itemising a number of Biblical examples of women whose scolding tongue showed that they did not know their place, Whately continues:

> Yet for all these warnings wee haue some women that can chafe and scold with their husbands, and raile vpon them, and reuile them, and shake them together with such termes and carriage, as were vnsufferable towards a seruant. Staines of woman-kinde, blemishes of their sexe, monsters in natures, botches of humane society, rude, gracelesse, impudent, next to harlots, if not the same with them. Let such words leaue a blister behinde them, and let the canker eate out these tongues.[19]

The injunction is quite clear, and with good Biblical authority — the husband's order to his wife is 'hold your tongue':

> *Paul* commands the woman to *learne in silence*. The worde is, *in quietnesse*: wherein he not alone inioynes a publicke, but euen a general silence to hold in the house and other like meetings: for why should that bee restrained without any neede, which doth well receiue a larger extent.[20]

In support of this case for silence as the domestic ideal in women, other authors produced even more reassuring Biblical precedent:

There is nothing that doth so commend, avaunce, set forthe, adourne, decke, trim, and garnish a maid, as silence. And this noble vertue may the virgins learne of that most holy, pure and glorious virgin Mary, which, when she eyther hard or saw any worthy and notable thing, blabbed it not oute straight wais to her gossips, as the manner of women is at thys present day, but being silent, she kept al thos sayinges seacreat, and pondered them in her hart.[21]

This emphasis on the need for women to control their tongue is hardly surprising, for within the tightly-knit Renaissance household the wife's tongue is her only weapon. Both gossiping and scolding give her a semblance of power, which threatens disorder without actually freeing her from her multiple obligations and constraints. Woman's power to disrupt is illusory: it is only 'telling tales' and 'calling names'. As Vittoria puts it, in Webster's *The White Devil*:

> Instruct me some good horse-leech to speak treason,
> For since you cannot take my life for deeds,
> Take it for words, – O woman's poor revenge
> Which dwells but in the tongue.[22]

No wonder it is so solidly in the interests of a 'quiet' life for the patriarchal moralists to insist that silence is the rule, speech in woman a deviation from that rule: 'By silence indeed women achieve the fame of eloquence.'[23] Silence is the final accolade in Bosola's stirring tribute to the imprisoned Duchess of Malfi's strength in adversity: 'She will muse four hours together, and her silence, / Methinks, expresseth more than if she spake.'[24]

In the final analysis, the patriarchy is driven to the absurd limiting case, in affirming that all speech in woman is intrinsically harmful: 'A Womans Tongue that is as swift as thought, / Is ever bad, and she herself starke Nought.'[25] In a number of traditional folk-tales (including 'the six swans') the ultimate test of the woman's devotion (be she wife, daughter or sister) is for her to keep silence for incredible periods of time in the face of extreme hardship and provocation; only thus can she break the charm or spell on her brother/husband/father. The *reductio ad absurdum* of this view is that the ideal wife is mute: physically incapable of speech. The tale of the man who married a dumb wife is to be found in numerous collections of witty tales of the late medieval period and the Renaissance, and is included in particular in the English translation of Erasmus's *Uxor Mempsigamos* or *Con-iugium, A Merry Dialogue Declaring the Propertyes of Shrowde*

Shrewes and Honest Wyues (1557).[26] A man is married to a woman who cannot speak at all:

> He obtains an aspen leaf from the Devil, which he places in her mouth instead of the tongue which she has lost or never had. But when she begins to fulfil her womanly destiny and fills the house with shrewish chatter, her husband repents and asks the Devil to have her dumb again. The answer of the Prince of Darkness (supplied from the jest-book version) rings down through the ages: 'Al be it yet I haue power to make a woman to speke but and if a woman begyn ones to speke, I nor all the deuyls in hell that haue the more power be nat able to make a woman to be styll, nor to cause her to leaue her spekynge.'[27]

King Lear opens with Cordelia's culpable silence:

> Lear   Tell me, my daughters –
>   Since now we will divest us both of rule,
>   Interest of territory, cares of state –
>   Which of you shall we say doth love us most?
>   That we our largest bounty may extend
>   Where nature doth with merit challenge. Goneril,
>   Our eldest-born, speak first.
> Goneril   Sir, I love you more than word can wield the matter;
>   Dearer than eyesight, space, and liberty;
>   Beyond what can be valued, rich or rare;
>   No less than life, with grace, health, beauty, honour;
>   As much as child e'er lov'd, or father found;
>   A love that makes breath poor and speech unable:
>   Beyond all manner of so much I love you.
> Cordelia (aside)   What shall Cordelia speak? Love, and be silent.[28]

To her father, Cordelia's silence is not a mark of virtue, but a denial of filial affection:

> Lear   What can you say to draw
>   A third more opulent than your sisters? Speak.
> Cordelia   Nothing, my lord.
> Lear   Nothing!
> Cordelia   Nothing.
> Lear   Nothing will come of nothing. Speak again.[29]

The audience must, I think, understand this as a moral mistake on Lear's part. Silence = virtue; excessive speech = disorder. Contrast, for instance, Greene's tale of exemplary female succinctness in *Penelope's Web*. The king, Ariamenes, blessed with three virtuous sons who have married three honourable women, decides to 'measure his affection by the conditions of their wiues'.

Each wife is given a chance to prove to the king that she is the most virtuous of the three. The two elder make elaborate speeches; the third and youngest cannot find it in herself to do so:

> The youngest Sister hearing how vnreuerently they babled before the King, began to blush: which *Ariamenes* espying, noting in her face the very purtraiture of vertue, demaunded of her why hearing her Sisters so hard by the eares for a Crowne, she sayd nothing: her answere was thus briefe and pithie. He that gaineth a Crowne getteth care: is it not follie then to hunt after losse. The king looking for a longer discourse, and seeing contrarie to his expectation that she was onely short and sweete, prosecuted still in questioning, and demaunded what vertues she had that might deserue so royal a benefite? This (quoth she) that when others talke, yet being a woman I can hold my peace.[30]

Naturally, the king and the nobility are unanimous in finding the youngest daughter the most virtuous:

> Therefore debating the matter betwixt them which of the three were most vertuous: although they found by proofe that the other Ladies were both obedient and chast: yet for that they wanted silence, which (sayd *Ariamenes*) comprehended in it all other vertues, they mist of the cushion, and the King created his youngest Sonne heire apparent to the Kingdome.[31]

The fundamental paradox is apparent in both stories: the woman is commanded to speak, to prove her virtue; yet to speak is to negate virtuousness.

Lear makes the wrong choice: he chooses 'not-woman', disowns the truly womanly Cordelia. By preferring voluble speech (anti-womanly) to silence (female virtue incarnate) he creates disorder, gives place to *misrule*. As the Fool chides him:

> Lear   When were you wont to be so full of songs, sirrah?
> Fool   I have us'd it, nuncle, e'er since thou mad'st thy daughters thy
>   mothers; for when thou gav'st them the rod, and put'st down thine
>   own breeches
>   Then they for sudden joy did weep,
>   And I for sorrow sung,
>   That such a king should play bo-peep
>   And go the fools among[32]

Goneril's husband Albany is also driven ultimately to acknowledge his choice of 'not-woman' as wife. She in turn captures the role-reversal pithily: 'I must change arms at home, and give the distaff / Into my husband's hands.'[33]

The man beaten by a woman (often lewdly illustrated in

woodcuts)[34] is a familiar emblem of disorder. In sixteenth-
century France and England, 'misrule' carnivals and mummings
included symbolic humiliations for the husband whose wife beat
him: in some places he was paraded through the streets riding
backwards on an ass.[35] According to the clergy and authorities
such cavortings

> repress the temerity and audacity of women who beat their husbands and
> those who would like to do so; for according to the provision of divine and
> civil law, the wife is subject to the husband; and if husbands suffer them-
> selves to be governed by their wives, they might as well be led out to pasture.[36]

This was the official version; to the participants in these riotous
street carnivals, the battered husband riding backwards on an ass
was a symbol for disorder in the ascendant: of women on top.
Curiously, Shakespeare appears to support this inversion theme
in *King Lear* when he has Lear succumb to 'a fit of the mother' –
hysteria, a rising up of the womb out of its place – quite
inappropriately for a man: 'O! how this mother swells up
toward my heart! / Hysterica passio – down, thou climbing
sorrow, / Thy element's below.'[37] Lear, subjected to the misrule of
his domineering and scolding daughters, responds with a peculiarly female malady:

> The womb is frequently subject to suffocation. Suffocation is the name
> doctors give to a constriction of the vital breathing caused by a defect in the
> womb. This hinders the woman's breathing. It happens whenever the womb
> moves from its proper place. [It was believed in antiquity and down to the
> sixteenth century that the womb could move about the body, lodge in the
> throat, and cause choking.] Then, as a result of a chill in the heart, women
> sometimes swoon, feel a weakness in the heart, or suffer dizziness.[38]

In his final enlightenment, the mad Lear, with his dead daughter Cordelia in his arms, recognises her as truly virtuous woman:
'What is't thou say'st? Her voice was ever soft, / Gentle and low –
an excellent thing in woman.'[39] The devilish scolds, Goneril and
Regan, are extinguished. Womankind is redeemed by Cordelia's
modest silence, now recognised for its true worth.

To bolster up the extreme position that all speech in woman is
intrinsically suspect (a sign of aggression, a symptom of 'woman
on top'), there was always the story of the Fall. It is Eve's dialogue
with Adam in mystery plays across the European continent
which seduces Adam into tasting the forbidden fruit. In the

twelfth century *Mystère d'Adam*,[40] Eve engages in animated debate with Adam which culminates as follows:

> *Eva* Or sunt mes oil tant cler veant,
> Jo semble Deu le tuit puissant.
> Quanque fu, quanque doit estre
> Sai jo trestut, bien en sui maistre.
> Manjue, Adam, ne faz demore;
> Tu le prendras en mult bon'ore.
> Tunc accipiet Adam pomum de manu Eva, dicens:
> Jo t'en crerrai, tu es ma per.
> *Eva* Manjue, nen poez doter.

[*Eve* Now my eyes are so clear-sighted, I seem like God, the Almighty. All that was, all that will be, I know entirely and am master of it. Eat, Adam, do not hesitate. You will take it in a fortunate hour.
Then Adam shall take the apple from the hand of Eve and shall say: i shall believe you. You are my equal.
Eve Eat, you have nothing to fear.][41]

When Adam realises how this female discourse has undone him he laments:

> Par ton conseil sui mis a mal,
> De grant haltesce sui mis a val.

[Through your advice I have been brought to evil, from a great height I have fallen into great depth.][42]

Just as the serpent in medieval and Renaissance representations of the Fall takes on female form,[43] so Eve's tongue, woman's tongue, becomes forked like the serpent's. Her punishment for this original disobedience (verbal and active) is the pain of childbearing, sexual dependence upon and subjection to the man: 'Unto the woman [God] said, I will greatly multiply thy sorrow and thy conception; in sorrow thou shalt bring forth children; and thy desire shall be to thy husband, and he shall rule over thee.'[44]

Katherina (Kate) in *The Taming of the Shrew*, and Beatrice in *Much Ado About Nothing* strike the primitive fear of disorder and misrule into the hearts of the men around them, although their witty dialogue seems to the modern audience charming and alert. Beatrice's uncle, Leonato, berates her for her sharp tongue in altogether familiar terms:

Leonato	Was not Count John here at supper?
Antonio	I saw him not.
Beatrice	How tartly that gentleman looks! I never can see him but I am heart-burn'd an hour after.
Hero	He is of a very melancholy disposition.
Beatrice	He were an excellent man that were made just in the mid-way between him and Benedick: the one is too like an image and says nothing, and the other too like my lady's eldest son, evermore tattling.
Leonato	Then half Signior Benedick's tongue in Count John's mouth, and half Count John's melancholy in Signior Benedick's face –
Beatrice	With a good leg and a good foot, uncle, and money enough in his purse, such a man would win any woman in the world, if 'a could get her good-will.
Leonato	By my troth, niece, thou wilt never get thee a husband if thou be so shrewd of thy tongue.
Antonio	In faith, she 's too curst.
Beatrice	Too curst is more than curst. I shall lessen God's sending that way; for it is said 'God sends a curst cow short horns'; but to a cow too curst he sends none.
Leonato	So, by being too curst, God will send you no horns.
Beatrice	Just, if he send me no husband; for the which blessing I am at him upon my knees every morning and evening. Lord! I could not endure a husband with a beard on his face; I had rather lie in the woollen.
Leonato	You may light on a husband that hath no beard.
Beatrice	What should I do with him? Dress him in my apparel, and make him my waiting gentlewoman?[45]

Any husband of mine, says Beatrice, would be a cuckold, therefore I thank God I have no husband. Or he would be an effeminate, and likewise to be deplored. It is Beatrice's shrewishness which guarantees that her menfolk would either be emasculated or cuckolded; the domineering wife brings shame and humiliation upon her husband.

City people from the fifteenth to the eighteenth centuries were even more concerned about husband-beating, and the beaten *man* (or a neighbour playing his part) was paraded through the streets backwards on an ass by noisy revelers. In the English Midlands the ride was known as a Skimmington or a Skimmety, perhaps from the big skimming ladle sometimes used by women in beating their husbands. In Northern England and Scotland, the victim or his stand-in 'rode the stang' (a long hobbyhorse), and a like steed was used in the *ceffyl pren* in Wales. In some towns, effigies of the offending couple were promenaded. In others, the festive organization mounted floats to display the actual circumstances of the monstrous beatings: the wives were shown hitting their husbands with distaffs, tripe, sticks, trenchers, water pots; throwing stones at them; pulling their beards; or kicking them in the genitalia.[46]

These figurative representations of male humiliation at the hands of the female exorcise the communal threat at the expense of the individual man. I do not think for a moment (*pace* Davis) that the floats depict actual bodily harm inflicted by wives on their husbands. Distaffs and tripe (like the rolling-pin in our own day) are the symbolic weapons of the housebound wife. What she actually does is scold; the disturbing and disruptive effect of the verbal drubbing is, for the patriarchy, as threatening as physical blows. The unfortunate Benedick is as bruised by Beatrice as if she had raised her distaff to his head.

But the literary shrew's moment of triumph is short-lived. Beatrice is forced to acknowledge that her tongue has no real power when her 'Kill Claudio' is registered as mere words – as not a command – by Benedick, provoking her indignant retort:

Is 'a not approved in the height a villain that has slandered, scorned, dishonoured my kinswoman? O that I were a man! . . . O that I were a man for his sake! or that I had any friend would be a man for my sake! But manhood is melted into curtsies, valour into compliment, and men are only turn'd into tongue, and trim ones too.[47]

At this moment she recognises the tongue as the symbol of impotence and inaction, of the threat which will never become a deed. When Beatrice and Kate are enclosed in matrimony to provide the plays with a 'happy ending' the sharpness of tongue which has marred their courtship is domesticated. Thereafter their active female wit will be accommodated without threat as the 'scolding' which men ruefully accept as the price of matrimony.

There is, of course, as critics point out, a heavy irony in the 'tamings' in these plays. But I think we are misled if we take that irony as some kind of benevolent approval for woman's verbal licence. The cultural deftness of touch which is involved in these dramatisations of popular topsy-turvy domestic situations has to do with the familiarity of the plot. Misrule is set to rights by astute sleight-of-hand. Beatrice charmingly capitulates; Kate wins for her husband a handsome wager.

In *Antony and Cleopatra* and *Troilus and Cressida*, by contrast, the dominion of women is political, not folkloristic; disruptive of public order, not domestic harmony. Women command, and the natural hierarchy is inverted, an inversion readily translated into female sexual predatoriness. North's *Plutarch* (Shakespeare's source for *Antony and Cleopatra*) characterises Antony's relations with women from the outset as unnaturally submissive on his part:

> [Antony] married Fulvia that was Clodius widowe, a woman not so basely minded to spend her time in spinning and housewivery, and was not contented to master her husband at home, but would also rule him in his office abroad, and commaund him, that commaunded legions`and great armies: so that Cleopatra was to give Fulvia thankes for that she had taught Antonius this obedience to women, that learned so well to be at their commaundement. . . . Fulvia was somewhat sower, and crooked of condition.[48]

In Shakespeare's play, Cleopatra's appearances on stage are associated with the emasculating (or at least undermining) of men: she teases the eunuch Mardian into admitting the sexual fantasies he cannot consummate, strikes the messenger who brings her unwelcome news, and in political confrontation after political confrontation is portrayed as directly responsible for Antony's failing judgement and misguided actions:

Cleopatra   O my lord, my lord,
              Forgive my fearful sails! I little thought
              You would have followed.
     Antony   Egypt, thou knew'st too well
              My heart was to thy rudder tied by th' strings,
              And thou shouldst tow me after.[49]

When Antony originally makes the (wrong) decision to fight Caesar at sea (because that is Cleopatra's wish) his soldiers complain: 'Our leader's led, / And we are women's men.'[50] Here, as in *Troilus and Cressida*, female sexuality has man unnaturally in its thrall. The need to justify Helen's rape warps Trojan judgement, therefore Troy must fall:[51] Antony is ravished by Cleopatra, therefore the heroic Antony must meet his end.[52]

There is only one area in which the unruliness and disruptiveness of the female voice achieves a kind of authenticity of its own, and that is prophecy. It is possible that articulate women were driven to claiming divine motivation for their public utterances by the patriarchal insistence both in antiquity and in the Middle

Ages that silence was the only acceptable mode of female public behaviour:

> The prominence of women among the religious prophets of this period is partly explained by the fact that the best hope of gaining an ear for female utterance was to represent them as the result of divine revelations. Women were forced into such postures because the more conventional vehicles of pulpit and printed sermon were denied them. . . . Before the Civil War recourse to prophecy was the only means by which most women could hope to disseminate their opinion on public events.[53]

But however expedient, such claims were well supported by precedent. Miriam and Deborah had prophesied in the Old Testament,[54] Cassandra had prophesied in antiquity, femaleness and the gift of spiritual tongues were compatible (possibly even linked with a Platonic enthusiasm for femaleness and spirituality as related qualities).[55] As the outsider, the person of no public status, traditionally unlikely to be heeded, the female prophet acquired a symbolic independence from authority.[56] And the inspired voice is, of its very nature, non-rational, non-cerebral, cryptic – qualities compatible with the traditional binary opposition between male and female qualities. Male is to female as rational to irrational, limited to unlimited, single to multiple, steadfast to changeable, and so on.[57]

The woman's voice as prophetic outsider links her with the traditional fool, and this brings us back to the unruly woman. Davis has argued that despite the conventional and regularised nature of the late medieval representation of the shrew and scold, husband-beater and emasculator of male antagonists, in the end these figures provided a genuine means of retaliation against the orthodox social structure:

> The ambiguous woman-on-top of the world of play made the unruly option a more conceivable one within the family. Ordinary women might also be disorderly in public. In principle, women could pronounce on law and doctrine only if they were queens, had unusual learning, or fell into an ecstatic trance. Virtually never were they to take the law into their own hands. In fact, women turn up telling off priests and pastors, being central actors in grain and bread riots in town and country, and participating in tax revolts and other rural disturbances. In England in the early seventeenth century (so Thomas Barnes has discovered), a significant percentage of the rioters against enclosures and for common rights were female. In Calvinist Edinburgh in 1637, the resistance to Charles I's imposition of the Book of Common Prayer was opened by a crowd of 'rascally serving women' at Saint

Giles' Church, who drowned out the Dean's reading, threw stools at the Bishop of Edinburgh, and when evicted, stoned the doors and windows. The tax revolt at Montpellier in 1645 was started by women, led down the streets by a virago named la Branlaire, who shouted for death for the tax-collectors who were taking the bread from their children's mouths. There are several reasons for this female involvement that we cannot consider here, but part of its background is the complex license accorded the unruly woman.[58]

I find this a plausible suggestion. Studies of female lawlessness for the early modern period show comparatively little independent crime by women,[59] and advance the view that woman's domestic dependence and enforced submissiveness prevented her from individual acts of lawlessness (female crimes tended to be domestic). On the other hand, the traditional figure of the disorderly scold provides an outlet for grievance in a female guise. And indeed, Davis goes on to suggest that it was the role of female shrew which protected the participants in such unruly activities from full responsibility for their anti-social actions:

> Sexual inversion also gave a more positive license to the unruly woman: her right as subject and as mother to rise up and tell the truth. . . . When Katherine Zell of Strasbourg dares to write an attack on clerical celibacy in the 1520s and claims 'I do not pretend to be John the Baptist rebuking the Pharisees. I do not claim to be Nathan upbraiding David. I aspire only to be Balaam's ass, castigating his master,' then Dame Folly is part of her tradition.[60]

Folly, misrule, the ship of Fools: these literary forms traditionally provide witty satiric comment on society.[61] Women are to be found prominently amongst these genre figures: Dame Folly is female in Erasmus's *Praise of Folly*, the Wife of Bath in Chaucer's *Canterbury Tales* is both widow/scold and commentator on society's mores.[62] Female figures are thus available to raise a dissenting voice – not *qua* women, since I have argued strongly that *qua* women they were in no position to do so, but as recognisable literary types of disorderly behaviour.

And the upshot of this is that, intriguingly, in the seventeenth century, we find *male* protestors rioting in female dress – transposing the fiction of the carnival of misrule into the political arena:

> It turned out that Dame Folly could serve to validate disobedient and riotous behaviour by men, too. They also could hide behind that sex. . . . The carnival right of criticism . . . sometimes tipped over into real rebellion. In

1630 in Dijon, for instance, Mère Folle and her Infanterie were part of an uprising in masquerade against royal tax officers. In fact, the donning of female clothes by men and the adopting of female titles for riots was surprisingly frequent, beginning (so our still scanty data suggest) in the seventeenth century.... In 1629, 'Captain' Alice Clarke, a real female, headed a crowd of women and male weavers dressed as women in a grain riot near Maldon in Essex. They sacked a ship thought to be exporting grain to the Netherlands. In 1631, in the dairy and grazing sections of Wiltshire, bands of men rioted and leveled fences against the king's enclosure of their forests. They were led by men dressed as women, who called themselves, 'Lady Skimmington'.[61]

The Skimmington ride was the parade through the streets ignominiously of the hen-pecked husband: Lady Skimmington is by implication his harridan wife. The female shrew/scold/prophet acquires, on this account, the verbal (and at times the physical) licence of the fool in motley, or the acerbic melancholic. She utters (and acts) with impunity, under the extended privilege of the Misrule carnival. Davis suggests that this is particularly the case where the 'female' scold is in fact a man in woman's dress: he retains the 'play' element which figuratively places his anti-social behaviour in the category of 'regularised disorder'. Once again it is worth pointing out that in the Elizabethan and Jacobean drama, female scolds also preserve this similarity to the medieval street carnival, since they too are played by male actors.

In Shakespeare's first tetralogy (*Henry VI Part I*; *Henry VI Part II*; *Henry VI Part III*; *Richard III*), the intelligent and articulate Queen Margaret, wife of Henry VI and model of female valour, becomes in the final play just such a privileged, carping voice, somewhere between witch and female prophet: uttering truths no one else dare voice, accompanied by the curses which wreak the actual bodily harm on the protagonists which in real life might have resulted from the tax riot or mob revolt:

Queen Margaret	Hear me, you wrangling pirates, that fall out
	In sharing that which you have pill'd from me.
	Which of you trembles not that looks on me?
	If not that, I am Queen, you bow like subjects,
	Yet that, by you depos'd, you quake like rebels?
	Ah, gentle villain, do not turn away!
Gloucester	Foul wrinkled witch, what mak'st thou in my sight?
Queen Margaret	But repetition of what thou hast marr'd,
	That will I make before I let thee go.
Gloucester	Wert thou not banished on pain of death?

> Queen Margaret   I was; but I do find more pain in banishment
> Than death can yield me here by my abode.
> A husband and a son thou ow'st to me.⁶⁴

Having heaped her incantatory curses on the assembled nobles, without regard for personal danger or the constraints of decorum, Queen Margaret closes her abrasive outburst:

> Queen Margaret   What, dost thou scorn me for my gentle counsel,
> And soothe the devil that I warn thee from?
> O, but remember this another day,
> When he shall split thy very heart with sorrow,
> And say poor Margaret was a prophetess!
> Live each of you the subjects to his hate,
> And he to yours, and all of you to God's!

As she sweeps out, Buckingham says with foreboding (soon to be fulfilled): 'My hair doth stand on end to hear her curses.'⁶⁵ In the man's world of the history play, the only power the woman can wield is her power to dismay through verbal abuse. The politically astute Margaret of the early plays becomes 'poor Margaret... prophetess'. The curse of the scold is feared almost as much as the drubbing she supposedly administers to her unfortunate man, as the records of the witch-trials remind us, but it achieves nothing.⁶⁶

The 'plain truths' uttered by female characters in Shakespeare (Emilia's chastising of Othello, Paulina speaking out against Leontes for wronging his queen) bear the mark of the scold's privilege. Indeed, the men concerned openly recognise them as such. As Paulina pours out before Leontes the words no one else dare utter (that his fears that his new born daughter is no child of his are grotesque and unfounded), Leontes calls her 'audacious lady', then 'a mankind witch! ... A most intelligencing bawd!', and: 'A callat [scold] / Of boundless tongue, who late hath beat her husband, / And now baits me!'⁶⁷ Finally, still failing to stop her speech by force, he accuses her of being a heretic (an 'explanation' for female unruliness evident from the Essex witch-trial records):

> Leontes   A gross hag!
> And, lozel, thou art worthy to be hang'd
> That wilt not stay her tongue.
>   ... Once more, take her hence.

Paulina	A most unworthy and unnatural lord
	Can do no more.
Leontes	I'll ha' thee burnt.
Paulina	I care not.
	It is an heretic that makes the fire,
	Not she which burns in't.[68]

When Iago cannot prevent Emilia from uttering the truths he has no wish to hear, he parries by calling her 'villainous whore' and 'filth'.[69] When Volumnia (Coriolanus's mother) turns on the Romans who have banished her son, they retaliate by terming her 'mad'.[70] In *Troilus and Cressida* the Trojans dismiss Cassandra's unwelcome prophecy that Helen will bring doom upon them as 'brain-sick raptures':

Hector	Now, youthful Troilus, do not these high strains
	Of divination in your sister work
	Some touches of remorse? . . .
Troilus	Why, brother Hector,
	We may not think the justness of each act
	Such and no other than event doth form it;
	Nor once deject the courage of our minds
	Because Cassandra's mad. Her brain-sick raptures
	Cannot distaste the goodness of a quarrel
	Which hath our several honours all engag'd
	To make it gracious.[71]

Cassandra's words run counter to the orderly Trojan view of manliness and honour; her privileged speech is judged 'insane'.[72]

I think the same note of charmed immunity to orderly demands for speech is sounded in the sharp altercations between female characters like Helena bantering with Parolles in *All's Well That Ends Well*, or Maria matching wisecrack for wisecrack with Sir Toby Belch and Sir Andrew Aguecheek in *Twelfth Night*, or Desdemona and Emilia baiting Iago in *Othello*. The female sharp tongue both entices and threatens. A number of critics find the 'shrewdness' of Desdemona, for example, incompatible for her supposed 'innocence'. For instance, M. R. Ridley, in the Arden *Othello*, footnotes II.i.109–66 as follows:

> This is to many readers, and I think rightly, one of the most unsatisfactory passages in Shakespeare. To begin with it is unnatural. Desdemona's natural instinct must surely be to go herself to the harbour [where Othello has just arrived], instead of asking parenthetically whether someone has gone. Then, it is distasteful to watch her engaged in a long piece of cheap backchat with

Iago, and so adept at it that one wonders how much time on the voyage was spent in the same way. All we gain from it is some further unneeded light on Iago's vulgarity.[73]

It is, of course, Desdemona's vulgarity which offends the critic. There is something too-knowing, too-independent about her tone and ready reply. But Desdemona's 'backchat' is 'licence to carp', subsequently to be withdrawn from her when comment gives way to action, in which she must inevitably be the passive victim. When a female character in the drama gives verbal thrust for verbal thrust as Desdemona does in this scene, she is acting out the paradoxes of patriarchy:

Desdemona	Come, how wouldst thou praise me?
Iago	I am about it, but indeed my invention
	Comes from my pate as birdlime does from frieze,
	It plucks out brain and all: but my Muse labours,
	And thus she is deliver'd:
	If she be fair and wise, fairness and wit;
	The one's for use, the other using it.
Desdemona	Well prais'd! How if she be black and witty?
Iago	If she be black, and thereto have a wit,
	She'll find a white, that shall her blackness hit.
Desdemona	Worse and worse.
Emilia	How if fair and foolish?
Iago	She never yet was foolish, that was fair,
	For even her folly help'd her, to an heir.
Desdemona	These are old paradoxes, to make fools laugh i' the alehouse; what miserable praise hast thou for her that's foul and foolish?
Iago	There's none so foul, and foolish thereunto,
	But does foul pranks, which fair and wise ones do.[74]

These 'paradoxes' are, in fact, the substance of the 'woman debate'.[75] Desdemona's sharp-tongued involvement in an exchange about womanish wiles (the feminine mystique) sets her up as active temptress, scold, 'husband-beater' and cuckolder: an appropriate talismanic threat. Iago's own insidious tongue has only to play on these traditional fears lurking beneath female 'mystery' to rouse Othello to full jealousy, and finally murder.

Coda: Scolding or Shrewing Around?

The tongue is the female weapon (*faute de mieux*); it is also (particularly in bawdy humour) a sexual instrument. In *Cymbeline*, the oafish Cloten puns lewdly on its double function as part of his wooing of Imogen:

> Cloten I would this music would come. I am advised to give her music a
> mornings; they say it will penetrate. (*Enter* Musicians.) Come on,
> tune. If you can penetrate her with your fingering, so. We'll try with
> tongue too. If none will do, let her remain; but I'll never give o'er."⁶

In *The Taming of the Shrew*, Kate's bantering tongue gets embroiled early on with Petruchio's lewd punning on its sexual function:

> Petruchio Come, come, you wasp; i' faith, you are too angry.
> Katherina If I be waspish, best beware my sting.
> Petruchio My remedy is then to pluck it out.
> Katherina Ay, if the fool could find it where it lies.
> Petruchio Who knows not where a wasp does wear his sting?
> In his tail.
> Katherina   In his tongue.
> Petruchio   Whose tongue?
> Katherina Yours, if you talk of tales; and so farewell.
> Petruchio What, with my tongue in your tail? Nay, come again,
> Good Kate; I am a gentleman."⁷

The two metonymic uses of 'tongue' get drawn together in its bawdy use as the specifically female sexual instrument – the female counterpart of the penis. The suggestion is not, I think, that women are actually supposed to practise fellatio! But the topological similarities are apparently irresistibly suggestive – two fleshy protuberances, one the source of male power, one of female. Throughout the literature of the period we find a willingness to slide provocatively from one sense to another: scolding = active use of the female tongue = female sexuality = female penis. Iago runs through the whole sequence as he banters vulgarly with his wife Emilia and Desdemona in the scene which I suggested critics find altogether unworthy of Desdemona. Cassio kisses Emilia and her husband quips:

Iago Sir, would she give you so much of her lips
   As of her tongue she has bestow'd on me,
   You'ld have enough.
Desdemona   Alas! she has no speech.
Iago I know, too much:
   I find it, I; for when I ha' list to sleep –
   Marry before your ladyship, I grant,
   She puts her tongue a little in her heart,
   And chides with thinking.
Emilia You ha' little cause to say so.
Iago Come on, come on, you are pictures out o' doors;
   Bells in your parlours; wild-cats in your kitchens;
   Saints in your injuries; devils being offended;
   Players in your housewifery; and housewives in your beds.
Desdemona O, fie upon thee, slanderer!
Iago Nay, it is true, or else I am a Turk,
   You rise to play, and go to bed to work.[78]

Iago insists that Cassio has the better of the deal than he: Cassio gets her lips, while he gets too much of her tongue. But there is no doubt that he is playing lewdly with the sexual favours Emilia's tongue might 'bestow'. And this is solidly confirmed when Iago goes on to talk exclusively of women's dedication to the work they do in bed – it is the only place where they are truly housewives, that is, where they work strenuously. Although he began by maintaining that in bed Emilia did nothing but scold ('when I ha' list to sleep – . . . / She puts her tongue a little in her heart, / And chides with thinking'), he now insists that the only strenuous activity that women are prepared to carry out is in bed. Desdemona's 'O, fie upon thee, slanderer!' confirms that this has to be taken to refer to their sexual activities. Her curious interjection, 'Alas! she has no speech' (on which I find no guidance in the critical editions of the play) provides another verbal link between the female tongue and sexuality. The tongue and the male sexual organ are the two 'parts of the body' without a bone in them; or, put another way (in the bawdy literature of the period), there are two parts of the body without a bone, one of which has speech while the other does not. Ferdinand puns lewdly after this fashion when he intimates that the Duchess of Malfi is hot and lusty:

Ferdinand And women like that part which, like the lamprey,
   Hath ne'er a bone in't.
Duchess   Fie sir!

Ferdinand   Nay,
        I mean the tongue.

There is a curious comparison in Francis Meres' *Palladis Tamia* (London, 1598; Garland reprint, 1973) which seems to support the association of lamprey with female sexuality. It is already linked to 'tongue' by a common etymological root – 'to lick':

> The Viper being the deadliest of all serpentes, desireth to engender with the sea lamprey, and by hissing doth bring y lamprey out of the vast ocean, and so the Lamprey engendereth with ye poysonfull viper: so a wife must beare with her husband, though he be rough and cruell, neither for any wrath or fury must shee breake the mariage bonds. Hee doth strike thee, thou must beare him: he is thy husband; he is a drunkard, but he is ioyned by nature vnto thee. He is fierce and implacable, but he is thy member, and the most excellent of thy members. But as the Viper doth vomite out his poyson for the reuerence of engendering: so a husband must put awaie all fiercenes, roughnes, cruelty, and bitternes towardes his wife for the reuerance of vnion.[80]

In any case, the literature of the scolding husband-beater is closely shadowed by that of the sexually predatory, lewdly dominating woman.[81] In the *Arabian Nights*, scolding and sexual aggressiveness go together (for instance in 'the Porter and the Three Ladies of Bagdhad', in which physical beating, verbal drubbing and general shrewish behaviour towards the porter are part of the ladies' sexual allure, and provide anticipation of sexual performance). And, of course, the narrative structure of these Thousand and One Tales of a Thousand and One Nights is determined by the relationship between female lasciviousness and the female ability to talk interminably. King Shahryar discovers that his beautiful and much beloved wife has been lewdly unfaithful (he discovers her ecstatically copulating with a huge blackamoor). The King vows thereafter (having summarily executed her) that to avoid such humiliation at the hands of future wives he will wed only certified virgins, and execute them the morning after he has deflowered them. The Wazir's daughter Shahrázád volunteers to marry the king to her father's dismay. Immediately the marriage has been consummated she embarks on telling a story so captivating that when it is incomplete at dawn, the king her husband spares her life in order to hear it completed the following night. And so on, on each successive night. The female tongue, endlessly voluble, has saved female sexuality (which, as the stories themselves show, is endlessly voracious and insatiable).[82]

Throughout the early modern period, the fantasy of the woman whose scolding even the devil cannot halt runs parallel with the fantasy that a woman once she has experienced the sexual act is insatiable. Shakespeare's Venus, in *Venus and Adonis* is 'red and hot as coals of glowing fire' in this tradition, as is Mistress Francis in Nashe's 'The Choice of Valentines':

> So fierce and fervent is her radiance,
> Such fiery stakes she darts at every glance,
> She might enflame the icy limbs of age,
> And make pale death his surquedy assuage:[83]

Saint Jerome, in a discussion familiar to Renaissance readers of Shakespeare's 'The Rape of Lucrece' maintained that Lucretia killed herself despite her technical innocence (Tarquin took her by force, therefore she was not guilty of adultery), because she, like all women, could not help enjoying the sexual act – rape or no.[84] English attempts to blacken the reputation of Joan of Arc concentrated on the charge of sexual aggressiveness:

> *Pucelle* I am with child, ye bloody homicides;
> Murder not then the fruit within my womb,
> Although ye hale me to a violent death.
> *York* Now heaven forfend! The holy maid with child!
> *Warwick* The greatest miracle that e'er ye wrought:
> Is all your strict preciseness come to this?
> *York* She and the Dauphin have been juggling.
> I did imagine what would be her refuge.
> *Warwick* Well, go to; we'll have no bastards live;
> Especially since Charles must father it.
> *Pucelle* You are deceived; my child is none of his:
> It was Alençon that enjoy'd my love.
> *York* Alençon, that notorious Machiavel!
> It dies, an if it had a thousand lives.
> *Pucelle* O, give me leave, I have deluded you.
> 'Twas neither Charles nor yet the Duke I nam'd,
> But Reignier, King of Naples, that prevail'd.
> *Warwick* A married man! That's most intolerable.
> *York* Why, here's a girl! I think she knows not well –
> There were so many – whom she may accuse.[85]

'Low-life' literature, a popular Elizabethan genre, purporting to give eye-witness accounts for the urban burghers of the unsalubrious goings on amongst villains and ruffians, is full of graphic tales of women of easy virtue and large sexual appetite.[86] The taboo aspect of this insistence on the voraciousness of female sexual appetite is fairly evident. It is presumably deeply linked with male anxieties about their own sexual performance: once woman is sexually aroused, so the tradition goes, it is the devil's own job to satisfy her. Nashe's 'The Choice of Valentines' – an unashamedly pornographic poem about an encounter with an energetic prostitute, in the course of which the man finds himself unable to perform at all – dwells in considerable detail on female enjoyment as at once gratifying and a source of anxiety:

> 'Oh, not so fast!' my ravish'd mistress cries,
> 'Lest my content, that on thy life relies,
> Be brought too soon from his delightful seat,
> And me unwares of hoped bliss defeat.
> Together let our equal motions stir;
> Together let us live and die, my dear.'[87]

It is the lady's insistence on equal enjoyment which reduces the bold lover to impotence. By no means solely a western preoccupation, this secret fear of humiliation in the face of female sexual demands is the theme of tale after tale in the *Arabian Nights*. In 'The Barber's Tale of his Third Brother' (to choose a single example), a merchant's wife and daughter lure Al-Haddár into shaving his beard, dyeing his eyebrows and rougeing his face, with the promise of sexual delights. Finally the daughter strips naked and instructs the barber's brother to do likewise:

Then she set out at a run and he ran after her while she rushed into room after room and rushed out of room after room, my brother scampering after her in a rage of desire like a veritable madman, with yard standing terribly tall. After much of this kind she dashed into a darkened place, and he dashed after her; but suddenly he trod upon a yielding spot, which gave way under his weight; and, before he was aware where he was, he found himself in the midst of a crowded market, part of the bazaar of the leather-sellers who were crying the prices of skins and hides and buying and selling. When they saw him in his plight, naked with standing yard [erection], shorn of beard and moustachios, with eyebrows dyed red, and cheeks ruddled with rouge, they shouted and clapped their hands at him, and set to flogging him with skins upon his bare body till a swoon came over him. Then they threw him on the back of an ass and carried him to the Chief of Police.[88]

Here we are with the Skimmington ride again – the man who cannot cope with the sexual scolding of the woman is publicly humiliated, and ridden through the streets on the back of an ass.[89]

It is, I think, nevertheless the case that female sexual enjoyment *was* better acknowledged in the early modern period than our own post-Victorian prejudices would lead us to expect. This is in part, ironically, precisely because the close association of sexual pleasure with Eve and the Fall led Elizabethans to expect women to derive evident physical pleasure from the sexual act.[90] It was also clearly asserted in the ancient medical works on which the Renaissance depended for their understanding of the biology of intercourse that women took an active enjoyment in sex:

> The woman feels pleasure from the beginning and throughout inter-course.... If she has an orgasm, she ejaculates before the man does and ceases to feel the same degree of pleasure; if she does not have an orgasm, her pleasure ceases at the same time as the man's.... Woman's sensation of heat and pleasure comes to a climax at the moment when the sperm falls into the matrix [used by the ancients to mean both vagina and uterus], then everything stops. If one throws wine on a flame, the flame flares and is momentarily increased by this affusion, then it dies away. In intercourse women feel a great deal less pleasure than men do, but they feel it longer. If men feel a more intense pleasure, it is because the discharge of liquid is brusquer in their case and provoked by a more acute excitement than that experienced by women. Another point should be borne in mind: if women are having sexual intercourse, their health is better for it.... One reason for this is that during intercourse the matrix becomes moist and ceases to be dry. Now, when the matrix is dry it contracts sharply and this contraction causes pain. A second reason is that intercourse, by heating and moistening the blood, makes it easier for the menstrual blood to flow; and when menstrual blood does not flow, women become sickly.[91]

What in the medical literature is described as 'equal enjoyment', with the man getting a distinctly larger share, becomes in literary representations an appetite which unashamedly increases with experience.[92] In *The Changeling*, the maid Diaphanta, a proven virgin, is substituted by her mistress Beatrice-Joanna for herself on her wedding night. (Beatrice-Joanna has given herself to her servant De Flores, and therefore needs a stand-in virgin for her wedding night.) When Diaphanta fails to leave the marriage bed on a pretext immediately after the consummation (as directed by her mistress), Beatrice-Joanna instantly assumes that she is enjoying copulation too much to leave:

One struck, and yet she lies by 't! – Oh, my fears!
This strumpet serves her own ends, 'tis apparent now,
Devours the pleasure with a greedy appetite.'³

De Flores is yet more forthright: all women are sexual gluttons, particularly on the occasion of their deflowering, and especially with a 'classy' man:

> Push! They are termagants,
> Especially when they fall upon their masters,
> And have their ladies' first-fruits; th' are mad whelps,
> You cannot stave 'em off from game royal.'⁴

Once again we have crossed the divide between experience and fantasy. Diaphanta is a 'termagant', that is, a scold and a shrew. Virgins are insatiable on the occasion of losing their maidenhead (and De Flores includes a sly pun on Diaphanta's lost virginity – her womanly first-fruits – and her theft of her mistress's enjoyment – her lady's first night). The rite of performance on so auspicious an occasion as the wedding night drives the patriarchal imagination to posit a threatening eagerness on the part of the bride, which common sense tells us can hardly have been matched by any reality. And in similar fashion, the widow (already sexually experienced) is represented as offering a particularly strong sexual threat. (Widows could be courted with greater sexual aggressiveness, according to the moralists, than maids.) Chaucer's Wife of Bath is sexually experienced and sexually exuberant:

> She was a worthy womman al hir lyve:
> Housbondes at chirche dore she hadde fyve.
> Withouten oother compaignye in youthe, –
> But therof nedeth nat to speke as nowthe. . . .
> Of remedies of love she knew per chaunce,
> For she koude of that art the olde daunce.'⁵

Ferdinand's bawdy remarks to the Duchess in *The Duchess of Malfi* express a commonplace view of the predatoriness of widows, as do Hamlet's insulting comments on his mother Gertrude's sex-drive, which, he claims, has driven her prematurely into an unworthy man's bed:

Hamlet Could you on this fair mountain leave to feed,
And batten on this moor? Ha! have you eyes?
You cannot call it love; for at your age

> The heyday in the blood is tame, it's humble,
> And waits upon the judgment; and what judgment
> Would step from this to this? Sense, sure, you have,
> Else could you not have motion; but sure that sense
> Is apoplex'd; for madness would not err,
> Nor sense to ecstacy was ne'er so thrall'd
> But it reserv'd some quantity of choice
> To serve in such a difference. . . .
>   O shame! where is thy blush?
> Rebellious hell,
> If thou canst mutine in a matron's bones,
> To flaming youth let virtue be as wax
> And melt in her own fire; proclaim no shame
> When the compulsive ardour gives the charge,
> Since frost itself as actively doth burn,
> And reason panders will. . . .
>   Nay, but to live
> In the rank sweat of an enseamed bed,
> Stew'd in corruption, honeying and making love
> Over the nasty sty!⁴⁶

The threat of female sexuality is here concocted out of a number of *topoi* we have already encountered: the transformation of the hideous 'moor' (here a pun) into fair-seemingness, because of his sexual prowess; the sensuality which in imperfect woman overwhelms reason; the corruption and lust which are the active aspects of mature womanhood. And in his comparison between the 'natural' ardour of youth and the 'unnatural' sexual drives of the mature woman, Hamlet touches on a theme which Natalie Davis considers to be a vital element in the misrule mockery of ill-matched couples:

> Why then the charivaris [carnivals of misrule]? First there was the dead spouse to be placated. He was sometimes present at the charivari as an effigy. Then there were the children from the first marriage to be thought about, psychologically and economically. Folktales about the wicked stepmother or stepfather express the former worry. . . . And last and most fundamental, there was resentment when someone had been inappropriately removed by an older widow or widower from the pool of young eligibles. . . . The air could be cleared and the community reminded of the imbalance by a noisy mocking laugh at the 'Vieille Carcasse, folle d'amour' ['Old baggage, crazy for love'], or at the old man surely incapable of satisfying his young wife.⁴⁷

Coupled as the threatening sexuality of widowhood was with some real power due to fiscal independence (as I discussed above), the widow is the paramount emblem of all that men cannot deal with in women. Thomas Deloney packs absolutely every *topos* of the threatening widow into his 'Jack of Newbury' (1597).[98] Jack is a well-liked fellow, a bit on the feckless side: '*Iack* could no sooner get a Crowne, but straight hee found meanes to spend it: yet had hee euer this care, that hee would alwaies keepe himselfe in comely and decent apparell.'[99] His master dies, leaving a widow 'who was a very comely auncient Woman, and of reasonable wealth'. The widow takes Jack into her confidence and discusses with him her (many) lovers: their drawbacks are that one is too old, one travels too much, the third, a cleric, 'will bee so bent to his books, that he will hàue little minde of his bed'.[100] By this time Jack's friends are gossiping, on the basis of no evidence, that Jack 'cannot liue without the smel of his Dames smocke [underwear]'. Like the Duchess of Malfi, Deloney's widow tries to entice Jack into treating her as an equal (all her other lovers are, of course, wealthy and of suitable estate), and hints that she prefers one 'nearer at hand'. Jack feigns total innocence, and avers that he intends to remain single, 'for as young maides are fickle, so are old women iealous: the one a griefe too common, the other a torment intolerable'.[101] Running out of patience, the widow actually extends a direct sexual invitation to Jack: she claims to have had a nightmare, and that in future, for comfort, she will not lock her bedroom door, 'till I am married'.[102] When this produces no result, she gets Jack drunk at dinner:

Bed time comming on, shee caused her maide in a merriment to plucke off his hose and shooes, and caused him to bee laide in his masters best bed, standing in the best Chamber, hung round about with very faire curtaines. . . . About midnight, the Widow being cold on her feet, crept into her mans bed to warme them. *Iohn* feeling one lift vp the cloathes, asked who was there?

O good *Iohn* it is I, quoth the widow, the night is so extreame colde, and my Chamber walles so thin, that I am like to be starued in my bed: wherefore rather then I would any way hazard my health, I thought it much better to come hither and trie your curtesie, to haue a little roome beside you.

Iohn being a kind young man would not say her nay, and so they spent the rest of the night both together in one bed.[103]

Having tricked him into an actual marriage ceremony, the widow now launches into a series of tactical taxings of his patience by 'gadding abroad', calculated to 'take him downe in his wedding shooes', and to 'trie his patience in the prime of his lustinesse' (this is supposed to make sure she keeps his love). Finally he locks her out of the house; she tricks him into letting her in again, and locks him out in his turn. When she does let him back she denies him her bed. He complains that he is 'troubled with a shrewe, who the longer she liues, the worse shee is: and as the people of *Ilyris* kill men with their lookes, so she kils her husbands hart with vntoward conditions', therefore he will 'leaue [her] to [her] own wilfulnes'. This settled she promises that from now on she will be like the pelican – emblem of maternal devotion. They live happily until 'she died, leauing her husband wondrous wealthie'.[104]

Medical treatises of the period pay special attention to the sexual demands of the widow. Fontanus's treatise on female diseases treats their need for sexual gratification as a serious problem:

> We must conclude that if they be young, of a black complexion, and hairie, and are likewise somewhat discoloured in their cheeks, that they have a spirit of falacity, and feele within themselves of frequent titillation, their seed being hot and prurient, doth irritate and inflame them to venery; neither is this concupiscence allaid and qualified, but by provoking the ejaculation of the seed, as Galen propounds the advice in the example of a widow, who was affected with intolerable symptoms, till the abundance of the spermatick humour was diminished by the hand of a skillful midwife, and a convenient oyntment, which passage will also furnish us with this argument, that the use of venery is exceedingly wholesome, if the woman will confine herselfe to the laws of moderation, so that she feele no wearisomenesse, nor weaknesse in her body, after pleasing conflicts.[105]

Like the scold, the female with a voracious sexual appetite fails actually to disturb the social order, despite the supposedly ever-present threat.[106] For in the case of sexual behaviour, the constraint upon women is a most straightforward one: in addition to the traditional double standard for sexual behaviour (men are expected to have extensive sexual experience; in women it is 'dishonest'), pregnancy was a serious inhibitor of female sex drive.[107]

Contraception was little understood and less practised in the early modern period. As a result, sex and pregnancy went hand in hand in the Renaissance imagination. One night with Bertram guarantees that Helena is with child by her errant husband in *All's Well That Ends Well*. When Isabella refuses to sleep with Angelo to save her brother's life in *Measure for Measure*, she states simply: 'I had rather my brother die by law than my son should be unlawfully born.'[108] The pregnant woman is the Renaissance image of female sexuality.[109]

Throughout the early modern period *coitus interruptus* was the only widely advocated method of birth control, and of course this relied entirely upon the good-will and self-control of the individual man. Even this method was frowned upon by the Church, which insisted that sexual intercourse and the desire to beget children must go together. In 1590 the Vicar of Weaverham in Cheshire was denounced as 'an instructor of young folks how to commit the sin of adultery or fornication and not 'beget or bring forth children'.[110] The condom was known and its use described in detail in medical treatises from Fallopius's *De morbo gallico* (*On syphilis*) onwards, but, as the title of that work suggests, its use was advocated as a protective against venereal disease, rather than as a contraceptive measure. In any case, it is unlikely that any but educated urban adults had access either to the literature, or to the condom itself. Even in the cities, it is not until the eighteenth century that we find condoms openly advertised for public sale.[111]

Folk beliefs about contraceptive measures were many and varied, testifying eloquently to the ever-present anxiety about unwanted pregnancy. In the early modern period in western Europe they range from drinking willow tea to suspending hare dung or mule's hide over the woman's bed.[112] Learned treatises were little more helpful. Albertus Magnus suggests that if a woman spits three times in the mouth of a frog, or eats bees, she will not become pregnant; other authorities suggest the wearing of macabre talismans like the finger and anus of a dead foetus.[113] There is a long tradition (traceable back to Hippocrates) that vigorous movement on the part of the woman during intercourse inhibits conception, and the Christian Church seized upon this in order to assert that passionate love is the more sinful on this account. In antiquity, on the other hand, it was held that simultaneous orgasm increased the likelihood of conception.[114]

Better-nourished, married younger and more frequently, it was middle-class women who bore the heaviest burden of childbearing.[115] In 1643 Ralph Josselin wrote in his diary: 'In Spring now my wife weaned her daughter and began to breed againe'.[116] The diary of a fifteenth-century Florentine merchant captures the rhythm of family sexual relations poignantly, and must remind us of the strongly repressive character of sexual activity for women before efficient contraception:

> I married my second wife, Betta on 22 June [1393] . . . On the 26th of that same June, I received a payment of 80 gold florins from the bank of Giacomino and Co. This was the dowry.
>
> On Sunday, 17 May 1394, Betta gave birth to a girl. . . .
>
> On Friday evening, 17 March 1396, the Lord blessed our marriage with a male son.
>
> 12 March 1397, Betta gave birth to our third child. . . .
>
> 27 April 1398, Betta gave birth to our fourth child.
>
> 1 July, 1399, Betta had our fifth child.
>
> 22 June 1400, Betta gave birth for the sixth time.
>
> On Wednesday, 13 July 1401 . . . the Lord lent us a seventh child.
>
> On 5 July 1402 . . . Betta gave birth to our eighth child.
>
> After that my wife Betta passed on to Paradise. . . .
>
> The [business] partnership is to start on 1 January 1403 and to last three years. . . . I have undertaken to put up 2,000 florins. This is how I propose to raise them: 1,370 florins . . . are still due to me from my old partnership. . . . The rest I expect to obtain if I marry again this year, when I hope to find a woman with a dowry as large as God may be pleased to grant me. . . .
>
> I record that on 8 May 1403, I was betrothed to Ginevra, daughter of Antonio Brancacci. . . . The dowry was 1,000 florins: 700 in cash and 300 in a farm at Campi.
>
> On Sunday morning at terce, 27 April [1404], Ginevra gave birth to our first-born son. . . .
>
> Altogether Ginevra and I had eleven children: four boys and seven girls. . . .
>
> After that it was God's will to recall to Himself the blessed soul of my wife Ginevra. She died in childbirth after lengthy suffering. . . . God bless her and grant us fortitude.[117]

Dati went on to marry again, and to have six further children before he himself finally died. No wonder Leantio can confidently promise his mother, in *Women Beware Women:* 'I'll prove an excellent husband, here's my hand; / Lay in provision, follow my business roundly, / And make you a grandmother in forty weeks.'[118]

In *The Duchess of Malfi*, the scene in which the Duchess exits to her marriage bed with her new husband, Antonio, is followed immediately by her pregnancy:

> Bosola   I observe our duchess
> Is sick o'days, she pukes, her stomach seethes,
> The fins of her eyelids look most teeming blue,
> She wanes i' th' cheek, and waxes fat i' th' flank.[119]

In a directly bawdy scene, Bosola tempts the Duchess with 'apricocks' (by traditional irresistible to pregnant women), and, as she eats greedily, informs her they were ripened in horse-dung. The Duchess 'troubled with the mother' (a blunt pun on hysteria / pregnancy) is made sick by the fruit, and rushes off in labour. There is little sympathy in this treatment, and a considerable amount of pointed humour at the expense of the Duchess's lust, which her pregnancy alludes to, and is a constant reminder of, in this scene. The pregnant Annabella receives no more sympathetic treatment in Ford's *'Tis Pity She's a Whore*.

In *Measure for Measure*, when the pregnant Juliet appears on stage as living evidence of Claudio's capital crime (extra-marital sex), the Duke asks: 'Repent you, fair one, of the sin you carry?' To which Juliet replies: 'I do; and bear the shame most patiently.'[120] The visible pregnancy is the representation of 'the sin [she] carries'; she will *bear* it – carry it to term, support the shame, and give birth in the pain which is woman's punishment for the concupiscence she acquired at the Fall. In Webster's *The Devil's Law-Case* the *topos* of the pregnant/lusty woman is compounded by disguising her as a nun. Once again, the scene is pure bawdy: Jolenta, not pregnant but feigning pregnancy, meets Angiolella, pregnant and in nun's habit. Jolenta engages in lively backchat about 'tumbling' (falling into bed), while Angiolella regrets her lost maidenhead.

In *The Winter's Tale*, all the sexual innuendo in the figure of the pregnant woman is invoked as part of Leontes' delusion that his chaste wife is unfaithful. It is a small step from Hermione's Ladies' good-natured banter about her swelling figure to Leontes' accusation of her irrepressible lasciviousness:

1 *Lady*	The Queen your mother rounds apace. We shall
	Present our services to a fine new prince
	One of these days; and then you'd wanton with us,
	If we would have you.
2 *Lady*	She is spread of late
	Into a goodly bulk. Good time encounter her![121]
Leontes	Bear the boy hence; he shall not come about her;
	Away with him; and let her sport herself
	With that she's big with – for 'tis Polixenes
	Has made thee swell thus. . . .
	She's an adultress; and I have said with whom. . . .
	A bed-swerver, even as bad as those
	That vulgars give bold'st titles.[122]

Notes

1 Aulus Gellius, *Noctes Atticae* I.xvii.1–4; see also Diogenes Laertius, *Lives of the Philosophers* II.35–7, in which Socrates makes a number of further witty remarks about the lessons to be learnt from Xanthippe's scolding.

2 e.g. J. Warrington (ed.), *Everyman Classical Dictionary*. One of the first speeches about Kate in *The Taming of the Shrew* likens her to Xanthippe.

3 Chaucer, 'The Wife of Bath's Prologue' III(D) 729. T. Heywood, *Gynaikeion, or Nine Books of Various History, concerning Women* (London, 1624), also gives Socrates two scolding wives, 'Zantippe' and 'Mirho'. For a woodcut version of the 'Phyllis and Aristotle', see N. Z. Davis, 'Women on top', in N. Z. Davis, *Society and Culture in Early Modern France* (London, 1975), pp. 124–51. See, in general, K. M. Rogers, *The Troublesome Helpmate: A History of Misogyny in Literature* (Seattle and London, 1966; 1973 edn), chs. I–IV.

4 See the *OED*.

5 For convenience I subsume gossips under scolds/shrews in this chapter.

6 A. D. J. Macfarlane, *Witchcraft in Tudor and Stuart England* (London, 1970), pp. 292, 288, 291. On the reality of shrews in societies repressive of women, see M. Wolf, 'Chinese women: old skills in a new context, in M. Z. Rosaldo and L. Lamphere (eds) *Woman, Culture, and Society* (Stanford, 1974), pp. 157–72.

7 See R. Masek, 'Women in an age of transition 1485–1714', in B. Kanner (ed.), *The Women of England* (London, 1980), pp. 138–82, 138. In fact we have a typical case of mistaken tone in comments on women and the 'woman question' in the early modern period here. The full *bon mot* runs: 'London (or Paris) is the paradise of women, the purgatory of men and the hell of horses', and is attributed sometimes to John Florio, sometimes to Richard Burton. It also occurs as part of the *Catechisme des courtisans ou les questions de la cour* (1668) said of Paris rather than of London, and prefaced by the question: 'What is a woman? A reasoning monkey.' For the shrew literature in the early modern period, see R. Masek, *op. cit.*, p. 150.

8 Noah's wife is not Biblical – but Noah's weakness (getting drunk and being seen naked by his sons) is. See K. Casey, 'The Cheshire Cat: reconstructing the experience of medieval women', in B. A. Carroll (ed.), *Liberating Women's History* (Urbana, Chicago and London, 1976), pp. 224–49, 237: 'If . . . we are to believe the diatribes of literature and of sermons, . . . the "average" woman was "Noah's wife," a stock character of street drama, or that Alice of a fifteenth-century song, drinking with her female friends in a tavern and boasting: "I dread no man!"' (p. 237) See Rogers, *op. cit.*, pp. 89–90.

9 Talkativeness is traditionally a peculiarly female attribute. Cornelius Agrippa ironically extols it as a 'special' female gift in his *Declamatio de nobilitate et praecellentia foeminei sexus* (Antwerp, 1529).

10 See Thomas Holcot, *In proverbia Salomonis*, in Bede Jarett, *Social Theories of the Middle Ages* (1926), p. 84. I am grateful to Mr A. C. Spearing for this reference.

11 See R. Kelso, *Doctrine for the Lady of the Renaissance* (Urbana, 1956).

12 Juvenal, *Satires* VI.268–70.
13 See *Henry VI Part III* I.iv.113–15, York to Queen Margaret: 'How ill-beseeming is it in thy sex / To triumph like an Amazonian trull / Upon their woes whom fortune captivates!' On the dramatic use of the threat of the female outsider see L. A. Fiedler, *The Stranger in Shakespeare* (New York, 1973), pp. 43–84.
14 fo. Cvii', in A. S. Cairncross (ed.), *King Henry VI Part I* (Arden, 1962), p. 145.
15 ibid., fo. Cxv'; Arden p. 152.
16 604/1/55; in Arden p. 167.
17 See M. Warner, *Joan of Arc: the Image of Female Heroism* (London, 1981), pp. 203–4, 139–58.
18 W. Whately, *A Bride-Bush: or a direction for married persons* (1619), p. 38.
19 ibid., p. 39.
20 ibid., p. 40.
21 Thomas Becon, in Kelso, *op. cit.*, p. 50. In *Ancrene Wisse* the Virgin Mary is especially commended because she is recorded only to have spoken four times in Scripture.
22 J. Russell Brown (ed.), *The White Devil* (Revels, 1960), III.ii.281–4.
23 Kelso, *op. cit.*, p. 101. And see I. Maclean, *Woman Triumphant: Feminism in French Literature 1610–52* (Oxford, 1977), p. 54: 'Leur honneur [des filles] se conserue mieux par le silence que par la parole. Celle qui a tant de discours, porte ordinairement l'affront dessus le front' (Artus Thomas, *Discours . . . qu'il est bien seant que les filles soynent scavantes* (1600), fo. 8'–8').
24 J. Russell Brown, *The Duchess of Malfi* (Revels, 1964), IV.i.9–10.
25 Kelso, *op. cit.*, p. 51.
26 Anonymous translation. See F. L. Utley, *The Crooked Rib: An Analytical Index to the Argument about Women in English and Scots Literature to the End of the Year 1568* (Columbus, Ohio, 1944), pp. 191–2, 296–7; the version quoted in Utley's synopsis is taken from *A. C. mery talys* (c. 1525), p. 297. See also Ben Jonson's *Epicoene, or The Silent Woman* (1609). In this version the mute wife who becomes a shrew subsequently turns out to be a boy in disguise. See also T. Heywood, *Gynaikeion*, p. 236: 'I desire to haue a woman to bee my wife that shall haue no more tongue to answer mee to a question than yea, or nay; or to haue more wit than to distinguish her husbands bed from an other mans' (witty riposte of a man trying to marry off a simple daughter).
27 Utley, *op. cit.*, p. 296.
28 I.i.47–61. The source story for this incident is the folk-tale 'Cap o' Rushes'. A version of the same story occurs in the story called by the brothers Grimm, 'The goose girl at the well'.
29 I.i.84–9.
30 A. B. Grosart (ed.), *The Life and Complete Works in Prose and Verse of Robert Greene, MA*, 14 vols (New York, 1964 reissue), V,231–2.
31 ibid., p. 232.
32 I.iv.169–76.

33 IV.ii.17–18.
34 See Davis, 'Women on top', *op. cit.*
35 See Davis, 'The reasons of misrule', and 'Women on top', *op. cit.*, especially pp. 116, 140; J. O'Faolin and L. Martines (eds), *Not in God's Image: Women in History* (London, 1979), p. 188.
36 Davis, *op. cit.*, p. 116. In *The Taming of a Shrew* (1594), a version of Shakespeare's *The Taming of the Shrew*, the play closes with Sly, the beggar's, evident incompetence at controlling his own wife. See G. Bullough, *Narrative and Dramatic Sources of Shakespeare*, I (London, 1957), p. 108. For the most recent view of the relation between the two plays, see Brian Morris's Arden edn (1981).
37 II.iv.55–7.
38 Nicholas Fontanus, *The Womans Doctour: or, an exact and distinct Explanation of all such Diseases as are peculiar to that Sex* (London, 1652), p. 1, in H. Smith, 'Gynecology and ideology in seventeenth-century England', B. A. Carroll (ed.), *Liberating Women's History* (Urbana, Chicago and London, 1976), pp. 97–114, 100. See also O'Faolain and Martines, *op. cit.*, p. 137.
39 V.iii.272–3. See Chaucer, *The Book of the Duchess*, ll. 919–20: 'And which a goodly softe speche / Had that swete, my lyves lech!' I am grateful to Professor John Stevens for bringing this passage to my attention.
40 In. E. Auerbach, *Mimesis*, transl. W. R. Trask (Princeton, 1953 edn), pp. 143–73.
41 ibid., p. 144.
42 ibid., p. 157. See Jerome, letter 52 (To Neoptianus): 'Always bear in mind that it was a woman who expelled the tiller of paradise from his heritage' (H. Wace and P. Schaff (eds), *St Jerome: Letters and Selected Works* (Oxford and New York, 1893), p. 92.
43 See M. Warner, *Alone Of All Her Sex: the Myth and the Cult of the Virgin Mary* (London 1976; 1978 edn), p. 58.
44 Genesis 3.16. See also Boccaccio, *De claris mulieribus*, transl. G. A. Guarino (New Brunswick, 1963), pp. 1–3; Warner, *op. cit.*, p. 52.
45 *Much Ado About Nothing* II.i.1–28.
46 Davis, 'Women on top', *op. cit.*, p. 140.
47 IV.i.299–318. On the difficulties in staging this scene if Beatrice is portrayed as 'charmingly' witty, see J. F. Cox, 'The stage representation of the "Kill Claudio" sequence in *Much Ado About Nothing*', *Shakespeare Survey*, 32 (1979), pp. 27–36.
48 In M. R. Ridley (ed.), *Antony and Cleopatra* (Arden, 1975 edn), p. 242.
49 III.xi.54–8.
50 III.vii.69–70.
51 Boccacio's version of Helen's story starts: 'Helen was known to the entire world as much for her lustfulness as for the long war which resulted from it.' He also makes Helen's treachery the direct cause of the fall of Troy. *De claris mulieribus*, *op. cit.*, pp. 73, 76. Helen and Cleopatra figure regularly in literature in the early modern period as 'bad' women bringing doom on mankind – 'war for a whore'. See A. J. C. Ingram, 'Changing attitudes to "bad" women in Elizabethan and Jacobean Drama' (unpublished Cambridge PhD dissertation, 1978), pp. 211–58.

52 Boccaccio makes Cleopatra whore and emasculator of men: 'To bring covetous Cleopatra to his embraces, effeminate Antony gave her . . . the captive king in all his regalia', ibid. (p. 194).
53 Keith Thomas, *Religion and the Decline of Magic* (London, 1973), p. 163, in M. Warner, *Joan of Arc*, p. 86.
54 Heywood makes Deborah one of his female worthies in *The Exemplary lives and memorable acts of nine of the most worthy women of the World* (London, 1640 edn). On the nine female worthies tradition see Warner, *Joan of Arc*, p. 205.
55 See ibid.; and C. C. Lougee, *Le Paradis des Femmes* (Princeton, 1976), pp. 31–40.
56 Warner, *Joan of Arc*, p. 86.
57 See I. Maclean, *The Renaissance Notion of Woman* (Cambridge, 1980), pp. 2–3. See B. M. Bolton, 'Mulieres Sanctae', in S. M. Stuard (ed.), *Women in Medieval Society* (University of Pennsylvania, 1976), pp. 141–58.
58 Davis, 'Women on top', pp. 154–6.
59 See B. A. Hanawalt, 'The female felon in fourteenth-century England', in Stuard, *op. cit.*, pp. 125–40.
60 Davis, *op. cit.*, p. 147; on Zell, see S. M. Wyntjes, 'Women in the Reformation era', in R. Bridenthal and C. Koonz (eds), *Becoming Visible: Women in European History* (Boston, 1977), pp. 165–91, pp. 174–5; O'Faolain and Martines, *op. cit.* pp. 216–19.
61 On the general theme of misrule and folly in Elizabethan drama, see C. L. Barber, *Shakespeare's Festive Comedy* (Princeton, 1959).
62 See J. Mann, *Chaucer and Medieval Estates Satire* (Cambridge, 1973).
63 Davis, *op. cit.*, pp. 147–8.
64 *Richard III* I.iii.158–70. See also the privileged outburst and ritual cursing of Constance in *King John* III.i.179–86; III.iv.17–105.
65 *Richard III* I.iii.297–304.
66 Heywood, who groups Amazon women (warlike and valorous) with scolds in his *Gynaikeion*, discusses Joan of Arc and Queen Margaret together in his chapter 'Of English Viragoes. And of *Ioan de Pucil*'. Both, in his view, were soldier-women.
67 *The Winter's Tale* II.iii.90–2.
68 II.iii.107–15.
69 *Othello* V.ii.232.
70 *Coriolanus* IV.ii.9.
71 *Troilus and Cressida* II.ii.113–25.
72 In Boccaccio's *De claris mulieribus*, Cassandra's gift of prophesying is explained by her sexual exploits with Apollo: she got the gift of tongues as a bribe to become his mistress; when she broke her word Apollo added the proviso that no one would believe her prophecies (*op. cit.*, p. 70).
73 M. R. Ridley (ed.), *Othello* (Arden, 1958; 1974 edn), p. 54.
74 *Othello* II.i.124–42 (Arden edn).
75 See below, p. 161.
76 *Cymbeline* II.iii.11–16.
77 *The Taming of the Shrew* II.i.208–16.

78 *Othello* II.i.100–15 (Arden edn).
79 *The Duchess of Malfi* I.i.336–8.
80 *Palladis Tamia* fo. 133ᵛ–134ʳ. The footnote to the Revels edition of *The Duchess of Malfi* links Ferdinand's remark about the lamprey to a quote from J. Maplet's *Green Forest* (1567), fo. N3ᵛ, to the effect that this eel-like fish with sucker mouth 'swimmeth all whole in flexible sort, and all alike bending hir bodie'. Nashe's wanton prostitute in 'The Choice of Valentines' 'wanton faints and falls upon her bed, / And often tosseth to and fro her head. / She shuts her eyes and waggles with her tongue: / O, who is able to abstain so long?' See J. B. Steane (ed.), *Thomas Nashe: The Unfortunate Traveller and Other Works* (Penguin, 1972), p. 461.
81 In Heywood, *op. cit.*, a compendious survey of stories and anecdotes about women, scolds and Amazons are grouped together in the fifth book.
82 See R. F. Burton (ed.), *The Book of the Thousand Nights and a Night* (London, 1885). Andresen-Thom points out that this is a theme which deserves consideration when thinking about representations of women in Renaissance drama, in M. Andresen-Thom, 'Thinking about women and their prosperous art: a reply to Juliet Dusinberre's *Shakespeare and the Nature of Women*', *Shakespeare Studies*, 11 (1978), pp. 259–76.
83 'The Choice of Valentines', *op. cit.*, pp. 463–4. See also Middleton's *The Family of Love*.
84 *Against Jovinian* I.
85 *Henry VI Part I* V.iv.62–81. In fact Joan's virginity was undisputed by her trial judges (see Warner, *Joan of Arc*), but stories of her sexual exploits circulated constantly amongst her enemies. In Ben Jonson's 'Conversations with William Drummond', he uses 'pucelle' as a synonym for 'whore': 'verses on the pucelle of the Court, Mistress Bulstrode' (G. Parfitt (ed.), *Ben Jonson: The Complete Poems* (Penguin, 1975), p. 463).
86 See, e.g., G. Salgado (ed.), *Cony-Catchers and Bawdy Baskets: an Anthology of Elizabethan Low-Life* (Penguin, 1972); E. J. O'Brien, *Elizabethan Tales* (London, 1937).
87 'The Choice of Valentines', p. 464. 'Die' is the standard Elizabethan euphemism for orgasm. See also the widespread belief that ejaculation shortens a man's life, e.g., Albertus Magnus, *De secretis mulierum*, in O'Faolain and Martines, *op. cit.*, pp. 136–7: 'men who copulate too much and too often do not live long'.
88 Burton, *The Book of the Thousand Nights and a Night*, I,328.
89 There is a standard popular tale of a roguish woman duping a man into being ridden around the room naked like an ass. Salgado, *The Elizabethan Underworld* (London, 1977), cities a supposedly true case of a 'witch', Judith Philips, who defrauded a Hampshire gentleman and then duped him into being bridled and ridden. A woodcut of this event is precisely like the traditional picture of Phyllis riding Aristotle. See G. Salgado, *op. cit.*, pp. 94–5.
90 On Eve, the Fall and sexuality see Warner, *Alone Of All Her Sex*, pp. 50–7.
91 Hippocrates, *Oeuvres* in O'Faolain and Martines, *op. cit.*, p. 136.
92 Acknowledgement of female sexuality and dread or awe at supposed

female insatiability are to be found curiously intertwined in vernacular medical treatises on midwifery and female diseases of the sixteenth and seventeenth centuries (all of which were written by male doctors). J. Duval's treatise, *Traité des Hermaphrodits, parties génitales, accouchemens des femmes et traitement qui est requis pour les relever en santé* (Rouen, 1612; reprinted Paris, 1880) typically combines the medical and informative with derogatory comment. See, for instance, his clear account of the clitoris and clitoral orgasm: 'D'autant que les plus pudiques des femmes et filles, quand elles ont donné permission de porter le bout du doigt sur cette partie, elles sont fort facilement submises à le volonté de celui qui le touche: leur causant l'attectation d'icelle une si grande titillation, qu'elles en sont amorcées et ravies, voire forcées au déduit vénéréen. Donnant l'exact sentiment de cette partie, pour petite qu'elle soit, une tant violente amorce au prurit et ardeur libidineux, qu'estant la raison surmontée, les femelles prennent tellement le frain aux dents qu'elles donnent du cul à terre, faute de se tenir fermes et roides sur les arcons. . . . Aussi a-t-on veu des femmes, qui ont promptement jetté leur semence génitale, quand elles ont senti toucher cette particule' (p. 67). Duval explains that the clitoris is called '*gaude mihi*' by voluptuous women ('give me pleasure'), and suggests that such women take inordinate pleasure in such titillation. He also informs the reader that 'quelques libidineuses femelles' 'en peuvent abuser les autres en la titillation qu'elles donnent par l'immission d'icelles' (p. 61).

93 N. W. Bawcutt (ed.), *The Changeling* (Revels, 1958; 1979 edn) V.i.1–3.
94 V.i.19–19.
95 *Canterbury Tales*, General Prologue ll.459–62, 475–6. See J. Mann, *Chaucer and Medieval Estates Satire* (Cambridge, 1973), pp. 121–7.
96 *Hamlet* III.iv.66–94.
97 Davis, 'The reasons of misrule', pp. 106–7.
98 M. E. Lawlis (ed.), *The Novels of Thomas Deloney* (Indiana, 1961), pp. 1–88.
99 ibid., p. 5.
100 ibid., p. 9.
101 ibid., p. 9.
102 ibid., p. 13.
103 ibid., p. 20.
104 Deloney's novel continues with Jack's career as an upstart nobleman of dubious status, 'clothier by trade', 'gentleman by condition'; the first his own rank, the second deriving from his wife. On the widow's careful assertion of her rank vis-à-vis Jack, see C. Jordan, 'The "art of clothing": role playing in Deloney's fiction', *English Literary Renaissance*, 11 (1981), pp. 183–93.
105 N. Fontanus, *The Woman Doctor: or, an exact and distinct Explanation of all such Diseases as are peculiar to that Sex with Choise and Experimental Remedies against the same* (London, 1952), in H. Smith, 'Gynecology and ideology in seventeenth-century England', *op. cit.*, p. 104. Remedies for 'hysteria' given by midwives similarly involve anointing 'the womb' with ointments, and cupping the groin and pubic hair. See N.

Z. Davis, ' "Women's history" in transition: the European case', *Feminist Studies*, 3 (1976), pp. 83–103, 101. See also B. Rowland (ed.), *Medieval Woman's Guide to Health: the First English Gynecological Handbook* (London, 1981), pp. 87–105, especially pp. 104–5.

106 *pace* Quaiffe, who seems to suggest some real threat in female promiscuity. See G. R. Quaiffe, *Wanton Wenches and Wayward Wives* (London, 1979).

107 On the double standard, see Stone, *The Family, Sex and Marriage*; K. Thomas, 'The double standard', *Journal of the History of Ideas*, 20 (1959), pp. 193–216.

108 *Measure for Measure* III.i.187.

109 See e.g. the extensive treatment of pregnancy alongside that of male and female sexuality in Duval, *Traité des Hermaphrodits*, *op. cit.*

110 In Stone, *The Family, Sex and Marriage*, p. 422, from E. A.'Wrigley, *Population and History* (London, 1969), p. 127.

111 See N. E. Himes, *Medical History of Contraception* (Baltimore, 1936; reprinted 1963; 1970 edn), pp. 188, 197–200.

112 Himes, *op. cit.*, pp. 171, 173.

113 ibid., pp. 161, 163.

114 ibid., p. 172. See Davis, ' "Women's history" ', p. 89; E. Shorter, 'Female emancipation, birth control and fertility', *American Historical Review*, 78 (1973), pp. 605–40, especially p. 626.

115 See Stone, *The Family, Sex and Marriage*, pp. 63–6. Putting children out to wet-nurses (rather than suckling them in person) may also have contributed to increased fertility, where nutrition was sufficiently low for breastfeeding to inhibit fertility. Stone is committed to this view, although there is now some doubt as to the actual inhibiting effect on menstruation and ovulation of under-nourishment and lactation.

116 A. D. J. Macfarlane (ed.), *The Diary of Ralph Josselin: 1616–1683* (London, 1976).

117 G. Brucker (ed.), *Two Memoirs of Renaissance Florence*, in O'Faolain and Martines, *op. cit.*, pp. 184–5.

118 *Women Beware Women* I.i.107–9.

119 *Duchess of Malfi* II.i.63–6.

120 *Measure for Measure* II.iii.19–20.

121 *The Winter's Tale* II.i.16–20.

122 II.i.59–94.

5

'Make thy doublet of changeable taffeta': Dress Codes, Sumptuary Law and 'Natural' Order

When Queen Margaret, in *Henry VI Part II*, wants to characterise the presumptuousness of Humphrey, Duke of Gloucester and his wife, she does so in terms of the Duchess's dress and retinue:

> Not all these lords do vex me half so much
> As that proud dame, the Lord Protector's wife.
> She sweeps it through the court with troops of ladies,
> More like an empress than Duke Humphrey's wife.
> Strangers in court do take her for the Queen.
> She bears a duke's revenues on her back,
> And in her heart she scorns our poverty;
> Shall I not live to be aveng'd on her?
> Contemptuous base-born callet as she is,
> She vaunted 'mongst her minions t' other day
> The very train of her worst wearing gown
> Was better worth than all my father's lands
> Till Suffolk gave two dukedoms for his daughter.[1]

This passage gives a curiously precise rendering of the 'dress game'. Dress, in the early modern period, was regulated by rank, not by income. That is to say, there was actual legislation to ensure that even if non-noble households had the cash to dress themselves like princes, with princely retinues of followers and servants, they were not entitled to adopt the manners and habits of dress of their hereditary betters. At the same time, the wealthy but 'base-born' could flout the regulations and exploit the extreme social sensitivity about dress to score political points, as Margaret records the Duchess of Gloucester as doing in this passage. She displays her lack of respect for the queen, and signals the power of her own husband, by boasting about the lavishness of her own dress, and wearing it ostentatiously.[2]

Nowhere is the tension between the old, outgoing feudal order and the new mercantile order more apparent than in the Elizabethan preoccupation with dress as status. In Deloney's *Jack of Newbury*, Jack, elevated financially by his marriage to the widow (now dead), sets out to improve his fortunes by, first, equipping himself and a whole army of men in 'white coates, and red caps with yellowe Feathers' (which duly brings him to the attention of the queen, who judges him 'though a Clothier by trade, yet a Gentleman by condition'):

> The Iustices and most of the Gentlemen gaue him great commendations for this his good and forward mind shewed in this action: but some other enuying heerat gaue out words that hee shewed himselfe more prodigall then prudent, and more vaine glorious then well aduised, seeing that the best Nobleman in the Countrie would scarce haue done so much.[3]

Jack correctly believes that to demonstrate his power (wealth) he must match the nobility in dress; the nobility in their turn recognise the sign, but resent the gesture as 'prodigall'.

Within a year of Elizabeth I's accession in 1559, her Privy Council had directed the lords of England to take in hand the dress of their servants. Henry VIII's reign had seen greater shifts in landownership (and hence in the composition of the peers of the realm) than any previous period in English history since the Norman Conquest. As often happens, it was these new peers who set their faces most firmly against any further social mobility during the reign of Elizabeth; control of dress (for individuals and their households) was seen as a significant control of real social power and influence.

Elizabethan sumptuary legislation (the laws designed to regulate the dress of men and women) makes so apparent the tension between rank and wealth that it is appropriate to offer a generous example. I reproduce here in its entirety the tabulated 1597 legislation.[4] There are exceptions to the rules given: officers and servants of the queen, for instance, might be licensed by her to dress as they wished (thus ensuring the superior status of her household). And gifts of old clothes to servants (or actors) were permitted.

If we try to sum up the consequences of this legislation, it is as follows: gold, silver and purple were jealously guarded for the use of the hereditary peerage; velvet was the mark of luxury for those who could only claim the rank of gentleman, and even then its use was severely restricted; only knights and those above that

Men's Apparel

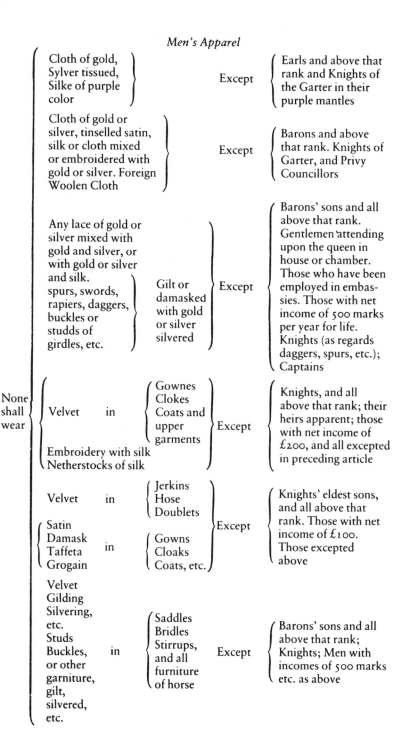

None shall wear				Except	
Cloth of gold, Sylver tissued, Silke of purple color				Except	Earls and above that rank and Knights of the Garter in their purple mantles
Cloth of gold or silver, tinselled satin, silk or cloth mixed or embroidered with gold or silver. Foreign Woolen Cloth				Except	Barons and above that rank. Knights of Garter, and Privy Councillors
Any lace of gold or silver mixed with gold and silver, or with gold or silver and silk. spurs, swords, rapiers, daggers, buckles or studds of girdles, etc.	Gilt or damasked with gold or silver silvered			Except	Barons' sons and all above that rank. Gentlemen attending upon the queen in house or chamber. Those who have been employed in embassies. Those with net income of 500 marks per year for life. Knights (as regards daggers, spurs, etc.); Captains
Velvet	in	Gownes Clokes Coats and upper garments		Except	Knights, and all above that rank; their heirs apparent; those with net income of £200, and all excepted in preceding article
Embroidery with silk Netherstocks of silk					
Velvet	in	Jerkins Hose Doublets		Except	Knights' eldest sons, and all above that rank. Those with net income of £100. Those excepted above
Satin Damask Taffeta Grogain	in	Gowns Cloaks Coats, etc.			
Velvet Gilding Silvering, etc. Studs Buckles, or other garniture, gilt, silvered, etc.	in	Saddles Bridles Stirrups, and all furniture of horse		Except	Barons' sons and all above that rank; Knights; Men with incomes of 500 marks etc. as above

Women's Apparel

Cloth of gold or silver tissued, purple silk	Except	Countesses and all above that rank

(Viscountesses may wear cloth of gold or silver tissued only in their kirtles)

Silk or cloth, mixed or embroidered with pearl, gold or silver	Except	Baronesses and all above that rank
Cloth of gold and silver only in linings of garments, etc.	Except	Wives of Barons' eldest sons and all above that rank. Barons' daughters
Cloth of silver in kirtles only	Except	Knights' wives and all above that rank
Embroideries of gold or silver Lace of gold or silver or mixed with gold, silver or silk. Headdresses trimmed with pearl	Except	Wives of Barons' eldest sons and all above that rank. Barons' daughters Wives of Knights of Garter or of Privy Councillors Maids of honor, Ladies, etc. of Privy Chamber Those with income of 500 marks a year
Velvet in upper garments Embroidery with silk Netherstocks of silk	Except	Knights' wives and all above that rank and those excepted above Those with incomes of £200
Velvet in { Kirtles Petticoats Gowns Satin in { Cloaks and other outer garments	Except	Wives of knights' eldest sons, and all above that rank. Gentlewomen attendant upon countesses, viscountesses, etc Those with incomes of £100
Satin in Kirtles Damask Tufte taffeta Plain taffeta Grograin } in Gowns	Except	Gentlemen's wives, bearing arms, and all above that rank, etc.

None shall wear any

rank were entitled to wear ornate arms or spurs or to furnish their horse with elaborate tackle.

Women's dress was determined by the rank of their husbands. Daughters of the nobility are included at the tail ends of lists of entitled wearers of lavish cloth and embroidery. Eldest sons are singled out, but not female heirs. The 'net income' categories stipulate that income should be 'per year for life', once again excluding those without income-producing investments, that is, landholdings.

But of course there is an obvious problem about any such legislation. The affluent burghers with ready money to dress like the gentry were also the purveyors of the commodity being legislated about: expensive fabrics. Various attempts were made during Elizabeth's reign to legislate from the other end, as it were, to prevent merchants from selling their most expensive cloths to anyone not 'entitled' to wear it. These met with fierce opposition, and, so far as one can judge, little success. Parliament (on whose benches the burghers did sit) was not inclined to legislate itself out of good business. A 1563 Act of Apparel 'against such as sell Wares for Apparel without ready money, to persons under £200 lands or fees' had a stormy passage through Parliament (in the course of which the £200 figure was amended to £3000, denying credit to a rather substantial portion of the gentry), and was soon revoked.[5] And the implication of this Act was that anyone who could produce ready money could buy cloth and fashionable accessories regardless of the laws controlling the wearing of such garments once acquired.

Puttenham gives a clear sense of the Elizabethans' equating of dress with rank in his discussion of poetical ornament at the beginning of the third book of his *The Arte of English Poesie* (1589). Poetry requires appropriate ornament, 'disguising it no litle from the ordinary and accustomed', to make it 'decenter and more agreable to any ciuill eare and vnderstanding'. Ornament appropriate to the occasion is part of the order which the civilised Elizabethan recognises as beauty and comeliness. 'Cloth of gold, sylver tissued, purple, silk' perform for the code of an individual's dress what figures of speech do for poetic speech:

> And as we see in these great Madames of honour, be they for personage or otherwise neuer so comely and bewtifull, yet if they want their courtly habillements or at leastwise such other apparell as custome and ciuilitie haue

ordained to couer their naked bodies, would be halfe ashamed or greatly out of countenaunce to be seen in that sort, and perchance do then thinke themselues more amiable in euery mans eye when they be in their richest attire, suppose of silkes of tyssewes & costly embroideries, then when they go in cloth or in any other plaine and simple apparell; euen so cannot our vulgar Poesie shew it selfe either gallant or gorgious, if any lymme be left naked and bare and not clad in his kindly clothes and coulours, such as may conuey them somwhat out of sight, that is from the common course of ordinary speach and capacitie of the vulgar iudgement, and yet being artificially handled must needes yeld it much more bewtie and commendation.[6]

'Kindly clothes and coulours', that is, the attire appropriate to one's kind, or rank, 'must needes yeld it much more bewtie and commendation', and 'conuey them somwhat out of . . . the common course of ordinary speach and capacitie of the vulgar iudgement'. If the apparel is appropriate to the status of the wearer it raises him/her above the common, and adds to his or her beauty. When Petruchio announces to Kate that they are to return to her father's house, he proposes that they dress so as to demonstrate their (elevated) marital status:

> And now, my honey love,
> Will we return unto thy father's house
> And revel it as bravely as the best,
> With silken coats and caps, and golden rings,
> With ruffs and cuffs and farthingales and things,
> With scarfs and fans and double change of brav'ry,
> With amber bracelets, beads, and all this knav'ry.[7]

It follows that the individual who adopts dress too elevated for his or her station in life is automatically to be perceived as grotesque – or so the committed supporter of the *status quo* would have it. In *Have With You To Saffron Walden*, Thomas Nashe mocks the social pretensions of Gabriel Harvey by insinuating that his dress is pretentious. Harvey rose from the class of burgher (he was son of a Saffron Walden ropemaker, a member of the wealthy mercantile class) to become, briefly, a Professor at Cambridge. This gave him the rank of gentleman when he was presented to Elizabeth I on one of her Royal Progresses. Nashe writes:

I have a tale at my tung's end, if I can happen vpon it, of [Harvey's] hobby-horse reuelling and domimering at *Audley-end* when the Queene was there; to which place *Gabriell* (to doo his countrey more worship & glory) came ruffling it out huffty tuffty in his suite of veluet. There be them in Cambridge that had occasion to take note of it, for he stood noted and scoared for it in their bookes many a faire day after.[8]

Nashe's malicious coinages capture what he sees as Harvey's temerity: he wears a large ruff (ruffles it out), affects 'tufte taffeta' (huffty tuffty), and a suit of velvet, running himself into debt with the clothiers of Cambridge. If we refer back to the sumptuary laws, however, it seems that Harvey was wearing no more than his entitlement as a senior member of the University. It is Nashe's class prejudice which is betrayed in his sensitivity over Harvey's attire. In 1582 a comparable effort to keep the *nouveaux riches* in their place was made when the Lord Mayor and Common Council of London enacted legislation prohibiting any apprentice, of whatever guild, from wearing 'ruffles', 'cuffs', 'loose collars', and in particular 'ruffs more than a yard and a half long'.[9]

Even in the moralising treatises of the period a clear distinction is made between ostentatious dress which befits the hereditary status of the wearer, and that which is mere presumption or affectation. In his *The Anatomie of Abuses* (1583; Garland reprint 1973), Philip Stubbes singles out 'the pryde of apparell' as the most widespread vice in Britain (or 'Ailgna', as he calls it, in a thinly-veiled pseudonym), and the one most offensive in God's eyes. He specifies this 'pryde of apparell' as follows:

> *Spudeus*: How is Pride of Apparell committed?
> *Philoponus*: By wearyng of Apparell more gorgeous, sumptuous & precious than our state, callyng or condition of lyfe requireth.[10]

Spudeus presses the point:

> *Spudeus*: Doe you thinke it not permitted to any hauinge store of other necessary clothing, to weare, silks, veluets, taffeties, & other such riche attyre, of what calling soeuer they be of?
> *Philoponus*: I doubt not, but it is lawfull for y⁽ᵉ⁾ potestates, the nobilitie, the gentrie, yeomanrie, and for euerye priuate subiecte els to weare attyre euery one in his degree, accordinge as his calling and condition of life requireth, yet a meane is to be keept. . . . And as for the priuat subiects, it is not at any hand lawful that they should weare silks, veluets, satens, damasks, gould, siluer, and what they list (though they be neuer so able to maintain it) except they being in some kind of office in the common wealth, do vse it for the dignifying and innobling of the same. But now there is such a confuse mingle mangle of apparell in *Ailgna*, and such preposterous excesse therof, as euery one is permitted to flaunt it out, in what apparell he lust himselfe, or can get

by anie mind of meanes. So that it is verie hard to knowe, who is noble, who is worshipfull, who is a gentleman, who is not: for you shall haue those, which are neither of the nobylitie gentilitie nor yeomanry, no, nor yet anie Magistrat or Officer in the common welth, go daylie in silkes, veluets, satens, damasks, taffeties and such like, notwithstanding that they be both base by byrthe, meane by estate, & seruyle by calling.[11]

It is striking how closely Stubbes sticks to the lists of fabrics and ornaments specified in the sumptuary legislation, in keeping with his frequently reiterated charge that it is the affecting of dress above one's class or calling which is 'unlawful'.[12] And it is also important for the modern reader to recognise that what is 'immoral' about the dress which Stubbes goes on to describe in fascinating detail is not, on the whole, its lewdness, but its flouting of 'natural' order and rank.[13] In this context it is *male* dress which Stubbes chooses to bear the main brunt of his assault on 'fashions', and chiefly ruffs and doublets:

They haue great and monsterous ruffes, made either of Cambrick, holland, lawn or els of some other the finest cloth that can be got for money, whereof some be a quarter of a yard deep, yea some more, very few lesse.

So that they stand a full quarter of a yarde (and more) from their necks hanging ouer their shoulder poynts, insted of a vaile. . . . The deuil, as he in the fulnes of his malice, first inuented these great ruffes, so hath hee now found out also two great stayes to beare vp and maintaine this his kingdome of great ruffes . . . the one arch or piller wherby his kingdome of great ruffes is vnder propped is a certaine kinde of liquide matter which they call Starch, wherin the deuill hath willed them to wash and diue his ruffes wel, which when they be dry wil then stand stiffe and inflexible about their necks.

The other piller is a certain deuice made of wyers crested for ye purpose, whipped ouer either with gold, thred, siluer or silk, & this hee calleth a supportasse or vnderpropper. This is to be supplyed round about their necks vnder the ruffe, vpon the out side of the band, to beare vp the whole frame & body of the ruffe, from falling and hanging down.[14]

The fashion in doublets, according to Stubbes, is similarly contrived and exaggerated:

Their dublettes are noe lesse monstrous than the reste: For now the fashion is, to haue them hang downe to the middest of their theighes, or at least to their priuie members, beeing so harde-quilted, and stuffed, bombasted and sewed, as they can verie hardly eyther stoupe downe, or decline them selues to the grounde, soe styffe and sturdy they stand vpon them. . . . Certaine I am there was neuer any kinde of apparell euer inuented, that could more disproportion the body of man than these Dublets w' great bellies hanging down beneath their *Pudenda* (as I haue said) & stuffed with foure, fiue or six pound of Bombast at the least: I say nothing of what their Dublets be made, some of Saten, Taffatie, silk, Grogram, Chamlet, gold siluer, & what not? slashed, iagged, cut, carued, pincked and laced with all kinde of costly lace of diuers and sundry colours, for if I shoulde stand vpon these particularities, rather time then matter would be wanting.[15]

Assured though Stubbes is as to the unnaturalness of affecting dress more sumptuous than your station in life allows, he remains (like the sumptuary legislation itself) uneasy about the relationship between sumptuousness and actual cost. Cloth of gold, silver tissued, tinselled satin, silk, tufte taffeta, are all supposed to be denoters of elevated rank. Yet Stubbes would like to argue that this is because of some intrinsic opulence – a richness 'which is aesthetic, perhaps – not just because they cost a lot. Only such an argument could justify the right of the nobleman to wear specified fabrics, not because he alone can afford them (which notoriously he cannot), but because he alone is made more gorgeous by them (the upstart looks outlandish). It is a perilous argument to maintain. As one contemporary observer wrote in 1598:

I hold this excessive costly apparel a great cause why gentlemen cannot maintain their wonted and accustomed bounty and liberality in hospitality and housekeeping – for whenas the mercer's book shall come *item* for so many yards of cloth of gold, of silver, velvet, satin, taffeta or suchlike ware; the goldsmith's *debet* for chains, rings, jewels, pearls and precious stones; the tailor's bill, so much for such a suit of laced satin and suchlike superflous charges, amounting in one year to more than the revenues of his lands.[16]

However, Stubbes does confess that one of the 'vices' attendant on lavish dress in England is that all these rich fabrics are imported, and enrich other countries at England's expense:

We impouerish our selues in buying their trifling merchandizes, more plesant than necessarie, and inrich them, who rather laugh at vs in their sleeues, than otherwise, to see our great follie in affecting of trifles, & departing w' good merchandizes for it. And howe litle they esteeme of silkes, veluets, satens, damasks, and such like, wee maye easely see, in that they sell them to vs for wolles, frizes, rugges, carzies, and the lyke, which they coulde neuer doe, if they esteemed of them as much as we doe.[17]

Likewise, Elizabethan sumptuary law betrays some anxiety about neglect of local products for more fashionable imported ones. Injunctions against the wearing of velvet, or velvet-covered caps (1566) were explicitly designed to protect the English cap-makers, whose trade was declining.[18] The intertwining of social and economic arguments is no accident: it betrays deep-seated Elizabethan uneasiness about the relation between innate and fiscal value.[19]

That there was indeed a correlation between the position up the social scale of fabric and ornament and its actual cost is shown by the bill submitted to Lady Lisle by Madame de Bours for expenditure on behalf of Lady Lisle's daughter by her first marriage, Mary Basset, then aged about sixteen, who had been placed in her care to learn French and to complete her education since she was eleven or twelve:

For the making of her gown of black cloth	viijs
For the making of a hood	viijs
For her kirtle of velvet	xs
Item For the lining of the said kirtle	xvs
Item, for white satin to make her sleeves	xxxs
Item, for *quenneval* [canvas?][20]	ijs
Item, given her at divers times to play	xs
Item, for gold thread	xvs
And for silk thread	vjs
Item, for a white girdle	ijs
Item, for a comb for her	ijs
Item, for a paternoster for her	ijs vj
Item, for furring her gown of satin with *rampans*	xxxvs
Item, for letice [another fur]	vll xvs
and for the making	xs
Item, given to her at three times to play	xvjs
Item, for an apron of satin for her	xs
Item, for taffeta to make her a cornette and a collar for her	xiijs
Item, for a pair of shoes	vijs
Item, for two pairs of hosen for her	xxijs
For two pairs of gloves, and for a scissors and for pins	vs
Item, given her divers times to play	xviijs
Item, for the making of her kirtle	xviijs
Item, for vj ells and a half of linen for her for making of smocks at three s. vjd. the ell	xxijs vjd
For a ribbon to put on her neck	ijs
Item, to the tailor who made her gown of worsted and repaired her gown of satin and for making a body for her	xvjs
Paid for silk thread	iijs
Maketh in all, these parties	xxjll xvs[21]

Gold thread (embroidery with gold thread is the item in Mary Basset's expenditure which comes highest up the sumptuary league table) cost more than twice silk thread (or five times the silk thread itemised lower – unfortunately we do not have the quantities). Embroidery with silk belongs one category lower on the list. Gold thread also costs half as much again as her 'kirtle of velvet' (one category lower again). Her hose, I take it, are silk, and cost the same as her velvet kirtle. Her kirtle lining is probably satin, and brings the total cost of her kirtle to twenty-five shillings. These expenditures suggest that the bottom three categories on the sumptuary legislation table have pretty much parity in financial terms, which is supported by the fine distinctions between the appropriate wearers of these specifications of garment and fabric. The white satin for Mary Basset's sleeves is particularly costly. We do not, however, know how much fabric they took. In any case, the satin costs more than about ten yards of linen, and four pairs of shoes. In Deloney's *Thomas of Reading*, he chooses white satin ('a gowne of pure white sattin, her kertle of the same, imbrodered with gold about the skirts') as the dress in which Lady Margaret, masquerading as a servant, reveals her true station as daughter of an earl.[22] Mary Basset makes no purchases from the top three categories of fabric on the sumptuary list; elsewhere in the letters we hear that she is given 'a headdress trimmed with pearl'.[23]

Dress denotes difference in degree, for the Elizabethan. And in two distinct ways Elizabethan anxiety about difference as projected through dress is focused in particular upon *women's* dress.

The first is a traditional argument: it is wives who covet the finery of women of higher rank than themselves; it is they who cajole their husbands into squandering their wealth on extravagant fabrics. As Stubbes says, quoting a contemporary proverb: 'Farre fetched, and deare boughte, is good for Ladyes.'[24] Throughout the Middle Ages, literature and homiletic writings had dwelt on the extravagance and addiction to finery of wives: an accusation given bite by the economic dependence of the wife on her husband, which enhanced her culpability.[25] Chaucer's comments on the Wife of Bath's headdress in the General Prologue to the *Canterbury Tales* is strictly in this tradition:

> Hir coverchiefs ful fyne weren of ground;
> I dorste swere they weyeden ten pound
> That on a Sonday weren upon hir heed. . . .
> Ywympled wel, and on hir heed an hat
> As brood as is a bokeler or a targe.[26]

J. Mann comments on this passage:

> There was a healthy satiric tradition of attacking women's head-gear which went back at least 200 years. Women's 'horns' provide a favourite target for attack, but English writers in particular seem to have featured veils, kerchiefs and wimples; Robert Mannyng refers contemptuously to 'wymples, ker-chyues, saffrund betyde' as items of female finery, and sees women 'wyp here kercheues' as baits of the devil. Some writers stress the excessive cost of the head-gear.[27]

Here again, economic anxiety is apparent: the wife's dress adver-tises her husband's status, but does it also impoverish him?[28] Stubbes claims that 'all be it, their poore Parents haue but one cow, horse, or sheep, they wil neuer let them rest, til they be sould, to maintain them in their braueries, past all tongue can tell'.[29] It might even be suggested that the fact of financial dependence encouraged women with time on their hands to spend irresponsibly; certainly it meant they had to ask for money for their clothes.[30] Sometimes husbands had to make a case in court for not paying their wives' excessive clothing bills:

> It was proved that [his wife] was very extravagant, and used to pawn her clothes for money, and tho' redeemed by the husband, she had pawned them again, and that she needed no clothes when she bought these goods; and further, that the defendant the last time he paid the plaintiff, warned his servant not to trust her any more[31]

In this case, because the husband had warned previously of his wife's irresponsible spending, he was absolved of responsibility; ordinarily the ruling was that 'while they cohabit together, the husband shall answer all contracts of hers for necessaries; for his assent shall be presumed upon the account of cohabiting, unless the contrary appear'.

Economic dependence makes women vulnerable to the charge of profligate and irresponsible use of resources. Where (less commonly) *men* are shown as thus dependent on others, the same charge is levelled against them. Nashe claims that Gabriel Harvey is extravagant at the expense of his indulgent father:

> His father he vndid to furnish him to the Court once more, where presenting himselfe in all the coulours of the raine-bow, and a paire of moustachies like a black horse tayle tyde up in a knot, with two tuffts sticking out on each side, he was askt by no meane personage *Unde haec insania?* whence proceedeth this folly or madness?[32]

In Middleton's *Women Beware Women*, the changed fortunes of both Leantio and his wife Bianca (he is the kept lover of the wealthy Livia, she the mistress of the Duke) are manifested prominently in their opulent dress, in which both dependent lovers take childish delight:

Leantio	Y' are richly placed.
Bianca	Methinks y' are wondrous brave, sir.
Leantio	A sumptuous lodging.
Bianca	Y' have an excellent suit there.
Leantio	A chair of velvet.
Bianca	Is your cloak lined through, sir?
Leantio	Y' are very stately here.
Bianca	Faith something proud, sir.
Leantio	Stay, stay, let's see your cloth-of-silver slippers.
Bianca	Who's your shoemaker? 'Has made you a neat boot.
Leantio	Will you have a pair? The Duke will lend you spurs.[13]

In the drama, the woman who grasps power fleetingly at the expense of the men around her is characteristically also of expensive tastes. Vittoria, in Webster's *The White Devil*, is presented as inferior rank sapping the masculinity of the rightfully noble:

Francisco	Some eagles that should gaze upon the sun
	Seldom soar high, but take their lustful ease,
	Since they from dunghill birds their prey can seize, –
	You know Vittoria, –
Bracciano	Yes.
Francisco	You shift your shirt there
	When you retire from tennis.
Bracciano	Happily.
Francisco	Her husband is lord of a poor fortune
	Yet she wears cloth of tissue.[14]

Vittoria's love of fine attire is part of her insidious draining of male strength; at her trial she herself confesses:

> Sum up my faults I pray, and you shall find
> That beauty and gay clothes, a merry heart,
> And a good stomach to a feast, are all,
> All the poor crimes that you can charge me with.[15]

And indeed, since these crimes sum to *luxury* – synonymous with lustfulness – that is crime enough.[16] Ferdinand's accusations of lasciviousness levelled against his sister, the Duchess of Malfi, include prominently her luxurious living:

I would have you give o'er these chargeable revels;
A visor and a mask are whispering-rooms
That were ne'er built for goodness.[17]

It is appropriate, therefore, that amongst Petruchio's devices for 'taming' his assertive wife, Kate, in *The Taming of the Shrew*, the most dramatically prominent should be his assault on her independent choice of attire, and on its explicit affluence. It will be remembered that I argued earlier that the final gesture of having Kate stamp on her cap makes no sense in real terms; we see now that it does in terms of an assumed relation between woman's lavish dress and her implied 'frowardness' – aggressiveness and social mobility:

> *Enter Haberdasher*
> Haberdasher Here is the cap your worship did bespeak.
> Petruchio Why, this was moulded on a porringer;
> A velvet dish. Fie, fie! 'tis lewd and filthy;
> Why, 'tis a cockle or a walnut-shell,
> A knack, a toy, a trick, a baby's cap.
> Away with it. Come, let me have a bigger.
> Katherina I'll have no bigger; this doth fit the time,
> And gentlewomen wear such caps as these. . . .
> Why, sir, I trust I may have leave to speak;
> And speak I will. I am no child, no babe.
> Your betters have endur'd me say my mind,
> And if you cannot, best you stop your ears.
> My tongue will tell the anger of my heart,
> Or else my heart, concealing it, will break;
> And rather than it shall, I will be free
> Even to the uttermost, as I please, in words.
> Petruchio Why, thou say'st true; it is a paltry cap,
> A custard-coffin, a bauble, a silken pie;
> I love thee well in that thou lik'st it not.
> Katherina Love me or love me not, I like the cap;
> And it I will have, or I will have none.[18]

The second Elizabethan preoccupation with dress and difference concerned its designation of *sex*. As men's fashions became increasingly elaborate and extravagant (a process intensified under the homosexual King James I), moralists and social commentators showed increasing alarm that the distinctions between male and female dress were being eroded. Stubbes had been incensed enough at the extravagances of men's doublets; he became even shriller in his denunciation when he drew attention to the fact that women were wearing identical doublets, thus obliterating the customary distinction between male and female costume. It was not that the doublet was indecent – it was actually more decorous than a 'feminine' low-cut gown. But it was morally indecent because it announced absence of difference between the sexes in a language only too readily understood by a contemporary:

> The Women also there haue dublets & Jerkins as men haue heer, buttoned vp the brest, and made with wings, welts and pinions on the shoulder points, as mans apparel is, for all the world, & though this be a kinde of attire appropriate onely to man, yet they blush not to wear it, and if they could as wel chaunge their sex, & put on the kinde of man, as they can weàre apparel assigned onely to man, I think they would as verely become men indeed as now they degenerat from godly sober women, in wearing this wanton, lewd kinde of attire, proper onely to man.
>
> It is written in the 22. of *Deuteronomie*, that what man so euer weareth womans apparel is accursed, and what woman weareth mans apparel is accursed also. Now, whether they be within the bands and lymits of that cursse, let them see to it them selues. Our Apparell was giuen vs as a signe distinctiue to discern betwixt sex and sex, & therfore one to weare the Apparel of another sex, is to participate with the same, and to adulterate the veritie of his owne kinde. Wherefore these Women may not improperly be called *Hermaphroditi*, that is, Monsters of bothe kindes, half women, half men.[19]

As a glance at any contemporary portrait will make clear, Stubbes here grotesquely overstates the case.[40] Male dress in the period became ornate, elaborate, contrived, and was openly called 'effeminate' by those of more modest tastes.[41] Its attractiveness proved irresistible to women also, who in any case followed a French vogue for female dress, hairstyles and manners which emulated those of young boys. In answer to the expanded case for monstrosity and unnaturalness in women based on their borrowed costume made by the author of *Hic Mulier: or The Man-Woman* (London, 1620), the author of *Haec-Vir* ('the womanish man') points out that the elimination of dress difference is the fault of men in the first place:

> What could we poore weake women doe lesse (being farre too weake by force to fetch backs those spoiles you have unjustly taken from us) then to gather up those garments you have proudly cast away, and therewith to cloath our bodies and our mindes; since no other meanes was left us to continue our names, and to support a difference?[42]

Hic Mulier is directed only accidentally, as it were, against women.[43] Actually the terms of its attack are Stubbes', and point an accusing finger equally at both sexes:

> From the first you got the false armoury of yellow Starch (for to weare yellow on white, or white vpon yellow, is by the rules of Heraldry basenesse, bastardie, and indignitie) the folly of imitation, the deceitfulnesse of flatterie, and the grosest baseness of all basenesse, to do whatsoeuer a greater power will command you. From the other, you haue taken the monstrousnesse of your deformitie in apparell, exchanging the modest attire of the comely Hood, Cawle, Coyfe, handsome Dresse or Kerchiefe, to the cloudy Ruffianly broad-brim'd Hatte, and wanton Feather, the modest vpper parts of a concealing straight gowne, to the loose, lasciuious ciuill embracement of a French doublet, being all vnbutton'd to entice, all of one shape to hide deformitie, and extreme short wasted to giue a most easie way to euery luxurious action: the glory of a faire large hayre, to the shame of most ruffianly short lockes.[44]

The only difference between this account and Stubbes' of twenty years earlier is in the length of the doublet: in Stubbes' day it was lewdly long and padded, suggesting private parts with indecent innuendo; in the 1620s it has become indecently short, allowing immodest access to those same private parts. Clearly fashion is a no-win wicket for the woman exposed to the relentless moralist.

In the natural order of things, the order which sumptuary law codifies in order of dress, woman is subject to man. The elimination of dress difference between men and women implies a narrowing of the gap between the man and his subordinate; that is the implied threat which is attacked in pamphlet after pamphlet addressed against fashionable excesses in the early seventeenth century. Intriguingly, we have a well-documented example of the way in which such a narrowing may actually take place in a period of strong signification of dress: the case of Joan of Arc.

Joan, a peasant girl from Domrémy, dressed throughout her brief period of public action as a man; and not just as a man, but as a *noble* man (a knight):

> The Maid, arrayed in white armour, rode on horseback before the King, with her standard unfurled. When not in armour, she kept state as a knight and dressed as one. Her shoes were tied with laces to her feet, her hose and doublet were shapely, a hat was on her head. She wore very handsome attire of cloth of gold and silk, noticeably trimmed with fur.[45]

So wrote a Burgundian around 1500. The description makes

clear Joan's sumptuary 'presumptuousness'. And in the charges laid against her at her trial, this feature of her dress figured prominently: it was not simply that she had adopted male dress, but that it had been dress well above her rank, and implied an assumed power which smacked of the secular:

> The said Jeanne put off and entirely abandoned woman's clothes, with her hair cropped short and round in the fashion of young men, she wore shirt, breeches, doublet, with hose joined together, long and fastened to the said doublet by twenty points, long leggings laced on the outside, a short mantle reaching to the knee, or thereabouts, a close-cut cap, tight-fitting boots or buskins, long spurs, sword, dagger, breastplate, lance and other arms in the style of a man-at-arms. . . . Not only did she wear short tunics, but she dressed herself in tabards and garments open at the sides, besides the matter is notorious since when she was captured she was wearing a surcoat cloak of cloth of gold, open on all sides, a cap on her head, and her hair cropped round in man's style. And in general, having cast aside all womanly decency, not only to the scorn of feminine modesty, but also of well-instructed men, she had worn the apparel and garments of most dissolute men, and, in addition, had some weapons of defence.[46]

The story that Joan was captured by being dragged from her horse by the dangling ends of her sumptuous cloth-of-gold surcoat is symbolic of the sense of affront afforded by her rich dress. By adopting male dress of a lavishness which signalled superior class and authority, Joan took upon herself a kind of visual authority which overrode her womanhood and her inferior class origins. As the charges against her show, *both* these functions of her dress were seen as a blatant and unforgivable challenge to social and political order. As Marina Warner puts it, 'transvestism does not just pervert biology; it upsets the social hierarchy'.[47]

We can see that Joan was aware of this desirable effect of her male dress, or at least that she was alert to the difficulties raised by discarding it, in the account of her conditions for reverting to female dress during her imprisonment. Bribed into putting on women's clothes with the offer that she might receive communion if she did so, she stipulated that she must be given 'a long dress reaching down to the ground, without a train', and later, 'give me such a dress as the daughters of your bourgeois wear . . . with a long surcoat and a hood'.[48] Here she tries to stipulate that the woman's dress she is given be of burgher's rank[49] – a rank well above her own. It must have been apparent to her that any authority residually accruing to her would be lost if she were to appear before her judges dressed as a little peasant girl.

To bear arms was a privilege of rank; to wear cloth of gold was equally a privilege. To adopt both when not entitled to them by birth was to usurp rank. For a woman to adopt male dress was correspondingly to shift position in the social hierarchy; to move from subordination into equality with men. Joan of Arc did both. Her judges read both as a deliberate challenge and denounced her transvestism in the strongest possible terms. The charge of immodesty lags far behind in their reckoning.[50]

In anti-women tracts of the sixteenth and seventeenth centuries, both in England and in France, the adopting of male fashions by women figures remarkably prominently. What it reiterates again and again is a sense of a breakdown of order between class and sex: male fashions are extreme and do not correlate with rank, turning acceptable lavishness into 'effeminacy' and 'dissoluteness'; female fashions are close enough to men's to give an uncomfortable sense of parity. In *Hic Mulier* one of the outrages in female dress treated is the wearing of spurs and ornamental daggers by women, that is, the bearing of arms (however figuratively). The woman 'wears the spurs' (like the cant 'wears the trousers', though on the whole she did not do that in this period),[51] raising herself to authority comparable with her male equivalent. At the same time, the man adopts dress-weapons so ornate and lavish that they suggest decorativeness, not use, reducing male authority:

> To these haue they their Rapiers, Swords and Daggers gilt, twise or thrise ouer the hilts, with scaberds and sheathes of Veluet and the like, for leather, though it be more proffitable and as seemely, yet wil it not carie such a porte or countenance like the other. And wil not these golden swords & daggers almost apale a man (though otherwise neuer so stout a *Martialist*) to haue any deling with them? for either to y' end they be worne or els other swoords, daggers and rapiers of bare yron and steele were as hansom as they & much more conducible to that end, whereto swoords and rapiers should serue, namely for a mans lawful and godly defence, against his aduersarie in time of necessitie. But wherefore they be so clogged with gold and siluer I know not, nor yet wherto this excesse serueth I see not, but certain I am, a great shewe of pride it is, an infallible token of vain glorie.[52]

Recognising the same symbolism a century and a half earlier, Joan of Arc had had a plain leather scabbard made for the sword she carried, in preference to those of crimson velvet and of cloth

of gold which she was given by the populace of St Catherine of
Fierbois of Tours.[53] Joan's sword represented her knightly authority; she furnished it with a 'manly' scabbard betokening its use,
by which it could not be confused with a courtly ornament.

Middleton's *The Roaring Girl* is tightly bound in with the
period's anxieties about dress and degree. Even the introduction
to the published play (1611) is couched as an elaborate dress
metaphor:

> The fashion of play-making I can properly compare to nothing so naturally
> as the alteration in apparel: for in the time of the great crop-doublet, your
> huge bombasted plays, quilted with mighty words to lean purpose, was only
> then in fashion. And as the doublet fell, neater inventions began to set up.[54]

The play has often been advanced as evidence for a 'real' vogue
for male attire amongst avant-garde and 'liberated' women of the
early seventeenth century. That is to say, it has been used to
support the view that a significant element in the female population broke sufficiently with female conventions to adopt male
dress and behaviour, live independently, and match men blow for
blow. Mary Frith (also known in real life as Moll Cutpurse) did
actually exist.[55] In fact, however, the transgressing of roles which
the play explores is elaborately stylised, and is couched in
precisely the terms of the 'dress code' with which the present
chapter has concerned itself.

The three main fashions to draw the abuse of the pamphleteers
provide the focusing context for the play: ruffs and feathers,
doublets and breeches, and tobacco smoking. Mistress Open-
work sells 'fine bands and ruffs, fine lawns, fine cambrics',[56] and
chides her husband at the suggestion that he might wear cambric
set aside for a countess's underwear (or make sexual advances to
her): 'Dare you presume to noblewomen's linen? / Keep your
yard to measure shepherd's holland.'[57]

Jack Dapper, out to buy a new feather,[58] is offered the latest in
up-market stock:

> What feather is't you'd have sir?
> These are most worn and most in fashion
> Amongst the beaver gallants, the stone riders,
> The private stage's audience, the twelfepenny-stool gentlemen:
> I can inform you 'tis the general feather.[59]

The scene in which Moll orders a pair of breeches from the tailor is made the occasion for a voguish discussion of breeches and doublet fashion:

Tailor	You say you'll have the great Dutch slop, Mistress Mary.
Moll	Why sir, I say so still.
Tailor	Your breeches then will take up a yard more.
Moll	Well, pray look it be put in then.
Tailor	It shall stand round and full, I warrant you. . . .
Sir Alexander	Here's good gear towards, I have brought up my son to marry a Dutch slop and a French doublet, a codpiece daughter."[60]

Although in this scene Moll orders herself a pair of breeches, and asserts her 'masculinity' by fighting and brawling (confirming Sir Alexander's proverbial observation that 'if the wife go in breeches, the man must wear long coats like a fool')[61] she first appears in fashionable female dress – that is, in 'masculine' doublet, ruff and short sword (probably spurs), with a *skirt*. The stage direction for her first entrance runs: 'Enter MOLL in a frieze jerkin and a black saveguard [skirt].' Later Laxton, who has set up an assignation with Moll at Gray's Inn Fields in order to seduce her, describes her as dressed in 'a shag ruff, a frieze jerkin, a short sword, and a saveguard'.[62] When Moll appears in breeches, Laxton fails to recognise her: there is, dramatically, a total gap between fashionably 'masculine' female dress, and man's dress, particularly on a boy player taking Moll's part, which is 'disguise', and transvestite disguise at that.

On stage, Moll is most believably the pushy, scurrilous, rascally female thief when she wears 'lewdly' masculine fashion – with a *skirt*. In breeches she is fantasy warrior-woman, to be set alongside Mary Fitz-Allard, also disguised as a boy, who is romantic page-boy lover disguised. When Mary's lover Sebastian embraces her, Moll quips: 'How strange this shows, one man to kiss another', returning us to the covertly homosexual fantasies of my first chapter. Sebastian retorts: 'Methinks a woman's lips taste well in a doublet', confirming the erotic male interest in 'transvestied' love.

Moll in breeches picks up and makes literal the pamphleteers' insistence that masculine dress in women is equivalent to role transgression. When Laxton is determined to rape her, she abandons her skirt for breeches and trounces him in a straight fight.[63] And her assertions of forceful activity are couched

throughout the play in terms of not succumbing to a husband,
like the 'shrewish' exchanges of disorder discussed in the last
chapter, and neither more nor less threatening:

> I scorn to prostitute myself to a man,
> I that can prostitute a man to me.

> I have no humour to marry, I love to lie o' both sides o' th' bed myself, and
> again o' th' other side; a wife you know ought to be obedient, but I fear me I
> am too headstrong to obey, therefore I'll ne'er go about it. . . . I have the head
> now of myself, and am man enough for a woman; marriage is but a chop-
> ping and changing, where a maiden loses one head and has a worse i' th'
> place.[54]

'Home truths' such as these are the prerogative of the misrule
figure who temporarily steps out of his or her customary role to
point a finger at the social hierarchy. Whether waxing indignant
at the fate of dominated wives, or abused women slandered by
loose men like Laxton, or those who are accused of thieving
merely because they are noisy and unruly ('How many are
whores in small ruffs and still looks!')[65] Moll in breeches has the
prerogative of free speech of the 'roaring girl' – the outspoken
spokesperson for disorder.

The figure of Moll Cutpurse combines comedy of fashions,
rich with allusions to contemporary 'anti-feminist' pamphlet
themes, romantic transvestism, and folkloristic misrule. Middleton's play concentrates the accumulation of uneasinesses which
for the period lurk behind the blurring of boundaries between
fashionable male and female dress. All the available literary
variants on the 'woman on top' theme come together in the
exuberant fantasising of *The Roaring Girl*. Moll is not Mary
Frith in the sense of documenting a contemporary figure's notorious career; she is appropriated as a figure representative of all
society's nervousnesses where the relations between men and
women are concerned.

What must remain curious, I think, is the extraordinary interest
in these potential ambiguities of social hierarchy during the late
sixteenth and early seventeenth centuries. 'The woman question'
produced something of a vernacular publishing boom in pamphlets and treatises, either extolling the virtues of women, or
scurrilously denigrating their shortcomings, between the 1550s
and the 1640s.[66] These 'paradoxes' concerning women (Hamlet's

'this was sometime a paradox' alludes directly to the controversy) apparently captured the imagination of the urban reading public.

'Controversy', however, is too strong a word for the stylised and rhetorical exchanges these publications contain. There is a solidity and a smugness about them (whichever camp the author attaches himself or herself to) which betrays a lack of real urgency in the debate.[67] It has, as readers fresh from the 'woman question' debates of the nineteenth century are likely to overlook, a strong traditional precedent in 'controversial' themes admitting of rhetorical elaboration on either side of the question.' And its rhetorical bias is betrayed by the ruthless borrowing by successive generations of pamphleteers from the major originals in the field (Boccaccio and Agrippa, somewhat ironically on behalf of women; the Church Fathers on the whole seriously against), and then from one another.

In trying to find an answer for why this particular issue should find so eager an audience in this particular period we must return, I think, to the highly symptomatic relations between women, their dress and behaviour, and their place in the social hierarchy. Women bore the brunt of a general social uneasiness, I believe, because the fear of the inversion of authority between men and women has a primitive force which is not to be found in the threat of the upstart courtier to usurp his 'rightful' lord. To point a finger at woman's affecting of the badges of male office – dress, arms, behaviour – was to pin down a potent symbol of the threat to order which was perceived dimly as present in the entire shift from feudal to mercantile society.

This view is supported by the prevalence in the 'anti-woman' tracts of attacks on female gaming and gambling: vices which were considered a major disruptive force in Elizabethan and Jacobean society, but which were certainly not peculiarly the province of women. As 'cash outlay' gambling can be linked with dress expenditure, as part of a 'subverting of established order' by women, draining resources which are not their own. The accounts for dress expenditure sent to Mary Basset's mother include both money for dress and money for gambling ('given to her to play').[68] K. Casey links the two activities as part of a perceived common 'emasculation', in her survey of attitudes towards city-women in the period:

Middle-class townswomen at dice served to illustrate Barclay's English version of the German *Ship of Fools* (1497), even though both sexes had been seized by the passion for gambling. When the typical woman was not called shiftless or immoral, she was accused of having devouring ambition. Dread of a polymorphous evil found a specific target: women who allegedly put money on their backs instead of on the table, driving their overworked men forward to material success or backward into debt. It was as if a vague awareness already was abroad of the pressures attending a growth economy, projecting anxiety upon a more traditional enemy and on an economic collaborator defined mythologically, if not experientially, as the inactive partner."⁹

Gambling is symbolic, as almost nothing else can be, of the random allocation of wealth and thereby power. For a society pledged to the equivalence of 'value' and social rank, the acquiring of large sums of money by pure chance at the gaming-tables is the ultimate subversion of order. It is the state of affairs codified in fairy tale by the good-for-nothing son's discovery of hidden treasure, or of the goose that lays the golden egg, or of the formula which gains a princess's hand in marriage. Female gamblers epitomise the disorder attendant for such a society on the severing of authority from birth, and its association with cash and ready money.

At the same time women, as my earlier chapter on inheritance tried to make clear, were themselves seen as very much part of the process of valuation and exchange. Any marriageable well-born woman possessed a number of attributes which gave her a 'value': her dowry prospects, her title, her looks, her ability to produce heirs. As the sixteenth century wore on, these attributes, and the parental bargainings that went on concerning suitable matches, came to be seen increasingly as worryingly akin to cash transactions. In Italian discussions of the high cash-value of dowries, the question is earnestly raised as to whether parents are in fact marketing their daughters' virginity to the highest bidder by providing a cash equivalent for the desired match.⁷⁰ I think this anxiety about the 'cash' value of women as against their 'real worth' is captured in the *topos* of 'vicious but beautiful', which is to be found throughout Jacobean tragedy (in Middleton and Rowley's *The Changeling*, Middleton's *Women Beware Women*, Webster's *The White Devil*). Once worth and intrinsic value are separated, and 'worth' becomes 'cash value', beauty and intrinsic virtue can no longer be comfortably assumed to go hand in hand.

For the Jacobean drama, the beautiful woman 'gambling' for the highest stakes without moral scruple is the emblem of the evanescence of all worldly estate.[1]

French treaties in defence of women, which proliferated in the early decades of the seventeenth century, make this correspondence between acknowledgement of the merits and abilities of the female sex, and acceptance of the right of all men to rise through wealth and ability explicit:

> Because women functioned publicly as the promoters of the social life which integrated new sources of status into the culture of the traditional social élite, the debate about the fitness of women for public roles centred on two essential topics: the legitimacy of the new sources of status themselves and the desirability of extending the life-style of the court aristocracy to persons who acquired status. Feminists broadened the theoretical basis of nobility to include new sources of status (venality of office, nonfeudal wealth, luxury, court favor, social refinement), while antifeminists aimed to abolish both venality and the institutionalized court and to negate both the ethic of social polish and the pursuit of luxury.[2]

The anonymous 'Plaintes des dames de la cour contre les marchandes ou bourgeoises de Paris' draws together the strands of this chapter's discussion: 'beauty' amongst the nobility is being outshone by the lavishness and excessive expenditure on dress of the women of the bourgeoisie; order and rank are threatened by the visible incursion of economic success and 'bought' *politesse* into the 'natural' order of the feudal aristocracy. The brilliant dress of the non-noble ladies is denounced as a symbol of the transgressing of social and economic mores:

> That has made a mockery of the court a hundred times and caused the ladies particular chagrin to see themselves so often eclipsed by these marionettes, and not being able to so much as equal them in the rich curiosity of their dress. Gold and silk are in such low esteem with them that they adorn with them their nurses and servants to inflate their own vanity, and if the fabrics are not very rare and very expensive they leave them, so they say, to the ladies of the court and the bourgeois ladies want nothing to do with them. But if a product of extraordinary beauty appears, they want to have it no matter what the price, then, not having one-hundredth enough supply to meet the demand, the price rises so high that the ladies and maidens of the court cannot afford it.[3]

Bourgeois women, hot in pursuit of status and influence beyond their 'natural' entitlement, force up the price of commodities which they identify with their upward progress. The analogy here with the charge that women of the same class 'market' their beauty (morals being left to one side) as a commodity with high social exchange value is clear. 'Feminism' and 'anti-feminism' in the treatises of the late sixteenth and early seventeenth centuries betray a deep uneasiness about order and economics, in which women are seen to play a central and symbolic role.

Notes

1 *Henry VI Part II* I.iii.73–85.
2 Elizabeth I levelled the same complaint against Leicester's wife in the latter years of her reign.
3 M. E. Lawlis (ed.), *The Novels of Thomas Deloney* (Indiana, 1961), pp. 30–1. C. Jordan has drawn attention to Deloney's use of dress to highlight the tensions between wealth and hereditary rank. See 'The "art of clothing": role playing in Deloney's fiction', *English Literary Renaissance*, 11 (1981), pp. 183–93. In *The Taming of the Shrew* Grumio explains to Petruchio the absence of his servants by the fact that they are not yet dressed fittingly for his newly elevated social status (he has just made a rich marriage to Kate): 'Nathaniel's coat, sir was not fully made, / And Gabriel's pumps were all unpinck'd i' th' heels; / There was no link to colour Peter's hat, / And Walter's dagger was not come from sheathing' (IV.i.116–9). On Elizabethan struggles between old and new power, see A. Esler, *The Aspiring Mind of the Elizabethan Younger Generation* (Durham, North Carolina, 1966).
4 F. E. Baldwin, *Sumptuary Legislation and Personal Regulation in England* (Baltimore, 1926), pp. 228–9.
5 ibid., p. 208.
6 In G. Gregory Smith, *Elizabethan Critical Essays* (London, 1971 edn), pp. 142–3.
7 IV.iii.52–8.
8 In R. B. McKerrow (ed.), *The Works of Thomas Nashe*, 5 vols (1910; reprinted Oxford, 1958), III,73.
9 Baldwin, *op. cit.*, p. 231.
10 fo. Bvii^r.
11 fo. Ci^v–Cii^v.
12 For earlier legislation see 'Proclamation enforcing statutes of apparel, 21 October 1559', in P. L. Hughes and J. F. Larkin (eds), *Tudor Royal Proclamations* (New Haven, 1969) ii,136–8, reprinted in J. Hurstfield and A. G. R. Smith (eds), *Elizabethan People: State and Society* (London, 1972), pp. 30–2.
13 There is, of course, a wealth of contemporary theological denunciations of ornament and lavish dress as incompatible with Christian humility. See, e.g., M. Bucer, *De regno Christi* (1557?), ch. 55, in W. Pauck (ed.), *Library of Christian Classics*, XIX (London, 1969), pp. 354–7.
14 Stubbes, fo. Dvii^v–Dviii^r.
15 ibid., fo. Eii^r–Eii^v.

16 I. M. 'A health to the gentlemanly profession of servingmen' (1598), in A. Nicoll, *The Elizabethans* (Cambridge, 1957), p. 30, reprinted in Hurstfield and Smith, *op. cit.*, p. 23.

17 Stubbes, fo. Ciᵛ.

18 Baldwin, *op. cit.*, p. 210. See also the inclusion of 'Foreign Woolen Cloth' in the 1597 sumptuary laws.

19 It is interesting to note that the freedom which critics like Dusinberre take to refer, in contemporary accounts, to English women's emancipation, is often specified as freedom in *dress*: 'The women have much more liberty than perhaps in any other place. They also know well how to make use of it, for they go dressed out in exceedingly fine clothes, and give all their attention to their ruffs and stuffs, to such a degree indeed, that, as I am informed, many a one does not hesitate to wear velvet in the streets, which is common with them, whilst at home perhaps they have not a piece of dry bread' (1592), in Hurstfield and Smith, *Elizabethan People*, pp. 34–5; see also p. 34.

20 M. St Clare Byrne's suggestion.

21 M. St Clare Byrne (ed.), *The Lisle Letters*, 6 vols (Chicago, 1981), III,213–4.

22 Lawlis, *op. cit.*, p. 342.

23 St Clare Byrne, *op. cit.*, vol. III, letter 579. Deloney's Lady Margaret wears 'gold pearles and precious stones' on her headdress as appropriate to an Earl's daughter (p. 342).

24 Stubbes, fo. Ciᵛ.

25 F. L. Utley, *The Crooked Rib: An Analytical Index to the Argument about Women in English and Scots Literature to the End of the Year 1568* (Columbus, Ohio, 1944), especially p. 217.

26 453–5, 470–1; in J. Mann, *Chaucer and Medieval Estates Satire* (Cambridge, 1973), p. 124.

27 Mann, *op. cit.*, p. 124.

28 For the 'virtuous' attitude, see 'patient' Griselda, who leaves all her fine clothes behind and goes home in her underwear when her husband discards her.

29 Stubbes, fo. Fviiᵛ.

30 See the endless requests for money for clothing which make up the major part of Mary Basset's correspondence with her mother (who was administering an annuity left by Mary's dead father, Lady Lisle having remarried). St Clare Byrne, *op. cit.*, vol. III, letters 570–627.

31 J. O'Faolain and L. Martines, *Not In God's Image: Women in History* (London, 1979), p. 245.

32 McKerrow (ed.), *op. cit.*, III,78.

33 *Women Beware Women* IV.i.51–7.

34 *The White Devil* II.i.49–54.

35 III.ii.207–10.

36 'Luxury' and 'lustfulness' are semantically closely linked. See, for instance the entry under 'luxuria' in Ravisius Textor's influential compendium *Epitheta* (1518), discussed in W. J. Ong, 'Commonplace rhapsody: Ravisius Textor, Zwinger and Shakespeare', in R. R. Bolgar (ed.), *Classical*

Influences on European Culture A.D. 1500–1700 (Cambridge, 1976), pp. 91–126, especially pp. 122–3.

37 *The Duchess of Malfi* I.i.333–5.
38 *The Taming of the Shrew* IV.iii.63–85.
39 Stubbes, fo. Fv'–Fv'.
40 See, for instance, the portrait of the young Charles I in the Cambridge Senate House, reproduced in R. Strong, *The English Icon* (London, 1969), p. 228, where the close similarity between the dress of a courtly young man and that of a woman is evident. L. Faderman comments on the hysterical note in these 'paper war' pamphlets condemning 'masculine' fashions for women in, *Surpassing the Love of Men* (London, 1981), p. 48.
41 For detailed descriptions of elaborate male court dress, see the accounts of Royal entertainments, in J. Wilson, *Entertainments for Elizabeth I* (Cambridge, 1980).
42 *Haec-Vir* fo. Cii, in J. Dusinberre, *Shakespeare and the Nature of Women* (London, 1975), p. 256.
43 See especially fo. Ci': 'Let therefore the powerfull statute of apparell but lift vp his Battle-Axe, and crush the offenders in pieces, so as euery one may be knowne by the true badge of their bloud, or Fortune.'
44 *Hic Mulier* fo. A3'–A4'.
45 D. Rankin and C. Quintal (eds), *The First Biography of Joan of Arc* (Pittsburgh, 1964), p. 118, in M. Warner, *Joan of Arc: The Image of Female Heroism* (London, 1981), pp. 160–1.
46 In Warner, *Joan of Arc*, p. 143.
47 ibid., p. 147.
48 ibid., p. 145.
49 And even so, such dress would be judged pretentious for a burgher's wife by some, at any rate by the time of Stubbes: 'euery marchants wyfe, and meane Gentlewomen, in her french-hood' (fo. Fiii').
50 France relegated women yet more decisively in the social order than England by denying them by law the right to rule – the Salic Law whereby male princes always take preference over any female princes in line to the throne or to major estates. See I. Maclean, *Woman Triumphant: Feminism in French Literature 1610–1652* (Oxford, 1977), pp. 58–62. The bearing of arms is registered as a symbolic gesture of considerable significance, since it implies the ability to give 'knight service', and thus to take a full place in the inheritance ranking. When anti-feminists argue against a woman's right to rule, it is their unsuitability to bear arms which is most frequently invoked, see e.g. Maclean, p. 60, n. 164: 'le sexe feminin estant vraysemblablement d'un corps moins propre aux armes, par la necessite du port et nourriture des enfans.'
51 Though she *did* in fantasy woodcuts of 'woman on top'. See N. Z. Davis, *Society and Culture in Early Modern France*, (London, 1975).
52 Stubbes, fo. Cvii'.
53 Warner, *Joan of Arc*, p. 164.
54 A. Gomme, *The Roaring Girl* (New Mermaids, 1976), p. 3. Gomme attributes the play to Middleton and Dekker.

55 For the scanty evidence of her real activities, see G. Salgado, *The Eliza-bethan Underworld* (London, 1977), pp. 42–4.

56 *The Roaring Girl* II.i.2.

57 II.i.153–4. There is a lewd pun on 'yard'.

58 Stubbes, fo. Dvii'.

59 *The Roaring Girl* II.i.131–5. See also III.1.12: 'May we safely take the upper hand of any couched velvet cap or tufftaffety jacket?'

60 II.ii.80–90. The great Dutch slop were wide and baggy breeches, much padded as Stubbes described; the French doublet and the pendant cod-piece were equally in vogue. Once again there is lewd punning on fitting 'yards' (penises) into Moll's breeches.

61 II.ii.75.

62 III.i.31–3.

63 Or, where Laxton would have sex with her, she gives him a beating, recalling the Skimmington rides again. Woodcuts of husband-beaters sometimes showed them in breeches (i.e., as Moll). See Martin Treu's engraving (c.1540–3), reproduced in Davis, *op. cit.* plate 9(c).

64 III.i.109–10; II. i.36–44.

65 V.ii.318.

66 See R. Masek, 'Women in an age of transition 1485–1714', in B. Kanner (ed.), *The Women of England from Anglo-Saxon times to the Present: Interpretive (sic) Bibliographical Essays* (London, 1980), pp. 138–82 for a competent bibliography of the English tracts; Maclean, *Woman Trium-phant*, for the French; Utley, *The Crooked Rib* makes a striking contrast, since this compendious survey of tracts and poems on 'the woman question' for the Middle Ages is of manageable size although it covers the entire period down to 1568. See also K. M. Rogers, *The Troublesome Helpmate* (Seattle, 1966).

67 See D. Bornstein (ed.), *The Feminist Controversy of the Renaissance* (Scholars' Facsimiles and Reprints, New York, 1980), Introduction, for the traditional element in these treatises.

68 See the bill reproduced above, p. 150.

69 K. Casey, 'The Cheshire Cat: reconstructing the experience of medieval women', in B. A. Carroll (ed.), *Liberating Women's History* (Urbana, Chicago and London, 1976), pp. 224–249, 237.

70 Saint Nicholas is invoked to rescue the practice of dowry-giving as compatible with chastity and 'real' worth. See J. Kirshner, *Pursuing Honor while avoiding Sin: the Monte delle Doti in Florence* (Milan, (1978). The *Taming of the Shrew* is centrally concerned with the market-ing of daughters for cash.

71 In medieval literature it is the effeminate and homosexual male who symbolises fraud and dishonesty in money dealings. See J. Mann, *Chaucer and Medieval Estates Sature* (Cambridge, 1973), pp. 146–8.

72 C. C. Lougee, *Le Paradis des Femmes: Women, Salons, and Social Strati-fication in Seventeenth-Century France* (Princeton, 1976), p. 213.

73 ibid., p. 76.

6

'She sat like Patience on a monument, / Smiling at grief': The Saving Stereotypes of Female heroism

I have deliberately postponed until a late stage any consideration of the significance for representations of women in the drama of the fact that from 1558 until 1603 a woman sat on the throne of England, as Head of State and as Head of the Church of England. In the present chapter I shall argue that it is of some importance that the public (literary) representation of one woman – Elizabeth I – was a matter of national concern. But I shall suggest that far from leading the Elizabethans to a forward-looking tolerance of active womanhood, it betrays all their uneasiness about the instrumental power accorded to women in the period. It led to their reaching back into the literary past in search of representations which could redeem and enhance the majesty of the sovereign, *in spite of* her femaleness. And when I refer to 'the Elizabethans', I include Elizabeth herself amongst them. In playing extremely adeptly the game of statecraft she did so according to the patriarchal rules. And that meant contriving, and conniving in the 'double bind' evaluations of her own actions. That is a game which 'token' women, achieving in men's terms, in a man's world, have played adeptly throughout history.

The reader is not likely to be surprised that I take this view, since in chapter 3 I have already considered in some detail the way in which women fortuitously given prominence within the inheritance structure could nevertheless continue to be deprived of significant personal freedom, or anything we might term 'liberation'. Elizabeth was a female pawn in the English Royal inheritance struggle, as were Mary Tudor, Mary Queen of Scots and Lady Jane Grey. Each was astutely supported and manipulated by family, followers and governments to political ends. Each acted out that power personally within clearly-defined limits – extending at best to wilful choice of an unsuitable spouse (Mary Queen of Scots). And their freedom to act was likely to be permanently undermined by an 'unwomanly' action – Anne Boleyn, Elizabeth's own mother, lost hers on the unsubstantiated claim that she had committed adultery with her brother.[1] As 'substitute men' none of the royal queens, or nearly-queens ever advanced (or even considered advancing) a woman to any position of prominence within her administration except the traditional one of lady-in-waiting.[2]

There is no doubt that Elizabeth I was sharp-witted and intelligent, and that this made her a surprisingly active and astute politician (surprising for a Renaissance monarch, male or female). She also benefited from a humanistic education of exceptionally high quality. Henry VIII's youthful interest in the new classical and linguistic studies, which he abandoned when the political situation produced more pressing concerns (to the disappointment of continental humanists like Erasmus), did lead him to encourage a distinctly 'modern' training for his children.

But as I suggested in chapter 2, the educating of girls in the Tudor period was consistent with the view that humanistic studies were elegant, civilised and decorative (a view which certainly helped recommend them generally to noble Englishmen like Henry). Elizabeth learnt modern and ancient languages to a high level of competence as part of her decorative accomplishments. The fact that they later proved valuable in her political affairs was, of course, an added bonus. And it is fascinating to see how *textually*, in contemporary descriptions of Elizabeth I, Queen of England, her intellectual accomplishments are susceptible to the kind of accommodating 'reading' which I earlier suggested enabled the patriarchy both to celebrate and to contain the achievements of individual gifted women.[3]

I suggested that female achievement in humanistic studies could be regarded in one of three ways by contemporary society. It could be denigrated as confirming indecorous forwardness in (inevitably sexually rapacious) women. But this was not a promising line in treating Elizabeth's proficiency, except as part of the kind of general attack on the government produced by the underground presses. (John Knox's attack on female rule, actually intended for Mary Tudor, by an accident of bad timing implicated the acceptably Protestant Elizabeth.) The other two alternatives were both celebratory. Female learning could be extolled as showing that the individual woman was 'beyond her sex', that as an exceptional and uncharacteristic woman she had transcended her femaleness (with its inevitable defects) altogether. Or female learning could be praised as displaying exactly the kind of 'feminine' accomplishment to be expected of the ornamental weaker members of society – a giftedness on a par with musical skill and skill with the needle and the spindle, which 'enrich' both the woman and her family. All three strategies accommodate female achievement without actually extending 'equal opportunity' to them.[4]

Contemporary accounts of Elizabeth I's intellectual accomplishments 'package' the queen's proficiency with languàges, and her incisive intellect, so that it conforms exactly to one of these celebratory (but containing) modes. Which one is selected will depend upon the precise occasion for praise. Two incidents related from contemporary documents by the historian J. E. Neale show this clearly. The first is designed to convey her exceptional nature – her transcendence of femaleness into triumphant majesty. In 1597, the queen received an ambassador from the King of Poland, supposedly with a peace proposal. Instead, however, in a public audience he made, in Latin, an extremely menacing speech:

> Rising lion-like from her throne, Elizabeth trounced him in extempore Latin for his insolence and audacity. If his king, she declared, was responsible for his speech, then it must be since he was a youth and not a king by right of blood but by election, and that only recent. 'As for you', said she to the ambassador, 'although I perceive you have read many books to fortify your arguments in this case, yet I am apt to believe that you have not lighted upon the chapter that prescribed the form to be used between kings and princes.' The Court rang with delighted admiration of the Queen's *tour de force*, and soon the news of it was spread through town and country. Elizabeth said to Cecil that she was sorry Essex was not present to hear the ambassador's and her Latin. He took the hint and wrote the whole tale to Essex, who did not need the suggestion to send back a pleasant word of praise. 'I was happy for her Majesty,' he answered, 'that she was stirred, and had so worthy an occasion to show herself. The heroes would be but as other men, if they had not unusual and unlooked for encounters; and sure her Majesty is made of the same stuff of which the ancients believed the heroes to be formed; that is, her mind of gold, her body of brass.' Queen Elizabeth's reply to the Polish ambassador lived on as a treasured memory through several generations.[5]

Here Latin eloquence connotes Elizabeth's heroic stature in Cecil's and Essex's complimentary accounts. By strong contrast, when the issue was the comparative (female) accomplishments of

Mary Queen of Scots and Elizabeth, Mary's courtier James Melville integrated Elizabeth's competence in a wide range of modern languages into his composite picture of her charming aptitudes. Basing his account on Melville's reports back to Mary, Neale writes:

> For the remainder of his nine days' stay, Melville was in demand every day, and sometimes thrice a day. He had spent many years in foreign courts and Elizabeth could therefore air her knowledge of French, Italian, and German – the last bad – and discuss the customs of other lands with him. Women's fashions being compared, each day she put on a different dress, one day English, another French, and a third Italian. She was delighted when Melville announced that the Italian style suited her best, as it showed her golden hair to advantage. She wanted to know what coloured hair was considered best, and how hers compared with Mary's. There followed a whole series of comparisons. . . . Did she play well on the lute and the virginals? 'Reasonably for a Queen,' answered Melville. Accordingly that night the Queen's cousin, Lord Hunsdon, took Melville along to surprise Elizabeth, alone in her chamber, playing 'exceedingly well' on the virginals.⁶

Her languages are amongst the ornamental skills – 'gifts', 'fashions', like dress and hair colour – which show off Elizabeth to her best advantage as exemplary woman. And significantly, they rank with musical skill (and skill at dancing).

It is actually impossible, I believe, at this distance to decide just how accomplished Elizabeth really was, since every source testifying to her learning is adapted to the conventions of its compatibility with her femaleness. Surviving examples of her translating and composing abilities show her to be about middling by the standards of the day.⁷ Historians who wish to establish Elizabeth I as the first truly 'emancipated' woman will be able to read her 'heroic' displays of linguistic ability as evidence for their case; whilst those who prefer to see her as shackled by the prejudices of her age can make use of the lightly complimentary testimonies to her skill with languages as truly 'feminine', equally persuasively.

But in either case, I think, we are watching the assimilation of the image of the female monarch to the exigencies of male statecraft. And this assimilation can deal with Elizabeth herself, *however* she behaves. It is in the interests of this assimilation, I suggest, that alongside the rich literature for keeping women in their traditional place, and attacking their many and varied supposedly innate vices, we find a thriving Elizabethan line in saving stereotypes: in portraits of female virtue so magnificent that they distract attention from their sex altogether. On all public occasions Elizabeth I herself was metamorphosed into a *female personification*, an emblem (who could acceptably be of the female sex without any sense of inferiority). Classical and medieval literature was rich in female graces, female muses, female saints and 'good women', and all of these were drawn by Elizabeth's circle of advisers into a complex and overlapping image of 'all virtue personified', which removed from Elizabeth the taint of her sex, and endowed her instead with abstract and generalised authority.

In the secondary literature of the reign of Elizabeth, this transmutation of the queen into a multi-faceted emblem or icon is known as the 'cult of Elizabeth'. Over the forty-five years of Elizabeth's reign this cult grew in sophistication, until in the final years of the old queen's rule – years in which she was disfigured, bad-tempered and gout-ridden – the gap between reality and the masque-like fictions of her celebration must appear to us quite absurd. Ben Jonson reported to William Drummond how in her late years the court laughed behind the queen's back at her participation in the increasingly discrepant celebration of her eternal youthfulness and beauty:

> Queen Elizabeth never saw herself after she became old in a true glass; they painted her, and sometimes would vermilion her nose. She had always about Christmas evens set dice that threw sixes or fives, and she knew not they were other, to make her win and esteem herself fortunate.[8]

Since Jonson goes on to an extremely scurrilous comment ('she had a membrana on her, which made her uncapable of man, though for her delight she tried many'), we should perhaps not take the fact of the story too seriously. But the spirit is, I think, representative. Experienced courtiers, like Sir John Harington, adeptly kept up the fiction of the queen as Queen of Faerie, Pastoral Shepherdess, and Cynthia, virgin goddess of the moon, till the very end, whilst negotiating in a very unfairy-like manner with James VI of Scotland who was waiting in the wings for Elizabeth's death. Harington's diary contains a number of entries testifying to the through-and-through fiction of Elizabeth as idealised lover on the model of Petrarch's Laura, and idealised shepherdess, recipient of pastoral adulation, which the court maintained. Both, of course, convert the queen from female monarch into symbolic virtuous womanhood:

> The Queene stoode up and bade me reache forthe my arme to rest her thereon. Oh, what swete burden to my next songe. – Petrarcke shall eke out good matter for this businesse.
>
> The Queene loveth to see me in my laste frize jerkin, and saithe tis well enoughe cutt. I will have another made liken to it.
>
> The Queene seemede troubled to daye; Hatton came out from her presence with ill countenaunce, and pulled me aside by the girdle, and saide in secrete waie, If you have any suite to daie, I praye you put it aside, The sunne doth not shine.[9]

On the day of the queen's death in 1603, Harington made the final entry in his diary in this 'cult of Elizabeth' vein:

> Here now wyll I reste my troubled mynde, and tend my sheepe like an Arcadian swayne, that hathe loste his faire mistresse, for soothe, I have loste the beste and fairest love that ever shepherde knew even my gracious Queene, and sith my good mistresse is gone; I shall not hastily put forthe for a new master.

However, just to be on the safe side, he had in the mean time sent a gift to James in Scotland: Latin and English verses and 'a curious perfumed lantern decorated with symbolic figures and bearing the legend of the thief on the cross, "Lord remember me when thou comest into thy kingdom"'.[10] Expediency was the name of the game at the English court.

I think, however, that we should be clear that expediency, in the case of Elizabeth, had a good deal to do with projecting her as a suitable Head of State for a powerful country in troublesome times – projecting her, that is to say, as not-woman. The 'cult', therefore, is to be viewed not as a game to flatter an ageing and spoiled woman. Indeed, that view, ironically figured in Ben Jonson's tale of painting the old queen's nose red, tells us how Elizabeth would have been regarded (and treated) if her womanhood had been allowed to obtrude over her queenliness. Individual women readily fell victim to male prejudice and the old chestnuts about their womanly failings (vanity, childishness, petulance and so on). Figurative virtue with a female gender was not thus vulnerable, and into such an invulnerable figure Elizabeth allowed herself to be converted.

Ben Jonson's own jottings illustrate the strategy at work in the metamorphosing of Elizabeth. His comments in conversation to William Drummond are scattered with male prejudice against women, and misogynistic wit:

> The conceit of Donne's 'Transformation' or 'μετεμψυχοσις' was, that he sought the soul of that apple which Eva pulled, and thereafter made it the soul of a bitch, then of a she wolf, and so of a woman.
>
> Of his own life, education, birth, actions. . . . He married a wife who was a shrew yet honest, five years he had not bedded with her, but remained with my lord Aubigny.
>
> A gentlewoman fell in such a fantasy or frenzy with one Mr Dod, a puritan preacher, that she requested her husband that, for the procreation of an angel or saint, he might lie with her; which having obtained, it was but an ordinary birth.[11]

But in his 'Timber: or Discoveries' (jottings on various intellectual topics in notebook form), we find entries in which 'femaleness' is acceptably integrated into his serious thought:

> *Natura non* I cannot think nature so spent, and decayed, that she can bring
> *effoeta* forth nothing worth her former years. She is always the same,
> [Nature is like herself: and when she collects her strength, is abler still.
> not effete] Men are decayed, and studies: she is not.
>
> Eloquence is a great and diverse thing: nor did she yet ever
> *Eloquentia* favour any man so much, as to become wholly his. He is happy,
> that can arrive to any degree of her grace.[12]

Ben Jonson retains the feminine pronoun which goes with the feminine gender of his Latin terms (*Natura, Eloquentia*) and worldly womanliness falls away from the figures he describes. Pure and unblemished, they can be contrasted squarely with the decadence and disappointment of worldly achievement.

The female personification on which the cult of Elizabeth finally centred was Chastity.[13] Throughout Elizabethan literature, and in the entertainments devised directly to celebrate her many visits to the homes of loyal noble subjects, the queen is addressed by one of a range of names connoting female virginity:

> Are you then travelling to the temple of Eliza?
>
> Even to her temple are my feeble limbs travelling.
>
> Some call her Pandora: some Gloriana: some Cynthia: some Belphoebe: some Astraea: all by several names to express several loves: Yet all those names make but one celestial body, as all those loves meet to create but one soul.
>
> I am of her own country, and we adore her by the name of Eliza.[14]

Gloriana is Queen of Faerie, chaste medieval symbol of English supremacy, celebrated most famously in Spenser's *The Faerie Queene* (1596), itself a tribute to Queen Elizabeth; Cynthia, goddess of the moon, is emblem of chastity; Belphoebe is 'beautiful as the sun', another maidenly protagonist of Spenser's English epic;[15] Pandora is 'all gifts', the female persona endowed with all gifts by the gods in ancient myth (Dekker chooses to overlook her Eve-like curiosity which released sin into the world when she opened 'Pandora's box').[16] Astraea is 'the just virgin of the golden age':

> Now when the world with sinne gan to abound,
> Astraea loathing lenger here to space
> Mongst wicked men, in whom no truth she found,
> Return'd to heauen, whence she deriu'd her race;
> Where she hath now an euerlasting place,
> Mongst those twelue signes, which nightly we doe see.
> The heauens bright-shining baudricke to enchace;
> And is the *Virgin*, sixt in her degree,
> And next her selfe her righteous ballance hanging bee.[17]

Virginity is the acme of female virtue.[18] It is to femaleness what valour is to maleness. As Ripa explains, in his influential *Iconologia*, glossing the emblem *Fortezza* – strength, an armed woman with a broken column and a lion at her feet:

> She should be a woman, not to declare that a strong man should emulate feminine ways, but to make the figure suit the way we speak ['fortezza' is feminine in gender]; or because, as every virtue is an image of the truth, the beautiful and the desirable, in which the intellect takes its delight, and as beauty is commonly attributed to women, one can use them to represent them conveniently; or, rather, because just as women, depriving themselves of those pleasures to which nature inclines them acquire and keep the reputation of special honour, so should the strong man, with the risks to his own body, with the dangers of his life, and with his spirit on fire with virtue, give birth to reputation and fame of high esteem.[19]

As Astraea, virgin queen, Elizabeth emblematically contained within her all other virtues: justice, fortitude, magnanimity, benevolence, wisdom. She did not have to show or perform these civic virtues in her statecraft; she represented virtue itself. Portrait after portrait of Elizabeth projects the same message: here is virtue personified, richly embellished with the supporting paraphernalia of such virtue, the moon, the phoenix, the pelican, the ermine, the pearl, the sieve.[20] Triumphal entries and royal pro-

gresses are all studded with interludes and entertainments re-
minding the Elizabethan public that the sex of their Prince is
properly to be submerged in the complex iconography of her
paradigmatic virtue.[21] Courtiers anxious for royal favour made
the most extravagant gestures, not just financially, but in terms of
time and ingenuity, to frame compliments to the queen which
drew on some hitherto unexplored aspect of the rich association
of 'virginal' attributes accruing to Astraea. Sir Francis Carew
devised an ingenious compliment to Elizabeth in the terms of the
traditional 'Cherry Tree Carol' (the cherry tree, which bends at
the request of the Virgin Mary to offer her fruit which Joseph will
not pluck for her out of anger at her pregnancy, symbolises the
immaculateness of her conception, her perpetual virginity):

> Here will I conclude with a conceit of that delicate Knight Sir Francis Carew,
> who, for the better accomplishment of his Royal Entertainment of our late
> Queen Elizabeth of happy memory at his house at Bedlington, led her
> Majesty to a cherry-tree, whose fruit he had of purpose kept back from
> ripening, at the least one month after all cherries had taken their farewell of
> England. This secret he performed by so raising a tent or cover of canvas over
> the whole tree, and wetting the same now and then with a scoop, or horn, as
> the heat of the weather required, and so by withholding the sun-beams from
> reflecting upon the berries, they grew both great, and were very long before
> they had gotten their perfect cherry colour; and when he was assured of her
> Majesty's coming, he removed the tent, and a few sunny days brought them
> to their full maturity.[22]

The Virgin Mary is another obvious 'saving stereotype' conveniently to be associated with Elizabeth's much publicised virginity (particularly since the Anglican Reformation had technically
outlawed the worship of Mary herself). Complex as the ancient
traditions of Astraea as the fruitful virgin, and overlapping
significantly with that tradition, is the rich celebration of the
Virgin Mary as female personification of all virtues. For a
running together of the two one may take, for instance, Duccio di
Buoninsegna's painting 'Maesta', in which the angel announcing
Mary's imminent ascension into the heavens holds out to her the
'spicifera' (ear of corn), the attribute of Astraea/Virgo as constellation, and topped by seven stars. The Reformation had
terminated the 'cult of Mary' in England; to a significant extent
the 'cult of Elizabeth' replaced it:

When others sing *Venite exultemus!*

Stand by and turn to *Noli emulari!*
For *Quare fremuerant* use *Oremus!*
Vivat Eliza! for an *Ave Mari!*[23]

As Frances Yates records:

> There is an engraving of the queen with her device of the Phoenix, below which is written 'This Maiden-Queen Elizabeth came into this world, the Eve of the Nativity of the blessed virgin Mary; and died on the Eve of the Annunciation of the virgin Mary, 1602.' This statement is accompanied by the following couplet:
>
> > She was, She is (what can there more be said?)
> > In earth the first, in heaven the second Maid.[24]

Positively buried under the accumulated weight of all this reassuringly affirmative symbolism, Elizabeth's femaleness fades into insignificance. The symbolism is to be felt in her elaborate masquerade of iconographic perpetual youth and unfading beauty when she was aged and infirm and barely capable of supporting the massive wigs, vast and bejewelled dresses, ruffs and weight of diamond pins, which she insisted on for public appearances.[25] It is likely that Elizabeth herself knowingly manipulated the emblems through which her court and counsellors perceived her. In the later years of her reign this enabled her to retain control over her own political destiny by insisting on actual virginity (refusing to marry), where her ministers had used iconographic chastity to connote purity and strength. Chastity is a notoriously double-edged quality, depending upon how it is 'read', as Margaret King has pointed out for the case of learned women who chose to remain chaste in the interests of pursuit of knowledge:

> Learning and chastity were indissolubly linked – for in undertaking the life of learning women repudiated a normal life of reproduction. *She* rejected a sexually active role for the sake of the intellectual life; *he* insisted on her asexuality because by means of intellect she had penetrated a male preserve. Chastity was at once expressive, I propose, of the learned woman's defiance of the established natural order and of the learned man's attempt to constrain her energies by making her mind the prison for her body. In the first case, chastity is a source of pride and independence; in the second, it is an instrument of repression.[26]

In Elizabeth's case, I suggest, the figurative strength which had been derived from youthful emblems of her physical purity enabled her to side-step the apparently inevitable moment of yoking her to a suitable male to take over the monarchy.

There is one Astraea reference familiar to Elizabethan readers which makes vivid the possibility of dichotomy exploited by the queen and her ministers and advisers between her symbolic value and her actual womanhood. It is a source which, curiously, I do not find mentioned in any of the now substantial discussions of Elizabeth as Astraea, as far as I have been able to ascertain. This is Juvenal's sixth satire, on 'The ways of women'. The satire is a lengthy and lively attack on female mores and the lewd and disreputable antics of women in the Rome of Juvenal's day. It is a goldmine of quotations for the anti-woman pamphleteers (we saw that Rainoldes also used it in his attack on cross-dressing on the stage). But it begins with a *proemium* derived from the *topos* in Virgil's celebrated fourth eclogue, which is then juxtaposed with the supposed moral decay of contemporary society:

> In the days of Saturn, I believe, Chastity [*Pudicitia*] still lingered on the earth, and was to be seen for a time – days when men were poorly housed in chilly caves, which under one common shelter enclosed hearth and household gods, herds and their owners; when the hill-bred wife spread her silvan bed with leaves and straw and the skins of her neighbours the wild beasts – a wife not like thee, O Cynthia [in Propertius], nor to thee, Lesbia [Catullus's mistress], whose bright eyes were clouded by a sparrow's death, but one whose breasts gave suck to lusty babes, often more unkempt herself than her acorn-belching husband. For in those days, when the world was young, and the skies were new, men born of the riven oak, or formed of dust, lived differently from now, and had no parents of their own. Under Jupiter, perchance, some few traces of ancient modesty may have survived; but that was before he had grown his beard, before the Greeks had learned to swear by someone else's head, when men feared not thieves for their cabbages and fruits, and lived in unwalled gardens. After that Astraea withdrew by degrees to heaven, with Chastity as her comrade, the two sisters taking flight together.[27]

Astraea and Pudicitia having withdrawn, Juvenal launches into his scurrilous and obscene descriptions of current female behaviour. Astraea stands magnificently isolated from the misogynistic outpourings against 'real' women. Unscathed in reputation, she waits to return to a freshly chastened earth, in the company of her sister, to reign over it. Female divinity presides over fleshly woman.

In the drama, female characters of anything approaching this stature are significantly absent. The dynamics of stage action make it unlikely that a female figure will be able to remain emblematically virtuous for long – once the tableau moves, she becomes a woman of character (and hence instantly capable of malice and vice), no longer a female figurehead. Shakespeare's queens are by turns, as we have seen, shrews, wanton seducers, female prophets and witches in their speeches and actions. When described in their absence they may rise to 'epitome of womanhood' (like Antonio's idealised picture of the Duchess of Malfi). Margaret, future wife of Henry VI, is described as above 'ordinary' women in her absence by Suffolk:

> Her peerless feature, joined with her birth,
> Approves her fit for none but for a king;
> Her valiant courage and undaunted spirit,
> More than in women commonly is seen,
> Will answer our hope in issue of a king.[28]

In Marlowe's *Tamburlaine*, however, Tamburlaine persistently translates his queen, Zenocrate, into paragon of all virtues, divinity more than human, female personification of the good, using the strategies of the Elizabethan court poet (strategies Marlowe clearly understood well):

> Then sit thou down, divine Zenocrate,
> And here we crown thee Queen of Persia
> And all the kingdoms and dominions
> That late the power of Tamburlaine subdu'd:
> As Juno, when the giants were suppress'd,
> That darted mountains at her brother Jove,
> So looks my love, shadowing in her brows
> Triumphs and trophies for my victories;
> Or as Latona's daughter [Diana] bent to arms,
> Adding more courage to my conquering mind.[29]

Zenocrate is female emblem of Tamburlaine's triumphs – 'shadowing in her brows / Triumphs and trophies for [his] victories'. She is his goddess of inspiration, Diana, goddess of chastity and the hunt. When she dies, Tamburlaine refuses to recognise this death as an intimation of mortality and once again metamorphoses his prostrate queen (silent on her death-bed of state, as she sat before silent on her coronation throne) into an icon of eternal promise:

> Now walk the angels on the walls of heaven,
> As sentinels to warn th' immortal souls

> To entertain divine Zenocrate.
> Apollo, Cynthia, and the ceaseless lamps
> That gently look'd upon this loathsome earth,
> Shine downwards now no more, but deck the heavens
> To entertain divine Zenocrate.
> The crystal springs, whose taste illuminates
> Refined eyes with an eternal sight,
> Like tried silver runs through Paradise
> To entertain divine Zenocrate.[30]

Zenocrate, like Astraea, withdraws from the earth, leaving it symbolically cast into darkness.

But if Shakespeare's noble-women cannot sustain a talismanic value in the manner of England's virgin queen, they echo and are supported by a panoply of figures of 'good women' who were well-tried favourites of the early modern period. These are the steadily enduring figures in Boccaccio's *De claris mulieribus*, in Christine de Pisan's *Le trésor de la cité des Dames*, in Chaucer's *The Legend of Good Women*, in Jacob de Voragine's *The Golden Legend*, Thomas Heywood's *Gynaikeion*, and a host of others.[31] And to works like these whose tales persist in communal memory should be added the more recent popular volumes of exemplary tales for the amusement and edification of women, like William Painter's *The Palace of Pleasure* (1566–7),[32] in which women are the main protagonists, rewarded for their virtue or chastened for their misdemeanours, and acquiescing with gratifying resignation to their (deserved) punishments. The first volume of this work was such a success that within a year Painter had published a sequel. The plots of a number of Elizabethan and Jacobean plays are to be found, in whole or in part, in Painter.

'Nobility in adversity' is the theme of the majority of these exemplary figures. Where they show 'manly courage', it is likely to be in courageously killing themselves to avoid shame or humiliation. (Ovid describes Lucretia as 'virilis animi', manly of soul, in the *Fasti* (ii.847).) If, like Queen Semiramis (in Boccaccio), she makes a spirited bid for power, she is ultimately brought low (and commended for a gallant effort). Semiramis took advantage of her close resemblance to her young son, and disguised herself as a man to reign in his place during his minority:

Having assumed royal majesty, she preserved it and the rule of the armies, and by pretending very carefully to be a man she achieved many things which would have been great and noble even for the strongest of men. She spared herself no labours, feared no dangers, and with her unheard-of deeds overcame the envy of all men. Finally she did not fear to reveal to everyone who she really was and how with womanly deceit she had pretended to be a man. It was almost as if she wanted to show that in order to govern it is not necessary to be a man, but to have courage. This fact heightened that woman's glorious majesty as much as it gave rise to admiration in those who looked upon her.[33]

However, the 'womanly deceit' which is already in evidence here gets the better of her; 'with one wicked deed this woman stained all the accomplishments worthy of perpetual memory' – she went to bed with her look-alike son. Chastened into ignominy she becomes a watch-word for the downfall which female sensuality inevitably brings.[34]

Probably the two most persistent symbols of patient female suffering of the early modern period are Lucretia and Griselda ('patient Griselda' and 'the patience of Griselda' figuring with comparable frequency to 'as false as Cressid'). Viola's description of her 'sister', languishing for love, alludes directly:

> *Viola* My father had a daughter lov'd a man,
>   As it might be perhaps, were I a woman,
>   I should your lordship.
> *Duke*   And what's her history?
> *Viola* A blank, my lord. She never told her love,
>   But let concealment, like a worm i' th' bud,
>   Feed on her damask cheek. She pin'd in thought;
>   And with a green and yellow melancholy
>   She sat like Patience on a monument,
>   Smiling at grief. Was not this love indeed?[35]

'Virtue' here is silent enduring of whatever patriarchal fortune brings. In Chaucer's *Clerk's Tale*,[36] Griselda is the supremely virtuous daughter of a poor man, admired from a distance, and then unexpectedly asked in marriage, by her local Lord Walter:

> But for to speke of vertuous beautee,
> Thanne was she oon the faireste under sonne;
> For povreliche yfostred up was she,
> No likerous lust was thurgh hire herte yronne.
> Wel ofter of the welle than of the tonne
> She drank, and for she wolde vertu plese,
> She knew wel labour, but noon ydel ese.

> But thogh this mayde tendre were of age,
> Yet in the brest of hire virginitee
> Ther was enclosed rype and sad corage.⁺

Here are the vital ingredients for this fantasy of female desirability: 'vertuous beautee', 'virginitee' and 'sad corage'. Griselda consents to marry Walter, and gratefully accepts the grand life-style her sudden elevation in rank brings her. She bears Walter a daughter. At this point Walter's 'herte longeth so / To tempte his wyf, hir sadnesse for to knowe'. To try her virtue he takes her daughter from her and tells her her child is to be killed (in fact he sends her to be fostered). Four years later she bears him a son, and when the son is two years old he too is taken from her, supposedly to be killed because Walter's family are afraid of such humble blood inheriting at Walter's death. Finally, Walter gets a counterfeit Papal Bull setting aside his wife Griselda, and summons home the now twelve year old daughter, as if to be his new bride (accompanied by her young brother). Griselda, ignorant of their identity, is dispatched home in a simple smock, then summoned once more to Walter's house to make ready for the new bride.

Throughout all this 'trying of her patience' Griselda utters not a single word of complaint, obeys every one of her husband's commands, gives up her children meekly (having done her best to ensure them Christian burial). Her resignation is terrifying:

> 'I have,' quod she, 'seyd thus, and evere shal:
> I wol no thyng, ne nyl no thyng, certayn,
> But as yow list. Naught greveth me at al,
> Though that my doughter and my sone be slayn, –
> At your comandement, this is to sayn.
> I have noght had no part of children tweyne
> But first siknesse, and after, wo and peyne.'

> 'Ye been oure lord, dooth with youre owene thyng
> Right as yow list; axeth no reed at me.
> For as I lefte at hoom al my clothyng,
> Whan I first cam to yow, right so,' quod she,
> 'Lefte I my wyl and al my libertee,
> And took youre clothyng; wherfore I yow preye,
> Dooth youre plesaunce, I wol youre lust obeye.'³⁸

At this point, having well and truly 'assayed hire wommanhoode', Walter reveals all, congratulates his faithful wife, and they live happily every after. It should, of course, be noted

that all Griselda's 'manly' courage in the face of so much wilfully
inflicted adversity is described in terms of the marriage-bond, and
her obligations to her husband. Griselda is the ultimate crystal-
lisation of all demands for wifely obedience and virtue, although
as Chaucer explains in conclusion:

> This storie is seyd, nat for that wyves sholde
> Folwen Grisilde as in humylitee,
> For it were inportable, though they wolde;
> But for that every wight, in his degree,
> Sholde be constant in adversitee
> As was Grisilde.[19]

The print of Griselda is to be found on Shakespeare's long-
suffering female characters, from Viola herself (as she ably
diagnoses), to Imogen in *Cymbeline*, Helena in *All's Well That
Ends Well*, Hero in *Much Ado About Nothing*, Julia in *The Two
Gentlemen of Verona*, Marina in *Pericles*, Hermione in *The
Winter's Tale*. At the moment at which they shift into patient
resignation and waiting, while the injustices done to them by
their menfolk are painstakingly resolved, they fall naturally into
the postures expected of them; they become patient Griseldas.

As Desdemona gives way under the accumulating pressure of
false accusation, she leaves aside sexual backchat and becomes
the patiently suffering spouse as she prepares herself for Othello's
unjust punishment. She is Griselda glorious in her resignation in
the face of husbandly chastisement, 'let nobody blame him; his
scorn I approve':

> *Desdemona* (sings)   The poor soul sat sighing by a sycamore tree,
> Sing all a green willow;
> Her hand on her bosom, her head on her knee.
> Sing willow, willow, willow.
> The fresh stream ran by her, and murmur'd her
> moans;
> Sing willow, willow, willow;
> Her salt tears fell from her and soft'ned the stones;
> Sing willow —
> Lay by these —
> willow, willow. —
> Prithee, hie thee; he'll come anon. —
> Sing all a green willow must be my garland.
> Let nobody blame him; his scorn I approve —
> Nay, that's not next. . . .

> O, these men, these men!
> Dost thou in conscience think – tell me, Emilia –
> That there be women do abuse their husbands
> In such gross kind?[40]

The shadow of sexual frailty hovers over Desdemona, unlike Griselda (who, as Chaucer said, was too good to be true). But at this crucial point in the play that past frailty (recapitulated in Emilia's banter) provides a foil for her present heroic fortitude – exemplary passivity in adversity:

Desdemona   Wouldst thou do such a deed for all the world?
Emilia   The world's a huge thing.
  It is a great price for a small vice.
Desdemona   Good troth, I think thou wouldst not.
Emilia   By my troth, I think I should; and undo't when I had done it. Marry, I would not do such a thing for a joint-ring, nor for measures of lawn, nor for gowns, petticoats, nor caps, nor any petty exhibition; but for all the whole world – ud's pity, who would not make her husband a cuckold to make him a monarch? I should venture purgatory for't.
Desdemona   Beshrew me, if I would do such a wrong for the whole world.[41]

The story of Lucretia, twin pivot with Griselda's as stereotypes of grandiose female heroism, skilfully involves the ever-present possibility of 'frailty overwhelmed' in the tapestry of unfaltering and courageous submission by woman to her fate. I take the story from Painter, though it is also to be found in Livy and Ovid, in Boccaccio, in Chaucer's *The Legend of Good Women*, and, of course, in Shakespeare's *The Rape of Lucrece*. At a gathering of Roman gentlemen the husbands begin vying with one another in praise of the virtue of their respective wives. Failing to agree, they ride post-haste back to Rome, where all but one of them find their wives 'sportinge themselves with sondrye pastimes' (not sitting chastely awaiting their husbands' return as was supposed). Only Collatinus finds his wife Lucrece (Lucretia) employed in suitably wifely pursuits:

From thence they went to the house of Collatinus, where they founde Lucrece, not as the others before named, spending time in idlenes, but late in the night occupied and busie amonges her maydes in the middes of her house spinni̅g of wool. The victory and prayse wherof was given to Lucretia, who when she saw her husband, gentlie and lovinglie intertained him, and curteously badde the Tarquinians welcome.[42]

Chaucer embellishes this description of Lucretia surprised to emphasise the full range of wifely virtues: his Lucrece leaves off spinning to lament the absence of her lord and master:

> And therwithal ful tenderly she wep,
> And of hire werk she tok no more kep,
> And mekely she let hyre eyen falle;
> And thilke semblaunt sat hire wel withalle.
> And eek hire teres, ful of honeste,
> Embelished hire wifly chastite,
> Hyre contenaunce is to hire herte dygne,
> For they acorde bothe in dede and sygne.[43]

Sextus Tarquinius is inflamed by this sight, not with admiration, but with lust. He returns to the house, and threatening Lucrece with a naked sword, rapes her. In case she might prefer to die rather than to yield, he tells her that in that case he would defame her by killing his own servant, and claiming he caught the two of them in bed together.

Early the next morning Lucrece summons her absent husband and her father. Weeping 'piteously' she tells them what has happened, and makes them vow to avenge her. They assure her that she herself has done no wrong, 'imputing the offence to the authour and doer of the same, affirming that her bodye was polluted, and not her minde, and where consent was not, there the crime was absente'. Unwaveringly, Lucrece continues along the path she has already decided upon:

> 'As for my part, though I cleare my selfe of the offence, my body shall feele the punishment: for no unchast or ill woman, shall hereafter impute no dishonest act to Lucrece.' Then she drew out a knife, which she had hidden secretely, under her kirtle, and stabbed her selfe to the harte. Which done, she fell downe grouelinge uppon her wound and died.[44]

Her family avenge her by banishing the Tarquins from Rome forever.

I think we have to face up to the fact that the most powerful stereotypes of female heroism for the Renaissance all involve sexuality chastened in one form or another. In the case of Lucretia, her sexual sin is committed under duress, as is Lavinia's in *Titus Andronicus*. In both cases, however, it is the female victims who make atonement for the crime; Lucretia by her suicide, Lavinia in a visible symbol of patient suffering, a silent, mutilated emblem:

> *Enter ... Lavinia, her hands cut off, and her tongue cut out, and*
> *ravish'd ...*
> Marcus   But sure some Tereus hath deflowered thee,
> And, lest thou shouldst detect him, cut thy tongue.
> Ah, now thou turn'st away thy face for shame!
> And notwithstanding all this loss of blood –
> As from a conduit with three issuing spouts –
> Yet do thy cheeks look red as Titan's face
> Blushing to be encount'red with a cloud.[45]

Nor is this combination of sexual frailty and spiritual strength confined to the secular stereotypes of female heroism. Heloise was the passionate lover of Abelard (a passion which ended in his castration by her uncle's servants in revenge for their secret marriage), before she became the devout and articulate nun of the *Letters*. The two facts are naturally juxtaposed by François Villon in his *Ballade des Dames du Temps Jadis* (c. 1460):

> Où est la très sage Hellois
> Pour qui fut chastré, puis moine
> Pierre Esbaillart à Saint-Denis?
> Pour son amour eut cette essoyne ...
> Mais où sont les neiges d'antan?

[Where is that learned lady Heloise, for whose sake Pierre Abelard was first castrated, then became a monk at Saint-Denis? It was through love that he suffered such misfortune. . . . But where are last year's snows?][46]

In *The Golden Legend* female saint's life after female saint's life involves a trial of sexual advance[47] – the saint in question is desired by a man, whose desire is further inflamed by her refusals, and finally leads to her martyrdom (Saint Agnes, Saint Agatha, Saint Catharine).[48] In another series of saints' lives, the maiden saint adopts male dress, and flees to a monastery to avoid the loss of her virginity. In each of these stories, the saint is subsequently accused of fathering another woman's child, remains silent until death, humbly and uncomplainingly accepting the punishment which her silence brings her. At her death, on the laying out of the body, it is discovered that she is female, and that she is therefore innocent of the sexual assault of which she has been accused.[49] In these stories also, sexuality is evidently closely bound up in the 'sainthood' of the female saint concerned. Active sexuality is implied in the fact that the accusation is laid against her in the first place – a kind of inverse rape. Female heroism is displayed in the saint's subsequent acceptance of the shame of a sexual sin committed not by her but against her. It is Lucrece and Lavinia all over again.

Finally, *The Golden Legend* contains two further stories of women who disguise themselves as male monks, and lead a life of endless penitence, having actually committed the sexual crimes of which their fellow female saints are only accused. Saint Pelagia is a woman 'first among the women of the city of Antioch for her wealth, for her beauty of form, for the pretentious splendour of her attire, and for her lewdness of mind and body'.[50] She is converted to Christianity, and flees incognito to become a hermit, Brother Pelagius. Significantly, she is not subsequently accused of any sexual misdemeanour (she has already committed them), but is honourably buried when at her death her corpse is discovered to be female.

Saint Theodora is a devout and chaste married woman, who is actually tempted into adultery (by the Devil himself):

> Coming to her at the appointed hour, he lay with her and then went away. Then Theodora, returning to herself, shed bitter tears, and struck herself in the face, saying: 'Alas, woe is me, for I have lost my soul and destroyed the beauty of my honour!' At his return, her husband found her desolate and mourning, and not knowing the reason thereof, sought to console her; but she would not be comforted.[51]

In her husband's absence Theodora cuts off her hair, dresses as a man, and enters a monastery as Brother Theodore. Her husband believes her to have run off with another man. Theodora 'fulfilled all her duties [in the monastery] with humility, and her service was pleasing to all'. When she encounters her husband in the street and passes unrecognised, she weeps inwardly: 'Alas, alas, my good husband, how much do I moil to expiate the sin I committed against thee!'[52] Theodora in her turn is sexually accosted by a woman – in her case quite explicitly:

> One day, as she was returning from the city with her camels, and took shelter in a certain house, a girl came to her and said: 'Lie with me!' Theodora repulsed her, and she went to another and lay with him; and when she became big with child, she was asked of whom she had conceived, and said: 'That monk Theodore slept with me!'[53]

Again, appropriately, in view of her mature sexual status, Theodora herself raises the illegitimate child:

When the child was born, they carried it to the abbot of the monastery. The abbot sternly rebuked Theodore, and, when the latter pleaded for pardon, laid the child upon his shoulders and drove him out of the monastery. Thereafter Theodora remained for seven years outside of the monastery, and nurtured the child with the milk of the flocks.[54]

As usual, when Theodora dies she is identified as female, her husband comes to weep over her remains, her foster-child becomes a holy monk (and subsequently abbot). She is buried 'with many praises'.

Shakespeare's chaste women falsely accused of sexual misdemeanours share a dignity and a female heroism with these female saints, withstanding nobly and in silence the tainting of their virginity – albeit only by repute.[55] Hermione faces her husband's false accusation that she has committed adultery with Polixenes, and its consequences (loss of her husband, removal from her of her young son, who subsequently dies, and of her baby daughter, taken from her breast) with Griselda's patience, and the saint-falsely-accused's silence:

> Hermoine Since what I am to say must be but that
> Which contradicts my accusation, and
> The testimony on my part no other
> But what comes from myself, it shall scarce boot me
> To say 'Not guilty'. Mine integrity
> Being counted falsehood shall, as I express it,
> Be so receiv'd. But thus – if pow'rs divine
> Behold our human actions, as they do,
> I doubt not then but innocence shall make
> False accusation blush, and tyranny
> Tremble at patience.[56]

Hero swoons away into silence when accused of unchastity by her husband-to-be at the altar. To her father she swears:

> If I know more of any man alive
> Than that which maiden modesty doth warrant,
> Let all my sins lack mercy! O my father,
> Prove you that any man with me convers'd
> At hours unmeet, or that I yesternight
> Mjintain'd the change of words with any creature,
> Refuse me, hate me, torture me to death.[57]

Hermione's patience, Hero's willing submission to martyrdom by torture, surrounds them with a halo of female heroism which shines out vividly from these scenes.

It is Isabella in *Measure for Measure* who, I think, most complicatedly incorporates the full range of possibilities latent in these admirably steadfast and courageous assaulted (or at least slandered) women. Isabella is a 'very virtuous maid', shortly to become a nun. She is, therefore, committed to a life of chastity. Her brother is condemned to death, under a harsh law of the country (freshly revived) which makes it a capital crime to have unlawful (that is, extramarital) intercourse. When Isabella goes to plead with Angelo, deputy in charge of enforcing the law in the Duke, his master's, absence, he, like Tarquin, and like the oppressors of innumerable female saints, is roused to unspeakable lust by her virtue and innocence. He determines to seduce her:

> Angelo O cunning enemy, that, to catch a saint,
> With saints dost bait thy hook! Most dangerous
> Is that temptation that doth goad us on
> To sin in loving virtue. Never could the strumpet,
> With all her double vigour, art and nature,
> Once stir my temper; but this virtuous maid
> Subdues me quite.[58]

He therefore tells Isabella that her brother will be saved only if she consents to sleep with him. Isabella absolutely refuses, and tells her brother he will have to die for his own sexual offence – she is not prepared to commit another. Fortunately an acceptable stand-in is found in the form of Mariana, to whom Angelo was betrothed (he broke the betrothal when her father lost his wealth);[59] Angelo has his way with her, breaks his word by nevertheless sending to authorise Claudio's execution, but is exposed. He is only saved from punishment by the intercession of the deflowered Mariana, and Isabella on her knees. Claudio is saved by the intervention of the Duke and marries his pregnant Juliet. Isabella consents to marry the Duke.

The entire play is rich with sexual banter, bawdy, and open enjoyment of exuberant sexuality. Only Angelo (enforcing the absurd and unenforceable law) and Isabella (refusing to sacrifice her virginity even to save her brother's life) seem to feel *guilt* for their sexuality. And in this context, I think, the expectations concerning saintly virgins whose virtue is assaulted are used to undermine Isabella's position during the crucial scenes in which she allows her brother to go to his death, rather than submit to Angelo.

Were Isabella Lucretia (and the similarities between the preliminary circumstances are extremely close in the two stories), she would submit to enforced sex, tell all afterwards, and kill herself. That is what the patriarchy expects of a female hero under such circumstances. Isabella does threaten to denounce Angelo, but she threatens to do so without giving in to him. Angelo is correct in taunting her with the promise that no one will believe her because of his own 'unsoil'd name, th' austereness of [his] life' (II.iv.155). She would only be believed, of course, if she had actually been raped: dishevelled and endlessly weeping, her testimony would then be impeccable, like Lucretia's.

Were Isabella a female saint of *The Golden Legend* (or one of the many romance female heroes who escape dishonour at the hands of a lord, like Greene's Cratyna)[60] she would flee in disguise and do interminable servile penance for the lust she has aroused. Or she would stand firm and submit to torture, ending only with her death and martyrdom (she is a novice nun, and therefore ideally cast in the role of 'maiden devoted to Christ', like Saint Agnes or Saint Agatha).

Shakespeare's Isabella is belittled by the stereotypes to whom she so flagrantly refuses to match up. Her stature is diminished, her virtue is placed in question:

> *Claudio*   Sweet sister, let me live.
> What sin you do to save a brother's life,
> Nature dispenses with the deed so far
> That it becomes a virtue.
> *Isabella*   O you beast!
> O faithless coward! O dishonest wretch!
> Wilt thou be made a man out of my vice?
> Is't not a kind of incest to take life
> From thine own sister's shame?[61]

Claudio is right: the deed 'becomes a virtue' in the tradition of *The Golden Legend*. To suffer humbly sexual assault is a step on the way to sainthood. When Saint Margaret reveals that she could not have fathered the child attributed to her, she maintains that suffering the sexual 'sin' (bearing the *accusation* of intercourse) adds to her virtue – 'I have the virtue of a man, and have virtue of that sin that was put on me.'[62] Isabella's crude accusation of 'incest', and the claim that her enforced sex would 'make a man' of Claudio does nothing to elevate her in the audience's eyes. Indeed, it suggests curiously that Isabella is accusing *Claudio* of wanting to rape her, betraying an obsessive fear of her own sexuality in general.

In the accumulation of supporting figures of memorable virtuous women it is not surprising to find a disproportionate number of those who lament, and adopt postures of penitence and mourning.[63] One of the schoolroom exercises familiar to the Elizabethan schoolchild (and based on antique school exercises) was the imaginary speech: the histrionic monologuè in the imagined persona of a famous figure from ancient literature.[64] The textbook example of such a speech was Dido's lament for the departed Aeneas; second to this came Hecuba's outpouring of grief for the fallen Priam. Both are based on episodes from the *Aeneid*, and both are familiar reference points in Elizabethan literature to invoke intense and majestic female suffering.

In *The Rape of Lucrece*, at the peak of Lucrece's distraught grief at the wrong Tarquin has done her, Shakespeare has her encounter the figure of the grieving Hecuba in a tapestry of the Fall of Troy. Looking upon this image of the tragedy brought to one woman by the desirability of Helen, Lucrece inveighs against female lasciviousness which incites male lust, in a speech which might come straight from a school exercise-book:[65]

> 'Poor instrument,' quoth she, 'without a sound,
> I'll tune thy woes with my lamenting tongue,
> And drop sweet balm in Priam's painted wound,
> And rail on Pyrrhus that hath done him wrong,
> And with my tears quench Troy that burns so long,
>   And with my knife scratch out the angry eyes
>   Of all the Greeks that are thine enemies.

> 'Show me the strumpet that began this stir,
> That with my nails her beauty I may tear!
> Thy heat of lust, fond Paris, did incur
> This load of wrath that burning Troy doth bear;
> Thy eye kindled the fire that burneth here,
>   And here in Troy, for trespass of thine eye,
>   The sire, the son, the dame and daughter die. . . .

> 'Lo here weeps Hecuba, here Priam dies,
> Here manly Hector faints, here Troilus swounds;
> Here friend by friend in bloody channel lies,
> And friend to friend gives unadvised wounds;

And one man's lust these many lives confounds;
Had doting Priam check'd his son's desire,
Troy had been bright with fame and not with fire.'[66]

Male lust and female suffering unite Lucrece and Hecuba in a compelling composite image of extreme guilt: the ultimate posture for the female hero.[67] And behind that image lurks the guilt imputed by the patriarchy to the female sex for the lust they passively arouse.

I do not pretend to have exhausted here the range of possibilities offered by female personifications and familiar female worthies to the dramatist and his audience. What I hope I have suggested is that the female figure in heroic pose on the stage owes her forcefulness and compelling presence to a web of associations conjured up by her likeness to other familiar figures. She is not an allegory or a cypher; but she lures us into expecting of her gestures and actions consistent with those of a collection of shadowy and unreal female figures she fleetingly evokes. I suggest that even today we are tempted into responding to Hermione and to Hero as most grand when most wronged; or to Shakespeare's Lucrece as shamed and shameful in her level-headed confrontation of (and ultimate capitulation to) Tarquin (lines 652–93), but superb in her despair (lines 762–1750). Lucrece 'frantic with grief' is, in patriarchal terms, most reassuringly the female hero.

What is disturbing about the recumbant, weeping woman as female hero is not her qualities as such, but the fact that precisely those qualities *negate* the possibility for heroism in the male. When Hermione and Hero swoon in the face of false accusation, when Lucrece weeps piteously, that is female heroism. When 'manly Hector faints' and Troilus 'swounds', on the other hand, it is the sign of the final breakdown of order, for male heroes are unmanned by weeping and swooning.[68] 'Manly Hector faints' is a tautology; Adonis's blush betrays his unheroic passivity, 'the maiden burning of his cheeks'.[69]

In the male hero, weeping and swooning are the signs of vulnerability, of his being 'all too human'. In Elizabethan and Jacobean drama they may touchingly enhance his dying moments, the point at which manliness comes up against the cosmic insignificance of mankind. The female hero, on the other hand, is defined by that weakness, by her being *other than* manly.

I have, however, come across one example of the inverting of these stereotypes in Elizabethan literature, which is provocatively associated with the iconography of Elizabeth I herself, and which may serve as a fitting close for the present discussion. In traditional iconography, the turtle-dove is female, the phoenix male. The turtle-dove is the bird who mates only once, and who, on the death of her mate, remains on her nest and pines inconsolably until her own demise. The phoenix is the bird which lives for five hundred years, and is then spontaneously reincarnated out of the ashes of his own funeral pyre. Passivity, loyalty, nurturing, devotion, weeping, commendable grief, belong to the turtle; promise, activity, generative force, vigour, to the phoenix.

In the later years of Queen Elizabeth's reign the phoenix became her emblem. It allowed England to celebrate her perpetual virginity, and thus her refusal to reproduce, whilst affirming in compliment to the old queen a confidence that at her death a suitable heir would miraculously emerge from the flames of her funeral pyre. Shakespeare's *The Phoenix and the Turtle* and Ben Jonson's *The Phoenix Analysed* belong to this last phase of Elizabethan iconography, in which, as I suggested earlier, Elizabeth's own manipulations of the tradition have added to its complexity. Both poems were contributions to Robert Chester's *Loves Martyr* (1601), a compilation of emblems of the outgoing Elizabethan age (which also includes a contribution by Chapman). In addition to the 'phoenix and turtle' poems it includes 'a description of the Nine Female Worthies, a chronicle history of King Arthur, a bestiary, and a treatise on birds, on plants and their uses, on precious stones'.[70] In its second edition (published after Elizabeth's death in 1603) it was retitled, *The Annuals [Annals] of great Brittain, or A Most Excellent Monument*.[71] And half a century of iconographic effort to convert a female monarch to 'manly' strength appears, in this 'monument' for a fleeting moment to have dislodged the weight of traditional assumptions about the polarising according to gender of active and passive qualities. The phoenix of both poems is *female* – a compliment to the queen. And so the turtle-dove becomes *male*, in spite of his loyal, grieving submissiveness.[72] In Shakespeare's verses the shift is implicit, and judged by critics to be 'mysterious':

> Hearts remote, yet not asunder;
> Distance and no space was seen
> 'Twixt this Turtle and his queen. . . .

> Death is now the Phoenix' nest,
> And the Turtle's loyal breast
> To eternity doth rest.[3]

Yet the poem turns on the shift in qualities – 'properties' in Elizabethan parlance – 'Property was thus appalled [impaired]':

> Property was thus appalled
> That the self was not the same:
> Single natures double name
> Neither two nor one was called.[4]

Ben Jonson's poem takes the phoenix's reversal of sex as its explicit theme:

> Now, after all, let no man
>   Receive it for a fable,
>   If a bird so amiable,
> Do turn into a woman.

> Or (by our turtle's augur)
>   That Nature's fairest creature,
>   Prove of his mistress' feature,
> But a bare type and figure.[5]

Sex and gender attributes have been transposed. Because the phoenix, with all its affirmative connotations, has become female, by Royal Command, the turtle, with all its disturbing passive dependency has become male. Vulnerability, dependence, loyal subservience all take the masculine gender. Either the courtier has been 'emasculated', or here is an iconic possibility of laudibly passive maleness.

I believe that Elizabeth I failed to make other than the impact of a 'token' woman on the patriarchal attitudes of the early modern period. She 'stood in' for the absent male (as inheritance law readily allowed in England), on the strict understanding that she took upon herself 'manly' activity, and the associated patterns of behaviour strictly as a stand-in (feudal ladies rode into battle at the head of their husbands' troops, while the lord was away at the crusades). But it does appear that the creative effort which had gone into her iconography succeeded, if only for a moment, in disrupting the sustaining tradition of patriarchal emblems enough to unsettle and perturb two of the age's leading male poets.

Notes

1 J. E. Neale, *Queen Elizabeth* (London, 1934), p. 17.
2 See e.g. N. Z. Davis, 'Gender and genre: women as historical writers 1400–1820', in P. H. Labalme (ed.), *Beyond Their Sex: Learned Women of the European Past* (New York, 1980), pp. 153–82, 160: 'When Queen Elizabeth had Cecil commission a historian for her reign, no female was entrusted with that task.' See also A. Heisch, 'Queen Elizabeth and the persistence of Patriarchy', *Feminist Review*, 4 (1980), pp. 45–78.
3 See above, p. 51.
4 See above, p. 56.
5 Neale, *op. cit.*, p. 345.
6 ibid., pp. 130–1.
7 ibid., pp. 23–6; R. H. Bainton, 'Learned women in the Europe of the sixteenth century', in Labalme (ed.), *op. cit.*, pp. 117–28, 118.
8 'Conversations with William Drummond', in G. Parfitt (ed.), *Ben Jonson: The Complete Poems* (Penguin, 1975), p. 470.
9 H. Harrington (ed.), *Nugae Antiquae* (London, 1779).
10 E. Story Donno (ed.), *Metamorphosis of Ajax* (London, 1962), p. 6.
11 Parfitt (ed.), *op. cit.*, pp. 464, 467, 475.
12 ibid., pp. 378, 387.
13 On the shift towards decisive use of this emblem in the course of Elizabeth's reign, see M. Axton, *The Queen's Two Bodies: Drama and the Elizabethan Succession* (London, 1977).
14 T. Dekker, *Old Fortunatus*, in F. A. Yates, *Astraea* (London, 1975), p. 29; and in R. Strong, *The Cult of Elizabeth* (London, 1977), p. 15.
15 '*Belphoebe* was her name, as faire as *Phoebus* sun' (*The Faerie Queene* 3.v.27).
16 On Elizabeth as Pandora, see M. Axton, *op. cit.*, p. 71.
17 *The Faerie Queene* 5.i.11, *cit.* Yates, *Astraea, op. cit.*, pp. 31–2.
18 See M. Warner, *Alone Of All Her Sex: The Myth and the Cult of the Virgin Mary* (London, 1976; 1978 edn), *Joan of Arc: The Image of Female Heroism* (London, 1981).
19 Ripa, *Iconologia overo descrittione delle imagini universali, cavate delle statue, e medaglie antiche* (Milan, 1602), in Warner, *Joan of Arc*, p. 229.
20 See Yates, *Astraea*, p. 78. On the iconography of these portraits see F. A. Yates, 'The triumph of chastity', *Astraea*, pp. 112–20; R. C. Strong, *Portraits of Queen Elizabeth I* (Oxford, 1963); Strong, *The Cult of Elizabeth*; R. C. Strong, *The English Icon* (London and New York, 1969). There is something of an industry in unravelling more or less plausibly, and more or less complicatedly, the imagery of these paintings; on the whole the simpler interpretations seem to me most plausible.
21 See E. C. Wilson, *England's Eliza* (Cambridge, Mass., 1939); J. Nichols, *The Progresses, and Public Processions, of Queen Elizabeth*, 3 vols (London, 1823); J. Wilson, *Entertainments for Elizabeth* (Woodbridge, 1980); M. Axton, *op. cit*; F. M. O'Donoghue, *Descriptive and Classified Catalogue of Portraits of Q. Elizabeth* (1894).
22 In Nichols, *op. cit.*, III,44; J. Wilson, *op. cit.*, p. 24.
23 John Dowland, in Yates, *Astraea*, p. 78.

24 Yates, *Astraea*, pp. 78–9. On the cult of the Virgin see Warner, *Alone Of All Her Sex*; on Elizabeth as phoenix see Axton, *op. cit.* This passage is also cited by Strong, *The Cult of Elizabeth*, p. 15. Strong comments: 'The cult of Gloriana was skilfully created to buttress public order and, even more, deliberately to replace the pre-Reformation externals of religion, the cult of the Virgin and saints with their attendant images, processions, ceremonies and secular rejoicing' (p. 16). I suggest that the skill was in exploiting the available idiom to *conceal* Elizabeth's (female) failings under a cloak of near-religious ceremonies.

25 On Elizabeth's wardrobe, see H. Norris, *Costume and Fashion*, 3 vols (London, 1938), II,484–98, 602–16.

26 M. L. King, 'Book-lined cells: women and humanism in the early Italian Renaissance', in Labalme (ed.), *op. cit.*, pp. 66–90, 78.

27 Loeb classics pp. 82–5.

28 *Henry VI Part I* V.v.68–72.

29 R. Gill (ed.), *The Plays of Christopher Marlowe* (Oxford, 1971), *Tamburlaine I* V.i.504–13.

30 *Tamburlaine II* II.iv.15–25.

31 Boccaccio, *De claris mulieribus*, transl. G. A. Guarino (New Brunswick, 1963); Pisan (Paris, 1536 edn); G. Chaucer, *The Legend of Good Women*, in F. N. Robinson, *The Works of Geoffrey Chaucer* (London, 1966), pp. 480–518; J. de Voragine, *The Golden Legend*, transl. G. Ryan and H. Ripperger (New York, 1941); T. Heywood, *Gynaikeion, or Nine Books of Various History, concerning Women* (London, 1624). See also Heywood's *The exemplary lives and memorable acts of nine of the most worthy Women of the World* (London, 1640 edn). For a good bibliography of Renaissance treatises on virtuous women, see R. Kelso, *Doctrine for the Lady of the Renaissance* (Urbana, 1956); C. Fahy, 'Three early Renaissance treatises on women', *Italian Studies*, XI (1956), pp. 30–55.

32 *The Palace of Pleasure*, 3 vols (1566/7; Dover reprint New York, 1966).

33 Boccaccio, *op. cit.*, p. 5.

34 See Painter on the Duchess of Malfi, above p. 91.

35 *Twelfth Night* II.iv.106–14.

36 Chaucer's tale is based on Petrarch's 'De obedientia ac fide uxoria mythologia', which is in turn a translation of Boccaccio's *Decameron* x.10. See Robinson, *op. cit.*, pp. 709–10.

37 IV.211–20.

38 IV.645–58.

39 IV.142–7.

40 *Othello* IV.iii.39–61.

41 IV.iii.66–76.

42 *The Palace of Pleasure* (1566), in Arden *Poems*, pp. 193–4.

43 ibid., p. 190.

44 ibid., p. 195.

45 *Titus Andronicus* II.iv.26–32. See, for example, the emblem of repentance (*Poenitentia*), a silent woman grieving and chastising herself, in H. Peacham, *Minerva Britanna* (1612), p. 46.

46 B. Radice (ed.), *The Letters of Abelard and Heloise* (Penguin, 1974), p. 49.

47 I take as understood the appallingly explicit sexual symbolism of the actual martyrdoms: breasts ripped off, impalements, and spread-eagled rackings.

48 In some of these cases the saint is actually exposed in a brothel, but God strikes down her assailants, like those of Marina in *Pericles*. See Saint Agatha, Saint Agnes.

49 See e.g. Saint Marina, Saint Margaret (8 October).

50 *op. cit.*, p. 610.

51 *op. cit.*, p. 540.

52 p. 541.

53 p. 541.

54 ibid.

55 Chastity of *reputation* was urged on Renaissance women as òf as much importance as bodily chastity; and treatises warned of 'the uncertain chastity of those who are chaste in deeds and reputation but lascivious in words, gestures, bearing'. See Kelso, *op. cit.*, p. 24.

56 *The Winter's Tale* III.ii.20–30.

57 *Much Ado About Nothing* IV.i.178–84.

58 *Measure for Measure* II.ii.180–6.

59 There is an extended literature on whether or not Angelo was guilty in breaking this betrothal. Angelo is in fact morally guilty (since Mariana is ruined), but technically innocent. The rich and powerful had always got round *de futuro* betrothal obligations when they wished.

60 See above, p. 25.

61 *Measure for Measure* III.i.134–41.

62 In Warner, *Joan of Arc*, p. 155.

63 See also the female figure of Consolation (from Boethius's *De consolatione philosophiae*). On the relation of this figure to Paulina in *The Winter's Tale*, see C. Asp, 'Shakespeare's Paulina and the *Consolatio* tradition', *Shakespeare Studies*, XI (1978), pp. 145–58.

64 See T. W. Baldwin, *William Shakspere's small Latine and lesse Greeke*, 2 vols (Urbana, 1944); Aphthonius, *Progymnasmata*, Latin transl. R. Agricola.

65 Or see Heywood's version of Hecuba's lament, *Gynaikeion*, *op. cit.*

66 *The Rape of Lucrece* ll. 1464–91.

67 See also *Hamlet* II.ii.

68 See *King Lear* II.iv.276–7: 'And let not women's weapons, waterdrops / Stain my man's cheeks!' But see J. Mann, 'Troilus' swoon', *The Chaucer Review* (1980), pp. 319–35.

69 *Venus and Adonis* ll. 33, 49–50.

70 In Arden *Poems*, *op. cit.*, p. xxxix.

71 Axton, *op. cit.*, p. 117.

72 Although I take Axton's point about the elision and confusion of the sexes of the birds in Shakespeare's *The Phoenix and the Turtle* (the theme of the poem), the fact remains that the turtle is referred to using masculine pronouns. See Axton, *op. cit.*, pp. 119–20.

73 *The Phoenix and the Turtle* ll. 29–31, 56–8.

74 ibid., ll. 37–40.

75 Parfitt (ed.), *Ben Jonson*, p. 341.

Index